POLITICIANS
AT WAR

POLITICIANS AT WAR

COMPILED BY

HENRY BUCKTON

LEO COOPER

First published in Great Britain in 2003 by
LEO COOPER
an imprint of Pen & Sword Books Ltd
47 Church Street
Barnsley, South Yorkshire, S70 2AS

ISBN 0 85052 907 7

A catalogue record for this book
is available from the British Library.

Typeset in 11/13 Sabon by
Phoenix Typesetting, Burley-in-Wharfedale, West Yorkshire.

Printed in England by
CPI UK

CONTENTS

MPs FEATURED

James Callaghan
Peter Smithers
Morgan Morgan-Giles
Patrick Duffy
Reginald Bennett
Edward du Cann
James Wellbeloved
James Davidson
Norman Wylie
John Smith

John Peyton
Anthony Kershaw
Francis Pym
Anthony Royle
Thomas Boardman

Edward Heath
Roy Jenkins
Gordon Campbell
Edwin Leather
John Hill
John Page
Charles Simeons
David Renton
Frederic Bennett

Denis Healey
Ivan Neill
Ronald King Murray
John Osborn

William Wilson
Robert Redmond

Paul Bryan
Clive Bossom
Eric Cockeram
Marcus Worsley
William Deedes
Quintin Hogg
James Ramsden
Philip Goodhart
James Spicer

William Whitelaw
Stephen Hastings
Anthony Meyer
David Gibson-Watt
Douglas Dodds-Parker
Robert Boscawen

James Allason
Oscar Murton
Airey Neave
Esmond Wright

Tony Benn
James Molyneaux
Hector Monro
George Mackie
Colin Turner
Peter Shore

INTRODUCTION

In Britain today the title 'Politician' is given far less respect by the general public than it was in former times. All too often the word is associated with sleaze, or corruption. The reality of this was reflected by the electorate's poor turn out at the polling stations during the 2001 general election: quite probably the worst turn out this century. In the minds of many people in Britain today, it's no longer a question of which individual should represent them in Parliament, or indeed, which political party, but whether it really matters any more who represents them.

This was not always the case, and there was a long period after the Second World War when our representatives seemed to be pillars of society, often representing the greatness of our nation both at home and on the world stage. When I was at school in the 1970s most children not only knew the name of the Prime Minister, but of all the major players in his cabinet, and in opposition. I wonder how many children today –even adults –can say the same?

It would be impossible to pinpoint exactly why the world of politics has changed, when politicians are all too often a sad reflection of the society that Britain has become itself. But the great figures that our parents and grandparents once discussed with such vigour and respect had at least one common bond: they had either served in the armed forces during the Second World War or experienced its horrors in some other way. This bond was also shared by most of the voters in their respective constituencies. These men and women had seen politics abused by evil men, who had used their power to inflict some of the cruellest inhumanities the world has ever known.

In war the hero generation of 1939–1945 did battle to rid the world of the political powers that perpetrated these atrocities. In peace, while as politicians, they sought to make the world safe and free, and to endeavour as best they could to ensure that such wickedness could never happen again on such a grand scale.

In the Royal British Legion's *Golden Book of Remembrance* former Prime Minister Edward Heath perhaps speaks for an entire generation of politicians when he wrote: 'When I fought across Europe in 1944 and 1945 whilst serving with the Royal Artillery, I witnessed at first-hand the destruction, carnage and misery of modern warfare. Cities across the continent were razed to the ground. Europe had once again destroyed itself. The devastation and despair which surrounded the Allied armies as they made their way across a shattered Europe was to make a tremendous impact on all of us involved. Confronted with such scenes, I became convinced of the deep belief that remains with me to this day: that the peoples of Europe must never again be allowed to fight each other. We can only hope that by remembering all those who made the ultimate sacrifice, future generations may be able to grasp firmly the ideals of peace and reconciliation.'

Since Mr Heath wrote those words, Europe has again witnessed scenes of mass murder, segregation and ethnic cleansing. It is noticeable that the resurgence of political regimes with the ability to sustain such evil have only occurred with the diminishing influence of these grand old statesmen, not only in Britain, but throughout Europe.

It would be naïve to suggest that politics during the post-war years were without blemish. Naturally there have always been scandals of one sort or another. For instance, in 1963, John Profumo resigned as Harold Macmillan's Secretary of War, following his much-publicized affair with Christine Keeler, who was also the mistress of a Russian diplomat, which at the time created a security risk. John Profumo, the MP for Stratford-upon-Avon, had served with the Northamptonshire Yeomanry during the war, reaching the rank of Brigadier; he had also been mentioned in dispatches.

And, of course, British politics during this period had its share of controversial figures, such as Enoch Powell, whose 'Rivers of Blood' speech in 1968 effectively curtailed the career of a potential Prime Minister. When war broke out he enlisted as a private soldier in the

Royal Warwickshire Regiment. Commissioned in 1940, he also rose to the rank of Brigadier.

In 1945 there was a general election in Britain, and it was from this point onwards that those who had witnessed the evils of the past six years began to slowly emerge in the House of Commons, and inevitably their collective experiences helped to shape the post-war life of the nation.

Polling Day, 8 July 1945, was the culmination of one of the most unusual campaigns in political history. For nearly six years the nation had been at war. The conflict in Europe had only ended two months earlier, while in the Far East British and Allied troops continued their desperate struggle against Imperial Japan.

On 8 July 1945 the embattled population of Britain, still reeling from the effects of Hitler's revenge weapons, were required to place their mark on a polling slip. Thousands of servicemen arriving home from the European war, or helping to keep the peace on the continent, were asked to elect representatives from a campaign they knew little about, and candidates they knew nothing about. Many of these servicemen were still in a state of shock, thanking God they had been spared and wondering whether their families, homes and friends were safe back in Britain. In the jungles of south-east Asia troops continued to face an unrelenting and savage foe, and the probability of an invasion of mainland Japan. Compared to this, thoughts of a general election at home must have seemed almost insignificant.

Predictably, in retrospect, the population did what they always do after a period of turmoil and hardship – they opted for a change. Winston Churchill had been a popular leader, still today the personification of Britain's bulldog spirit of defiance. Yet for the populace at the time he represented the past, which they simply wanted to forget.

Sir Paul Bryan, who ended the war as a Lieutenant Colonel in the Royal West Kent Regiment and who became an MP in 1955, says in his autobiography *Wool, War and Westminster*: 'The general election of 1945 took place between VE Day and the end of the Japanese War. It was the greatest turnover in parliamentary history since the time of the great Reform Bill of 1832. The Conservatives were reduced to a parliamentary strength of 213; only twice before had they been reduced to less, in 1906 and 1932. This came as a surprise to many. As Churchill toured the country Union Jacks came out everywhere.

The VE spirit seemed everlasting. But when it came to voting people were thinking of the peace. Their minds were on housing and food, employment and pensions. The Conservative Party had been in power for virtually the whole period between the two wars so all the evils of that unhappy period could be put at their door.'

Many young men with political ambitions had done well in the armed forces and they were now ready to follow the career that had been put on hold for over five years. Consequently, at the 1945 general election, some of those elected were still in uniform. Others who had already been MPs at the outbreak of war, felt they could serve their country better in uniform than in the House of Commons. For instance, Captain Ronald Cartland, the brother of Dame Barbara Cartland, was the MP for Birmingham. He enlisted in the Army and was killed at Dunkirk, becoming the first serving Member of Parliament to be killed in the Second World War.

So, from 1945 onwards and at consecutive general elections, this new breed of politician was elected to the House of Commons, men with this common bond, that they had served in the Second World War. The last of them, Sir Edward Heath, Tony Benn, Sir Peter Emery and Sir Geoffrey Johnson Smith, finally relinquished their seats at the general election of 7 June 2001.

In this book I have outlined the military careers of several of these men. It is by no means a complete list, and other –equally famous – politicians could have been included, if there had been enough material about their military service to warrant an entry. Indeed, many people who subsequently became household names through their political achievements had served in the armed forces. These could have included James Chichester-Clarke, who later became Lord Moyola of Castledawson. He joined the Irish Guards in 1942 and was wounded at Anzio. He remained in the Army after the war and from 1947–1949 was ADC to the Governor General of Canada, Field Marshal Earl Alexander of Tunis. He retired from the Army in 1960 with the rank of Major and in the same year was elected as the Unionist MP for South Derry in Northern Ireland. His political career culminated as Prime Minister of Northern Ireland between 1969–1971, an office that was abolished when Northern Ireland converted to direct rule in 1974.

One might have included the Liberal MP Clement Freud, who served with the Royal Ulster Rifles, and was a Liaison Officer at the

Nuremberg War Trials; Bernard Weatherill, Speaker of the House of Commons from 1983–1992, who served with the 19th King George V's Own Lancers; or Labour Home Secretary Merlyn Merlyn-Rees, who served in the RAF.

There are also those, not quite so famous politically, who had outstanding military careers, such as Bill Anstruther-Gray, who had been the MP for North Lanark before the war, and who served in the Coldstream Guards. Bill Anstruther-Gray became famous for leading a squadron of Shermans into the sea at Hammam Lif, in order to outflank the Germans and force their surrender in Tunisia. He chose to use the beach because there were two German 88s firing down the village street and one 88 firing down the railway line. The railway and the street were separated from the beach by a line of beach villas, which hid the tanks from the Germans. For his part in this action Bill Anstruther-Gray was awarded the MC. On returning to England he informed the House of Commons that our Sherman tanks were no match for the Germans, much to the annoyance of P.J. Grigg, the War Minister. Anstruther-Gray later became Deputy Speaker.

Another thing that many of the politicians from the generation in question had in common, as several of the following accounts will show, are the physical scars they received. Many of those recorded here were wounded, some seriously. Again, there could have been others mentioned who sustained terrible injuries during the war and who would later serve in the House of Commons. For instance, Richard Wood (now Baron Holderness), who was the Member of Parliament for Bridlington, joined the King's Own Yorkshire Light Infantry as a private soldier in August 1940. In February 1941 he was commissioned in to the King's Royal Rifle Corps. His regiment left England as part of 1st Armoured Division in September 1941 and served in Egypt and Libya. In December 1941 he was very severely wounded and lost both his legs above the knees. Later, after adapting to the use of artificial legs, he went to America to join his father Lord Halifax, who was the British ambassador, where he was involved in PR work until the end of the war.

Undoubtedly there were others, but from the sources available to me the only lady I have discovered who did wartime military service and was later an MP was Lady Pike of Melton, the Conservative MP for Melton between 1956–1974, who served in the WAAF.

The individuals I have included in the book are grouped, not by political ideology, but by their area of military service. However, the parts tend to overlap, as men were posted away from their original branch of the service. For instance, former Home Secretary and Chancellor of the Exchequer Roy Jenkins can be found under Gunners, as he was commissioned into the Royal Artillery. Later, he was sent to Bletchley Park where he helped to interpret coded messages sent by the German Enigma Cipher machine.

The idea for writing this book was inspired by several political autobiographies, which included accounts of the author's war service. I felt certain that many other politicians had equally important and interesting tales to relate, which would be lost for ever, unless someone took the trouble to record them. Hopefully, you will agree that I was right.

The following book is therefore a combination of new material, specially written for the project, or in a few cases, the condensing of exisiting war chapters from political autobiographies. Between them, those represented here served in every branch of the armed forces, in every theatre of war, and at various levels of rank and responsibility. These are just a few of the individuals, whose common bond based on their experiences during the Second World War, both with other Members of Parliament and many of their constituents, helped to create the political and social make-up of post-war Britain.

Henry Buckton

Part One

THE ROYAL NAVY

Those studied in this opening section belonged to the 'senior service', the Royal Navy. They served in every field from traditional sailors on the high seas to pilots in the Fleet Air Arm. Some took part in the Battle of the Atlantic or accompanied the Arctic convoys to Russia; others served in more tropical zones. There were also those who worked in naval intelligence. Collectively, they represent the many facets of the wartime Royal Navy and illustrate why it was crucial to the ultimate Allied victory.

JAMES CALLAGHAN

Of those who served in the Royal Navy the most significant in political terms was James Callaghan, who was Prime Minister and First Lord of the Treasury between 1976–1979.

James Callaghan was born in Portsmouth in March 1912, where his father was serving in the Royal Navy, as an ordinary seaman aboard the Royal Yacht *Victoria and Albert*. At the start of the First World War the ship's company was dispersed and his father joined the battlecruiser HMS *Agincourt*. The family moved to Brixham, Devon, when his father was discharged from the Navy in 1919 and was accepted by the Coastguard Service. His mother and her young children returned to Portsmouth in 1923, after the death of her husband, where they lived in rented rooms. It was during this time that the young James Callaghan first became involved with politics. Mrs Long, one of the ladies they stayed with, was a member of the Independent Labour Party and during the 1923 and 1924 general elections she pressed him into service to run between the polling station and the Labour Party committee rooms, carrying the numbers of those who had voted.

He began his working life with the Inland Revenue Service in 1929 and eventually became Assistant Secretary of the Inland Revenue Staff Federation. He was married in 1938 and volunteered for service in the Royal Navy in May 1940, serving both at home and in the Pacific.

As my father and one of my grandfathers had both served in the Royal Navy, it was my hope to follow in their footsteps. But when I registered at a Labour Exchange in London I was told that I could be accepted only for the Army. Indignantly, I at once wrote a strong appeal to the Admiralty and, somewhat to my surprise, for it was the time of Dunkirk, within a few days I received a formal reply, saying that Their Lordships would accept me as an ordinary seaman.

But I had reckoned without my boss, Douglas Houghton, who was rather cross when I gave him the news, and insisted that my work with the Inland Revenue Staff Federation came first. He put a spoke in the wheel by getting the Ministry of Labour to declare that my job as Assistant Secretary was a 'reserved occupation,' which meant that I could neither volunteer nor be conscripted. So for the time being I joined the Local Defence Volunteers, which soon became the Home Guard. We practised our shooting at Bisley, dealt with a few Molotov Cocktail bombs with a stirrup pump and a bucket of sand, and guarded our local railway bridge, which had a convenient pub close by.

Eventually Douglas Houghton was persuaded that he could do without me, and I carried my precious Admiralty letter to a retired Marine colonel in the Naval Recruiting Office in Liverpool. I told him I was volunteering for Motor Torpedo Boats, which were small, fast craft for intercepting and sinking enemy ships in the English Channel. He sent me to Lowestoft, saying I would find the MTB base there. But when I arrived there was no sign of it.

The old Marine colonel had mistakenly recruited me to serve instead in the Patrol Service, whose main task was minesweeping in trawlers. It was too late to try to change, and some weeks of training followed, after which I joined a ship at Lamlash on the Isle of Arran, from which we patrolled the Irish Sea, the Minches and on occasion, northabouts around Cape Wrath and the Orkneys to the North Sea and Methil in Fife.

In due course, the ship's captain recommended me for a commission, but after I had left the ship in a Scottish base and was medically examined in Portsmouth, the doctors decreed that I was suffering from TB and I spent a dreary period in Haslar Hospital, Gosport. A few months later I was discharged but told I must serve a further six months ashore before I could go back to sea, and meantime I was to report to the Admiralty. I was still an ordinary seaman, but at the Admiralty became part of a team which was preparing the Navy for the war against Japan. My small part was to help to write a history of the war against Japan so far. I was also promoted to Lieutenant RNVR.

This work was completed within the required six months, but, instead of going back to sea at once, I was ordered to join the British Pacific Fleet in Australia, with the intention of becoming a Liaison Officer with the United States Navy when the Allies invaded Japan. I joined an aircraft carrier which was about to sail for Colombo in Sri Lanka, thinking that this would be a good jumping off place for Australia. But once in Trincomalee, I found it more difficult than I had expected to find a ship to take me on to Australia.

Whilst waiting, I was still determined to get to sea, and persuaded Captain Ellis, the Commanding Officer of the First World War battleship *Queen Elizabeth*, to take me aboard as a supernumary until I could find some means of getting to Sydney. I was aboard her somewhere in the Indian Ocean, off the Andaman Islands, chasing two Japanese cruisers when VE Day was announced.

Shortly afterwards, a signal arrived saying that a general election had been called and, as a Parliamentary candidate, I was to be returned home. I had as much difficulty getting transport back to England as I had had going out, and only just made the last date for handing in my nomination papers.

The election ended my service with the Navy except that in December 1945, after I had been elected, I was recalled and put on a naval uniform for the last time to become one of a young team of servicemen and women chosen to visit the Soviet Union to meet the Russian people and tell them of Britain's role in the war. During more than two months we had the never-forgotten experience of witnessing the wartime sufferings of the Russian people as we travelled from Leningrad to the Black Sea throughout the Soviet Union, and memorably watched the trial of Nazi generals in Kiev in the Ukraine.

As you can see, I cannot claim an heroic experience of war. It was mostly a case of the normal run of the mill dangers shared by all servicemen, and I may add by the citizens of the East End. However, I saw enough on the lower deck and in the wardroom to know what the Navy expected when the war was won and men and women came back to Britain after four or five years abroad. In the Commons in 1945 and 1946 I made sure that their voices were heard.

James Callaghan was elected as the Labour MP for Cardiff South at the 1945 general election, and stayed in the Commons until 1987, after which he was appointed a Knight of the Garter and created a life peer, as Lord Callaghan of Cardiff. His political career has been unique, as no other British politician has held the four great posts of Chancellor of the Exchequer, Home Secretary, Foreign Secretary and Prime Minister.

PETER SMITHERS

Peter Smithers was Conservative MP for Winchester from 1950–1964, when he was appointed Secretary General of the Council of Europe. He was knighted in 1970.

Although he began his naval career at sea, illness put an end to his active service, and he eventually became involved with various levels of naval intelligence.

History at school had been taught in a manner certain to bore an unfortunate schoolboy: the memorization of dates and places and names, until in the history fifth at Harrow I chanced upon a true teacher. As he spoke of great men and great events the past suddenly opened before me. This was the greatest of all games, the story of man's struggle to survive and to excel. I would be a player in it, come what may. At the end of ten days I had finished the books for the term and came back for more. Then I went to my housemaster to say that I wanted to compete for a history demyship at Magdalen College Oxford. Doing me a good turn, he laughed in my face. 'You, a scholar! I never heard such a thing'. Furious, I persuaded my parents to let me leave Harrow at age 16 and read for a year with a distinguished Tudor historian, Arthur Innes. There was a very numerous entry for the three demyships available in history and I got the second of them. Life had begun!

Three years later with a 'First' in history – in those days a 'First' opened a great many doors – I wrote to the Chairman of the Conservative Party to say that I wanted to enter politics. He replied that I was much too young and should think about it again in ten years time. Of course he was right. I embarked upon the 'Life of

Joseph Addison' for a D.Phil degree in history. And then Hitler burst upon the scene and I applied to join the RNVR. The naval board examining candidates asked why with a distinguished academic record I wanted to do that, and I replied, 'Because I love the sea' –as I still do. That did it, and I became a lieutenant overnight and began training. My aim was to be a navigator.

A friend had command of a 'whale catcher', HMS *Juniper*, a small craft of robust construction designed for North Atlantic patrol. He asked me to join his ship's company as second navigator to learn the trade at sea, a wonderful opportunity. And then higher authority intervened, ordering me to Cardington to learn to fly a barrage balloon from the quarterdeck of a destroyer. I was to be a 'BB Officer'! Winston had a project to sail a squadron into the Baltic and it was thought that this might be feasible with barrage balloons aloft. So HMS *Juniper* sailed into the winter mists without me and was never heard of again. Then the Baltic adventure was cancelled and I was posted to an auxiliary yacht, testing experimental devices in the Channel and the North Sea.

In the bitter January of 1940 I fell ill at sea, was hospitalized and narrowly escaped death. The Haslar Hospital board was emphatic: there was no more sea service for me. With an Oxford 'First' any government department would be glad to have me, they said. Perhaps, but I had a girl friend who had another boy friend, in the Admiralty, and I rang her up. Shortly afterwards Commander Ian Fleming telephoned the hospital. Lieutenant Smithers was not to be discharged. The Director of Naval Intelligence wanted him at once. A week later I was on my way to become naval member of MI6 Paris. I was in time to witness the shameful collapse of the French Government and Army. Both were political failures on the grand scale.

After acting as movements officer conveying our staff from Paris to Bordeaux, I embarked them in HMS *Arethusa*. Then I was ordered to stand by to become Acting ADC to the First Lord of the Admiralty, A.V. Alexander, who had arrived to negotiate for the French fleet to sail to Britain. Admiral Darlan bluntly refused to consider this, and the fleet was to slink off into inactivity for the rest of the war. I flew back with the First Lord in a Sunderland Flying Boat to Plymouth. A special train took us to Paddington where his Parliamentary Private Secretary awaited him. Cabinet was sitting and expecting his report. This was politics in action on the grand scale.

Through the summer and autumn I was seconded by the Admiralty to MI5 to assist in picking up German parachutists. We had broken their codes and knew where to wait to welcome them. Then there was a mission to study the danger posed by partly submerged wrecks in the North Sea and Western Approaches, in case they were used to station German radio operators who could observe shipping and report.

When this was completed DNI ordered me to the British Embassy in Washington as Assistant Naval Attaché in charge of the exchange of intelligence with the Navy Department. This included handling the material which the Americans were obtaining from Japanese intercepts. One day, to my astonishment and delight, I carried back to the Embassy the message from Oshima, the Japanese Ambassador in Berlin, to Tokyo, reporting that Hitler was about to attack the USSR. I had absorbed enough history to be convinced that Britain, still fighting alone, would survive.

At this point a British joint staff mission at the highest level was sent to Washington and my work was taken over by five intelligence officers. But at this point there were serious sinkings in the Yucatan Channel and I was sent as Assistant Naval Attaché in charge to the British Embassy in Mexico, to the Legations in the Central American Republics and the Embassy in Panama. There was no naval attaché in the area, so I was on my own. My task was to set up and run a reporting network which would watch for signs that U-boats were being fuelled from the area, and to work with the various governments in intelligence and service matters when necessary. I must just make myself as useful as possible. There was a large German colony throughout the area, and this involved many surprising activities, often in co-operation with MI6.

After the collapse of Germany and the general election which returned the Labour Party to power, the Rt Hon Leslie Hore-Belisha, the War Minister, was out of Parliament. He was now visiting Mexico. Our ambassador, a somewhat irascible man with whom, nevertheless, I always remained on very good terms, sent for me. 'Take away this (expletive) man and stop him wasting my time'. I picked up Hore-Belisha at his hotel to take him sight-seeing, but asked if he would mind my going to the Embassy to see if there was any urgent matter. There was nothing, except a telegram from my mother. I opened it in the car. It said that the Winchester Division

Conservative Association wished to know whether I was available as Prospective Parliamentary Candidate for the constituency. 'Good Lord! Sir. Look at that. What would you do?' And I handed the telegram to Hore-Belisha. Having read it, he turned round in his seat to face me, looked me in the eye and spat out the words, 'Young man, I would go on my bended knees for anything half as good'. I went back into the Embassy and sent the one-word answer 'Yes'. Back in Washington Lord Halifax wrote a letter to the Winchester Conservatives strongly endorsing my candidature. An exciting chapter in life had ended and another had begun.

Throughout my time in the House of Commons and the Government I retained my commission as lieutenant commander in the reserve. In the event of a 'flash' war my posting was to be Naval Attaché Madrid to release a deck officer serving in that capacity for sea duty. This would indeed have been a fascinating posting. But there was no 'flash' war, and when I was elected Secretary General of the Council of Europe, it was thought that it might be difficult for Her Majesty to call me up for duty. So with great reluctance I severed my connection with a wonderful service, receiving as consolation a 'clasp' to my Volunteer Reserve Decoration.

As for navigation, as owner of a succession of three small ocean-going yachts, 'Europa,' 'Europe II' and 'Europa III', I learned it after the war.

During his time in Washington working with Lord Halifax, Peter Smithers had been in charge of the movements when Winston Churchill made his famous visit to President Roosevelt. The plan was for the Prime Minister to sail straight to Baltimore, but when the engines of the battleship which carried him got indigestion, she put into Bermuda instead. It was then arranged for Winston to sail from Bermuda with a party of fifty in destroyers. In the end, however, his party flew from Bermuda to Norfolk Virginia, where they took a train to Washington DC. The President had indicated that he wanted to get Churchill into the Oval Office before anybody realized his presence in the USA. Accompanied by such a party, this was not an easy task. With all the changes of plan, the Press had realized that something important was about to happen in Baltimore. They went to see Peter Smithers to ask him for the Baltimore story. He managed to look as embarrassed as possible and said that there was nothing about to happen that he could tell them about. They leaped into their cars and left for Baltimore. Peter Smithers thereafter hurried to the Union Station, just in time to see Winston stumping down the platform. The Americans whisked him off at high speed to the White House, and President Roosevelt had his wish.

MORGAN MORGAN-GILES

When Sir Peter Smithers became Secretary General of the Council of Europe in 1964 he was succeeded as MP for Winchester by another naval officer, Rear Admiral Morgan Morgan-Giles DSO. Morgan-Giles at the time was still serving as the youngest flag officer in the Navy. As a professional sailor, he began his naval career in 1932 and served throughout the war. During this time he was attached to both the Army and the RAF and worked with Tito in Yugoslavia. He was the Conservative MP for Winchester from 1964–1979 and was made a Knight in 1985.

When asked to describe something of his war service, he explained that, as a young commander in the Royal Navy in 1947, he was a student at the newly formed Joint Services Staff College at Latimer. Graduates from this college were known collectively as 'Cormorants' after the sea bird which can fly long distances, but also spends much time on the ground. In an article published in the Staff College Magazine, which he called *Fifty Years a Cormorant*, he gives an overview of his feelings as a result of his service and wartime experience.

> The students who arrived at Latimer in September 1947 for JSSC No 2 all had a great deal of practical war experience. Some of them might have spent their war years in a single branch of a single Service: others would have been more variously employed. But there had been inter-Service misunderstandings . . .
>
> The captain of HM Submarine *Thrasher*, damaged and unable to dive, made a signal 'ETA Alexandria 1400 hours subject to cessation of attacks by friendly aircraft.' At that moment he, (Rufus Mackenzie,

a very distinguished submariner), might have wished that the Royal Air Force knew more about the Navy.

Similarly RAF pilots protecting convoys might often have wished that the Navy's anti-aircraft gunners could more readily distinguish a Beaufighter from a Ju 88. But by and large relations between all three British and Commonwealth Services during the war were excellent at junior officer level.

Perhaps I was lucky in the Mediterranean (1940–1945) to be part of the Tobruk garrison for most of the seven months of the siege. Soldiers and sailors formed a garrison strongly united under constant air attack by Stukas, and shelling too from 'Badia Bill'. My own admiration for the Army, and I hope understanding of them, developed beyond all measure. The Australians and the Poles defended the perimeter against all odds. The unflappable Australian Colonel 'Gaffer' Lloyd (Chief of Staff to General Morshead) had his HQ inside a small, narrow very overcrowded cave. One day six enemy tanks broke through the perimeter and headed down the harbour road. A despatch rider saw them, raced down to the docks and rushed into the cave to report them to Gaffer Lloyd. His reply was, 'Well, tell the bastards not to come in here. There are too many people in here already!'

Naval losses on the 'Tobruk run' were appalling – but the Army got their beef and spuds and ammunition. 'Lord Haw-Haw' on German radio referred to the Tobruk garrison as 'those voluntary self-supporting prisoners of war'.

Later that year I was again fortunate in being lent to the RAF to a Wellington squadron based at Shallufa in the Canal Zone. Every ship which arrived at Suez from the UK brought a dozen or so pink-faced boys, only a year out of school, who had learned to fly twin-engined bombers. Within a few weeks in the desert they had brown knees, within a few weeks more they had become flight commanders; within a further few weeks they would be missing at breakfast time. But they were endlessly light-hearted and they never faltered. In addition to its normal bombing role, 38 Squadron flew daily mine-sweeping sorties the length of the Suez Canal. This involved flying at less than 100 feet, in a Wellington equipped with a huge unwieldy magnetic coil 70 ft in diameter, attached under the aircraft from wingtip to wingtip. This was the famous 'flying wedding ring' – and it worked. This mine-sweeping effort made a great contribution to keeping the Canal open to shipping at a vital phase. Another achievement of 38 Squadron was to convert some of its aircraft for the torpedo dropping role –so that enemy shipping could be attacked at greater ranges, beyond the reach of the Fleet Air Arm's old Swordfish and Albacore biplanes. This worked successfully too; but it involved the pilots flying at less than 100 ft whereas their training was to bomb from 10,000 ft. They did not enjoy it – but they did it. After several months and three aircraft crashes I was left with an abiding admiration for the RAF, which will remain with me to my deathbed.

Certainly all three Services worked very closely together throughout the campaign in the Western Desert. I think incidentally that this campaign witnessed perhaps the last flickers of chivalry in the history of warfare. The Eighth Army and the Afrika Korps fought like tigers but had the greatest respect for one another. The desert war was a 'gentleman's war'. Once into Europe, with bombed cities and civilian refugees and dead babies, it became as squalid as war always is.

So in 1947 the principal object of the JSSC was to consolidate inter-Service understanding rather than to create it.

One must remember the circumstances of those days. It was before NATO existed; the Cold War was in the future; there was no British 'Atom Bomb'; India had just become independent a few weeks previously; Admiral Mountbatten was Viceroy; Churchill was still in Parliament, although no longer Prime Minister, and the unified MOD was still a matter for discussion. The armed forces were being reduced and dismantled as fast as was administratively possible. Soldiers, sailors and airmen were 'group happy' i.e. waiting only for the date of their demobilization group.

The students of JSSC2, all regular officers, were mostly in a state of euphoria; no more fighting (we thought); and of course domestically blissful. I had been married in Australia the previous year and during those six months at Latimer lived in my first 'permanent' married house.

The course was magnificently broad in its scope. We were lectured a lot on international affairs – once by Ernest Bevin the Foreign Secretary. The Chiefs of Staff at the time were Lord Cunningham, Lord Montgomery and Lord Tedder – all household names. The struggle between the Services for financial resources had not yet become as tough as it subsequently became. The Americans in effect assumed world leadership in 1947 –with the Truman doctrine for the containment of Communism, and the Marshal Plan for economic aid to Europe (UNRRA).

We were lectured by Lord Montgomery. I was so impressed that I rang my wife to bring our new baby to see the departure of 'the greatest man of our age' as I thought at the time. The baby waved its chubby fist and Montgomery gave a wave from the back of his special personal Rolls Royce. This car had been given to him by the Rolls Royce Company at the end of the war. Its distinguishing feature was a forward-sloping windscreen, as fitted to the vehicles of the Eighth Army in the desert –to avoid the reflection of the sun betraying their whereabouts to the enemy.

Curiously enough nobody mentioned a single word about 'ULTRA'. There was very little talk about Service intelligence –except for one Naval story told in the Mess. At the outbreak of war an elderly retired rear admiral had been recalled and was employed in the Naval Intelligence Division of the Admiralty. One cold winter's night this old chap was found in very compromising circumstances with a young WRNS in St James' Park. The scandal somehow reached the ears of the Prime Minister. Churchill's comment was '62 years of age. 5 degrees of frost in the Park. It makes one proud to be British.'

The JSSC qualification after Latimer led to my next appointment as NLO Trieste. Trieste was at that time (1948-9) a free state with a military governor –the British General Sir Terence Airey. There was a garrison of 5000 British troops and 5000 Americans. Thus I was lucky to have yet another job with the Army, and it was a particularly enjoyable couple of years.

We lived in a magnificent large house where a German admiral had shot himself in 1945, where Tito's Partisans had lived for a short time and painted hammers and sickles in every room and where the Royal Engineers had punched holes in all the walls and installed enormous hideous heating stoves in the cold winter of 1947.

It is a very different world now. This article is no place to pontificate upon present or future defence policy. But, swinging in the hammock of my recollections, it is interesting to compare the problems which now face the students of JSSC No 1 with those of 50 years ago.

Post-war British Services have acquitted themselves with remarkable success in campaigns such as the Falklands and the Gulf. Servicemen are still popular with the public when on display –for instance at the Royal Tournament, Navy Days, the Red Arrows, Royal Marine Band Concerts etc. But a Treasury-led defence policy produces terrible personnel problems. And if it is true that the Services as a whole are at present 10,000 short even on the numbers which they are allowed to recruit, one must wonder why.

Television, which entirely dominates the thinking of the whole population, churns out entertainment night after night with little reference to the existence of the armed forces. In addition the very ease and comfort of life under the Welfare State makes the more disciplined alternative of Service life appear less attractive.

Then there are all the problems of Internationalism. Would British soldiers 'die for Europe'? Or would the servicemen of any other country? Would a Federal Army ever function?

There is another problem which greatly troubles my octogenarian soul –that is the question of women's place in the Services. My generation knows what absolutely splendid work was done in the past by WRNS, ATS, WAAF etc. But I personally cannot come to terms with the idea of sending women to sea in warships – or indeed using women in the front line of any of the Armed Services. Despite all the many arguments, surely the fundamental moral dimension must be this –that no woman should ever be required to kill another woman's son.

One other thing. In crabbed old age one is sometimes apt to ask 'Where are the great names of yesterday? Where are the public figures? Where are the men like Monty, Alexander, Slim, Cunningham, Tedder, or Eisenhower?' The answer is, of course, that 'The moment produces the man'.

NIL DESPERANDUM.

PATRICK DUFFY

Patrick Duffy, who was made a Knight in 1991, was Labour MP for the Colne Valley Division of Yorkshire from 1970-1992. He was Parliamentary Private Secretary to the Secretary of State for Defence from 1974-1976 and Parliamentary Under-Secretary of State for Defence (Navy) MoD from 1976-1979. Later, he was opposition spokesman on defence between 1979-1980 and 1983-1984.

My first request on an official visit to Devonport Barracks in 1976 must have puzzled the Commodore. It was to be taken to the then redundant railway platform from which I had departed at midnight in mid-1940 –kit-bag under one arm and hammock under the other – on draft to the battle-cruiser *Repulse*. After a prolonged train journey due to bombing, I arrived a week later at the Home Fleet base at Scapa Flow. My ship was at sea, so I was berthed temporarily in the Fleet depot ship *Iron Duke*.

After initial training at HMS *Royal Arthur*, formerly the Butlin's holiday camp at Skegness, I was about to join this Devonport-manned ship. I had been called up at the beginning of the year under the National Service (Armed Forces) Act, 1939, after registering under-age. Accordingly, I was the youngest member of the draft reporting to *Repulse*, where my duties included peeling potatoes and acting as a 'cook to the galley' for my mess –No 49, starboard, fo'c'sle –and scrubbing daily at sea as well as in harbour the space occupied at the top of the foremast from which the six 15" guns were controlled. That was also to be my defence and action station. As a teenage ordinary seaman I felt privileged to join the gunnery team, though my duties never exceeded the fetching of cocoa from the galley during night watches. *Repulse* was then engaged on the Northern Patrol and the possible interception of German capital ships and raiders seeking transit to and from the Atlantic. That was before the destruction of HMS *Hood*, which unhappily confirmed the thin armoured protection of all battle-cruisers.

I did not know then that I was under surveillance for officer-training, and subsequently appeared before a Fleet Selection Board in the cruiser *Naiad* and an Admiralty Selection Board in Portsmouth Barracks. I survived both to my surprise. Once the fateful question (as I believed) concerning my father's occupation (he was a coal-miner) had been posed, I had expected rejection. Yet, I never knew discrimination whilst serving in the Royal Navy, unlike experience elsewhere. That was the first instalment of a great store of indebtedness I owe to the Royal Navy.

I owed much to my divisional officers at Devonport and in *Repulse*, to my chief petty officer on board and those other senior ratings in whose charge I often found myself as a member of working parties detailed daily to a variety of tasks ranging from painting ship and receiving stores over the side to working ashore on the new canteen. I was especially taken with Captain W G Tennant, who often cleared lower deck for pep-talks and whose outstanding leadership prior to assuming command had made possible large-scale evacuations from Dunkirk harbour. I was also impressed by some senior ratings on my mess-deck, whom I found widely read and still subscribing in wartime to book clubs ashore. Yet, intense bitterness lingered among many others from the events at Invergordon ten years earlier. I quickly sensed the precious brand of comradeship in this elegant big ship, and left her with some reluctance a year before her ill-fated deployment to the Far East in Force Z. That is why I was anxious to return to the railway platform at Devonport, in order that I could pay tribute to those friends who left with me in 1940 to join the ship and went down with her in the South China Sea the following year. And the echo of that moment's stillness was more evocative than any wartime memories of action stations and conflict.

After training at HMS *King Alfred* on Hove's sea-front, I was involved for the rest of the war in flying duties with the Fleet Air Arm. I served in the escort carrier *Biter* and the fleet carriers *Formidable* and *Implacable,* and also filled staff appointments. Finally, I was given command of the Naval School of Air Radar. My experience of naval aircraft covered the Swordfish, Albacore, Barracuda and the Firefly. *Biter* – among the first converted merchantmen – was remarkably cost-effective thanks to an excellent Swordfish squadron, No 811. She was responsible for the destruction of U-boats and enemy aircraft on convoy protection in the Atlantic and on the Russian run, and engaged in U-boat hunting in the Bay of Biscay in the company of Captain Walker's renowned *Black Swan* class of sloops. She was among the first to deploy the homing or accoustic torpedo; unfortunately, she quickly became its victim when the new weapon became detached from an aircraft that had pitched over the side and homed in on the ship's propellers.

Formidable was also engaged in Russian convoy support whilst I served in her, but principally in anti-shipping operations along the Norwegian coast and, in particular, strikes on the battleship *Tirpitz* lurking in Alten Fjord. I was obliged to leave *Formidable* when she left for the Far East, because of a three-monthly medical check imposed on me by the Air Medical Board at Lee-on-Solent, which effectively confined me to home waters. This was the result of a crash which left me lying on a Scottish mountain in mid-December and fortunate to escape frostbite. I was again fortunate to come into the care of Sir Harold Gillies, the leading plastic surgeon, whose patients appeared to be drawn largely from tank crews and naval aviators, whereas his son-in-law, Sir Archibald McIndoe, looked after the RAF at East Grinstead. I managed to return to front-line squadron work after a year, however, and served with naval air squadrons 817 and 822.

I nearly made it to the Far East in the summer of 1945 with 822 Squadron – another fine unit, well commanded and motivated – which was about to leave for the Far East in August, 1945, to take part in the coming campaign in South-East Asia. Its designed role – for which it had worked up over several weeks in Lough Foyle – was an assault on naval installations in Singapore. The squadron's Barracudas and stores were already embarked in *Campania* moored in Liverpool Bay, with its personnel on embarkation leave, when the atom bomb was dropped.

It was not possible for many post-war years to avoid periodic corrective surgery from Sir Harold Gillies at his unit in the grounds of the Hampshire Mental Institution outside Basingstoke, or to secure official discharge from the Navy whilst it was going on. I was only released when my 100% disablement status had been reduced to a permanent 30%. By that time, in the early 1950s, I had taken degrees at the London School of Economics and Columbia University, New York, fought two parliamentary elections and started lecturing at Leeds University.

Before taking extended leave to join the first post-war term at the LSE in October 1946, I had participated as commanding officer of the Naval School of Air Radar in airborne radar trials at sea in *Implacable*. Those trials pointed to exciting developments in detection, surveillance and target acquisition; it was a revolution in naval warfare. They also made me realize that in terms of naval technology my span of activity over just six years measured a greater advance on Admiral Jellicoe's World War One flagship *Iron Duke*, where I started afloat, than the *Iron Duke* represented on Nelson's *Victory*.

REGINALD BENNETT

Reginald Bennett was Conservative MP for Gosport and Fareham from 1950–1974 and Fareham from 1974–1979. Before the war he studied medicine at New College Oxford and St George's Hospital Medical School. While at Oxford he belonged to the University Air Squadron, where he learned to fly. He was also very keen on sailing and was an Oxford Sailing Blue from 1931–1934. His talents could well have suited the RAF, but he chose to join the RNVR instead. Before the start of hostilities, he had already 'signed on' as a doctor, on the liner *Cheshire,* which was going to Rangoon as an auxiliary merchant cruiser. The story of Reginald Bennett's war service was originally pieced together by his daughter Belinda, using a mini tape recorder, and reproduced in a little book about her father's life, entitled *Three Chousing Reers!*

We started the war in HMS *Cheshire,* at Rangoon in the rainy season. She was a Liverpool ship with Liverpool men, stiffened in due course by a few experienced lieutenant commanders from the RNR.

We went on from there shortly afterwards to Calcutta up the coast, up the Hoogly River to a yard at Kidderpore where they started converting us into a warship, putting in ancient 6" guns, and we started pretending to be a man-o-war. From Calcutta we went down to Trincomalee on the east coast of Ceylon, where we went on 'working up,' getting accustomed to the weapons and shooting at targets, and getting the ship as a running concern. In due course we went round to Colombo, where we sat in the main commercial harbour like any other liner. I was there as a doctor.

It was from Colombo that we were despatched, under sealed

orders, for an unknown destination. We ended up in Freetown and were appointed to escort a convoy back to England. That was the first time we arrived in England during that severe winter of 1939–1940. We went on, going on the Northern Patrol right up by Iceland, or escorting transatlantic convoys for the rest of the summer.

After we had refitted we went out to sea again to more of these patrols. I'm afraid that our ships were getting knocked off in appalling conditions. Sometimes a whole battery of torpedoes would blow out the bottom of one of these liners where all the fuel tanks would be lit up and she would sink in a sea of blazing oil, a prospect which wasn't very inviting for any of us. Anyway, in due course, on one evening just after dinner we were going out on patrol and passing a place called Tory Island on the north-west of Donegal and bang, we were hit. We were hit below the bridge under which the wardroom was and I nearly spilt my drink! Then there was this eerie hissing and howling noise as all the spaces below decks filled up with water and the air came squealing up through all the decks, all the orifices and cracks between plates and that sort of thing, as we settled in the water. A couple of salvage tugs came out and towed us into Belfast Lough, where in due course we were mined in. A terrific explosion one night; nothing seemed to have happened, but we were told that aircraft had been dropping mines around us.

We went on being salvaged and eventually steamed across the Irish Sea on our bottom row of portholes, very deep in the water, because we had flooded all the tanks aft to balance the damage forward, where the holds were full of water and mud. We lay in Gladstone Dock for a while and then, after we'd been partially repaired, went across the river to Birkenhead, where we went into Cammell Laird's Yard to be more extensively repaired.

After Christmas 1940 I got an appointment to another ship back in Belfast. The ship was an old cargo boat called *Springbank* which had been converted into a flak ship, covered with anti-aircraft guns. In addition, a battleship's catapult had been put on board, so that a fighter aeroplane could be projected into the air. This ship was due to go around with convoys fighting off air attack. If one of these Focke-Wulfs came along the fighter aeroplane was fired off to pursue it and shoot it down. Then it either had to splash down in the sea alongside some ship or make its way to shore, if within reach. Very brave guys they were who flew those aircraft.

When the ship was fitted out she had four pairs of 4" high-angle guns and a lot of pom-poms and heavy machine guns, so she was really armed to the teeth. We finished getting her ready and went on to Scapa Flow to 'work up'. Every single one of the officers in that wardroom was a survivor from some other ship that had been torpedoed or sunk in some other way.

We started off by doing a few coastal convoys round the north of Scotland, round to Methil in Fife, where the convoys used to assemble for coming round to the Liverpool side. We got into the Forth and anchored with all the merchant ships which were waiting to make up convoys.

After that we went on some Atlantic convoys and one of them was very notable. We were escorting a convoy out west, just south-east of Iceland. We were to drop the convoy and pick up an incoming convoy the next day or so. Suddenly the signals coming in on cipher began to bear some curious information. They said to all ships that extreme priority was to be given to anything coming from Akureyri, a minute place in Iceland, not far from us. Then, of course, the truth came out. This was being given huge priority because, on the other side of the island, the *Norfolk* and *Suffolk* were shadowing the *Bismarck* which was on its way down to massacre the two convoys, the one we were bringing and the one we were expecting to pick up.

I went to bed that night not feeling too content. But, I am happy to say, when I woke up the next morning those ships that had been swinging idly in Scapa Flow for years, grounding on their own empty bottles, the mighty *Hood* and the *Prince of Wales*, came steaming by and got between us and the *Bismarck*.

We were then sent down on a Gibraltar convoy. Things were getting very hot in the western ocean by then and return convoys from Gibraltar were absolutely bound to get trouble, because the obliging General Franco was letting the German observers watch Gibraltar from Algeciras opposite.

The first area we came through on that convoy was for Italian submarines who didn't bother us very much. One submarine had been sunk by one of our old destroyers called *Hesperus* and I think they'd scuttled themselves and abandoned ship. When we had finished with the Italian submarines area we got into a much nastier situation. Night after night we were losing ships. They were being torpedoed by submarines which came in on the surface from ahead, dashed down through the columns of the convoy, firing off torpedoes at likely targets and shooting out at the back end long before people had recovered from the explosion of the torpedoes. So we were fairly easy meat. In the end we had the unpleasant experience of seeing, in the dark of course, our convoy commodore ship torpedoed next to us and going straight down. She was full of scrap iron, or something like that, and went straight under. So we were expecting trouble –we were the biggest ship left now –and here we were, a Grey Funnel Line ship with a heavy escort of merchant ships all round us.

It was a dark night, with a big 30 to 40 Atlantic sea running. There'd been a northerly gale blowing for days, so here was a big sea coming down against us. I think our speed of progress was four knots over the bottom and so we weren't really a highly elusive target. One unpleasant thing was that we had Asdic, and we were actually able to detect a submarine underneath the ship behind us. So if we dropped depth charges we'd simply blow up our other ship. Anyway, they got us in the end. One torpedo came in just under the bridge and the other one got into the engine room and blew that up, so we came to a grinding halt and lay wallowing in the huge swell in the pitch darkness. We had to abandon ship. The two whalers on either side were lowered and I was supposed to get into one of them. I went around to see if anybody had been damaged in the torpedo explosions but we could find nobody and I went over the side in the whaler. She was on the leeside and the ship was drifting sideways so we couldn't get away from the ship, grinding 30-40' up and down the ship's side in the swell.

There we were, fending off with oars, the oars being driven through the bottom of the lifeboat, so it was very disagreeable, but not so disagreeable as what happened to the other whaler which simply vanished into one of the torpedo holes and was never seen again. In the end we pushed our way along and got clear of the bows, with the anchors coming slamming down into the water as she pitched, but missing us; so we didn't get damaged that way. We lay off in the swell.

A little merchant ship called *Coxwold* fell out of the convoy very bravely, and went round picking us up first because we were the biggest object visible in the dark. The Skipper put me as quartermaster at the wheel, so that his able seaman could go around the deck helping to pick people out of the water. This little coaster was open from end to end, no bulkheads, and was full of scrap iron so anybody could send her to the bottom. We knew there were plenty of submarines around because, right before we were sunk, we'd had the signal that three fresh U-boats had sighted the convoy. Anyway, when dawn came up we had picked up all the people we could find and we went pounding along following the convoy, about 40 miles behind it. We fortunately managed to escape observation and caught up with the convoy, fell in with it and landed in Liverpool, survivors for the second time.

This brings us to the autumn of 1941 and so, after a bit of survivor's leave, I was told to report to Lee-on-Solent and there I was given a course of aviation medicine. As airmen in general are not prepared to listen to anybody who isn't an aviator, the Navy needed doctors who were airmen. So, as I'd got plenty of time in as a pilot, I was clearly likely to be credible at least to the flying part of the ship's company. I was given a choice, to go to Penang or to Sandbanks. Well, it's perhaps no surprise to know that I chose Sandbanks. There I was posted to a nice Walrus aircraft training station where young sub lieutenants and midshipmen were being trained as amphibian pilots in Poole Harbour. The Royal Motor Yacht Club had some admirable buildings and a modern clubhouse and some big hangars next door where the aircraft could be stowed. Being the only doctor around, I found myself being asked to look after naval and even Army personnel in Poole itself, so I always had a most interesting responsibility.

The summer was coming up and I got a summons from the Admiralty to go to 780 Squadron at Lee-on-Solent and convert back onto bi-planes. I was just about completing my course when suddenly the Admiralty intervened again. They sent me up to Oxford to do my final degree without any preparation at all. All I can say is the examiners were very kind.

I was next posted to the Royal Naval Air Station in Nairobi in Kenya. I was then switched from Nairobi down to the hot and sweaty coast to a place called Tanga, where we occupied the former Nazi headquarters and other buildings in the town, as we were waiting for the completion of a camp suitably dispersed for its protection against enemy aircraft. It was to be up amongst the jungle and the coconut palms, amongst which the grass runways had already been created.

We had three doctors; I was the senior one. I took the local hospital section of the medical work, looking after the hospital patients, while my mates did the work up in the camp. I used to borrow squadron aeroplanes to take anybody who required treatment in the bigger hospital up in Mombasa, and sometimes collect patients from the naval aerodrome.

It was a nice run up and down the coast and occasionally I was having to fly up and down through the intertropical front in the course of it all. Of course not only patients came in the Albacores or Swordfish. I remember one Christmas my logbook shows that I transported three sucking-pigs in my other cockpit. These were for the Christmas dinner in the wardroom.

In time I was also able to fly the Walrus. That was an interesting one. We had a pilot for the air-sea rescue work for that Walrus, but he got very fed up with everything and wouldn't fly the weekly test flights just to see that the thing was still working, so I volunteered to do that. I had a great time cavorting around the harbour landing on the water and coming back to the aerodrome. Of course one had to be very careful to remember whether one's wheels were up or down. It was an amphibian and looked very strange flying off an aerodrome.

The other thing that I remember about the flying there was when we had a problem about night flying. We also had a problem about late morning 'dummy-deck landings', which meant that you fly along and land on the runway as if it's the back end of a carrier. At the beginning of the runway was the 'batsman' waving you up or down so as to tell you whether you were on the right angle of approach for landing on. Some of the chaps were making very bad landings just before lunch-time, so I went up and did a few myself. I found it was because the sun was glinting off the grass behind the batsman at that angle of incidence just about that time of day. The pilots were dazzled and prevented from seeing the batsman properly, so they were not obeying the batsman and were bashing the aeroplanes. That was easily solved, but another problem, the night flying one, was not so easily solved. In the end I had to fly an Albacore full of young midshipmen and sub lieutenants, which they thought was a bit odd – that the doctor should be flying and they should be passengers –down to Dar es Salaam, where there was an eye specialist, and he found that they had the beginnings of a rather unpleasant tropical eye disease. But the really diverting part of that trip was that the moment I finished taxiing up onto the tarmac at Dar es Salaam and stopped the propeller out from the gun ports came a whole swarm of tropical bees which had been taking passage with us. They had nested inside the aeroplane and I had been carrying far more passengers than I had expected, and very lethal ones.

The malaria problem was frightful. Hyper-endemic means that you have more than one expectation of a fresh infection with malignant malaria each year, and although the local civil servants scoffed at my insisting on making sailors wear long trousers after dark and doing all sorts of other things to try to stop it, they said, 'Take no notice of that, it doesn't matter, look at us; we are all right,' most of them were dead by the time I left East Africa –blackwater fever. This was a very dangerous thing and when the order came from the Captain that we were to move the whole affair up into the new buildings up in the jungle, which were not finished, I thought this was an extraordinarily dangerous thing to do and I put in a request to be relieved because I was being put into a situation I was not prepared to take responsibility for.

In due course I was relieved and went to Mombasa, where I did a bit of useful flying for the anti-aircraft gunners, letting them practice trying to get their sights on me in an old Swordfish from the local general purposes squadron at Port Reitz Aerodrome in Mombasa. When we got to Bombay I did similar things, dive-bombing the Towers of Silence, while the anti-aircraft people tried to register on me.

Then I went on another ship down to Colombo, from where I was appointed to a naval air station 30 miles south called Katakurunda, which was a big aircraft repair establishment.

I took passage back to England in a large P&O liner called the *Strathnaver*. There, after a due piece of leave, I was appointed to the north of Scotland, living in Nissen huts in six feet of snow in winter. It was a hell station, commanded by a captain called Brownrigg who was a great tyrant, an ambitious captain and really quite a bully, calling court martials all the time. I used to be a spare pilot, because we already had a full regular surgeon commander RN. So I used to fly into Inverness sometimes several times a month to fetch deputy-judge advocates for the numerous court martials that took place on the station.

I wasn't by any means sorry when the news of an election came up and my Christmas leave was just in time for me to make enquiries about this. I managed, against considerable competition, to get a hopeless candidature to my old stamping-ground East Woolwich.

After my selection I went north again, but rejoicing, knowing that I was going to be free the moment the general election was announced. Suddenly the word came and I was off. I had the great pleasure of informing some poor wretched surgeon lieutenant of the pleasures which were awaiting him.

VE Day cropped up and we had a lot of celebrations in the Mess at Lee and a lot of thunder-flashes were being let off in the wardroom; stockings were being blown off the Wrens' legs, it was really quite appalling. That was the end of my attention to naval matters for the rest of the summer. I went down to Woolwich and started campaigning. I got some digs in Ebury Street and went down to Woolwich daily. Woolwich was in a terrible state; it had been bombed very badly. I remember I had the longest poster in London, I think it was 78ft, along Plumstead High Street, surrounding a bomb site, exhorting the readers to vote for me and support Winston Churchill.

It was a good-humoured fight and I had the great pleasure of preserving my deposit. It was a long period, not only the campaign up to polling day, but of course we had to wait for all the votes from overseas troops to come back and be counted. And so I came to the end of that particular campaign and the end of the war, which I seemed to have survived after all.

After the war Reginald Bennett remained in the Navy until 1946, working at a psychiatric hospital on the outskirts of Fareham. Although he continued to work in civilian medicine, his political ambitions steered his subsequent career and he was duly elected as the Conservative MP for Gosport and Fareham in 1950.

When Winston Churchill's government was re-elected in 1951, he became Parliamentary Private Secretary to David Maxwell Fyfe, the Home Secretary. He later served as PPS to Geoffrey Lloyd, the Minister of Fuel and Power, and Iain Macleod, at the Ministry of Labour. He was knighted –Sir Reginald Bennett –in 1979. His other main interest was painting and his work has been exhibited at the Royal Academy.

EDWARD DU CANN

Edward du Cann, who was made a Knight Commander of the Order of the British Empire in 1985, was Conservative MP for the Taunton Division of Somerset from 1956–1987. He studied Law at St John's College Oxford, joining the RNVR in 1943. During his time in Parliament, he was both Commodore and Admiral of the House of Commons Yacht Club and, continuing a military connection, he was Honorary Colonel of 155 (Wessex) Regiment RCT (Volunteers) from 1972–1982.

I well remember the day the war began, 3 September 1939. I was with my mother and grandmother at our cottage in Sussex. When Prime Minister Chamberlain finished his mournful broadcast, my mother said, 'Thank God the boys (my younger brother and myself) won't be involved this time.' I had just turned fourteen.

No doubt she had in mind the horrors of the first war in which my father had been an infantry officer in France and Greece. These we were certainly spared, but even the youngest civilians had to endure the bombing which was to come a year later. I put out my share of incendiary bombs. The King was right when he told the nation that same evening that war would not be confined to the battlefields.

When France fell in 1940 Anthony Eden announced the formation of the Local Defence Volunteers in England. I enlisted at once. Later, at Churchill's suggestion, the LDV became the Home Guard, now parodied in the Dad's Army television programmes. It was a deadly serious body at the time. I had learned military discipline and how to shoot in the Officers' Training Corps at school. I was far and away the youngest member of the Home Guard in our village. We planned ambushes, made petrol bombs to throw at tanks and kept a nightly watch for parachutists. All the time I was a member of the Home Guard I never had a weapon.

Living within twenty miles of the south coast, we expected invasion at any time in the late summer and autumn of 1940. The Battle of Britain was being fought in the skies overhead. I sewed a sharp knife into the lining of my raincoat and just prayed that I would never be expected to use it. Looking back on those days it was pitiful to think that we local volunteers believed we might have had some military success in defending our homes. But the spirit was there. That is undoubted and Churchill's broadcasts confirmed it.

As early as I could I put my name down for the Royal Navy and eventually I was called up in April 1943 as a naval airman, second class. (There are only two classes). I spent fourteen months on the lower deck, did some sea time in an aircraft carrier, in a training cruiser and across the Atlantic and back in troopships. I was promoted to able seaman which meant a rise of threepence a day in pay. I was commissioned in June 1944, shortly after the Allied landings in France. I volunteered to serve in MTBs and I am happy to say that my wish was granted.

The boats in which I served in the Channel and the North Sea were based on the east coast port of Great Yarmouth, then in Ostend in Belgium. The roles of MTBs and MGBs were both defensive and offensive. We protected the inshore convoy routes against attack by E-boats and the like and we made forays to the coasts still occupied by the Germans. MTBs were also involved in clandestine operations and mine laying. We were always busy and, though the boats were manned overwhelmingly by volunteer seamen we were extremely efficient and effective. Coastal forces were credited with taking part in over 1000 actions worldwide and sinking some 500 enemy vessels. Most of those actions, as in olden times, were fought at close quarters.

At the end of the war my flotilla went up to Shetland. From there we sailed to Norway. We were the first British forces to arrive in our area and take the surrender of the Germans. It was a wonderful moment when we were greeted by the brave Norwegian people who had endured so much. The war was over, but we had casualties nonetheless.

Looking back, I rejoice at the friendships I made in those days. Sometimes our paths crossed after I was elected to Parliament. Tim

Bligh, who had a most distinguished time in the Mediterranean with MTBs before his equally distinguished career in the Civil Service, was one such: Bobby Allan, an MP who also was highly decorated for his leadership on the Mediterranean, was another: Alan Lennox Boyd was a third: David James, the eccentric MP for Brighton, was a fourth. David's MTB was sunk in an action in the English Channel. Rescued, he escaped from prison camp disguised as an officer in the Bulgarian Navy, his papers made out in the name of I. Buggeroff.

Many of my pals, alas, have now fallen off their perches, but some, happily, still endure. I spent three and a half years in the Navy and was lucky before I was demobilized to have command of an MTB. It must be the most marvellous experience in the world to be the Captain of a sea-going warship, even if it was not the largest one afloat.

It all seems like yesterday. Now, if one dresses for a formal occasion and medals are worn, it seems extraordinary to observe how many other guests have lacked the formative experiences that my contemporaries and I had. It is paradoxical to me that my late mother, who was Civil Defence Officer for the county of London in the Red Cross during the war, sleeping night after night underground in the tube stations and working all day, had fewer ribbons to show than me; my military service, even if proud, was short and undistinguished.

There is a postscript. It was wonderful to be elected to Parliament in 1956 and find myself on the same benches as Churchill and Eden. It was not so wonderful to find myself subject again to a military discipline through the Conservative Whips' office. They were all ex-Army men. And yet, maybe my party has lately suffered from a lack of the discipline and loyalties which my generation took for granted as a necessary part of daily life: and maybe our nation does also.

JAMES WELLBELOVED

James Wellbeloved was Labour MP for Erith and Crayford from 1965–1981, after which date he represented the same constituency for the SDP until 1983. He served in the Royal Navy from 1942–1946.

The outbreak of the Second World War had an early effect on me as a 13-year-old schoolboy, most of my schoolmates were evacuated from London to the countryside. For those of us who remained at home school became a half-day experience. It was a few years later before I commenced my military service as a boy seaman in the Royal Navy.

In the intervening period I acted as an ARP messenger and was on the scene of a number of air raid incidents rushing around on my bicycle with messages for the emergency services whenever bombing disrupted the telephone system. I have an abiding memory of acts of bravery by the men and women who served in the ARP, Fire, Ambulance & Police Services, heavy rescue squads and many other civilian wartime organizations. They were the unsung heroes who fought on the home front, received few medals but probably saw more enemy action than many who served in the armed forces.

I was inducted into the RN at HMS *Royal Arthur*, the former Butlin's holiday camp at Skegness. Now clad in naval uniform in place of my old ARP uniform, it was a little ironic that one of my earliest military jobs was to patrol around the flat roof of a huge building on fire-watching duty armed with a stirrup pump and a bucket of sand.

Basic training completed, I moved on to HMS *Cabot* based on Wetherby Race Course. Physical training consisted among other things of a daily run around the racecourse. Here ill fortune combined with good fortune. I caught a cold running around the racecourse that developed into a mild bout of pneumonia with the result I missed most of the square bashing. On my return to duty I joined my group for the passing out parade and in the time-honoured language of the Navy I was declared 'fit in all respects to proceed to sea.'

After various short postings, I eventually received a draft to an LST (Landing Ship Tanks), which was to be my home for the next couple of years and to be my first taste of active military service – the D-Day landings, then continuous voyages, sailing back and forth from Britain to Normandy with troops and equipment. In the early stages of the Normandy invasion we carried wounded men back from the beachhead, their stretchers laid out in the tank hold –sights and sounds that ended forever any lingering thoughts about the 'glory of war'. We next had the task of carrying German PoWs across the Channel. After our previous experience with our own wounded troops, we could not summon up much compassion for the PoWs.

Then it was off to the Far East: Christmas 1944 was spent at sea. One of the problems of flat-bottomed LSTs is that they roll wildly from side to side as well as being tossed up and down in heavy seas, making the journey a somewhat uncomfortable experience.

Soon after arriving at our area of operations we were busy carrying soldiers of the British and Indian Armies to various locations. For a young lad it was an interesting and exciting time – foreign ports, strange sights and a mix of cultures. We were among the first LSTs to reach Rangoon. Remnants of the Jap Army were still fighting in parts of the city. Our own guns picked off a sniper lurking in the cab of a dockside crane.

Now the war was over, our last duty was to ferry British PoWs from Changi Jail to India. I remember, when we first entered Singapore harbour, we virtually emptied our stock of food to send ashore for the released prisoners and detainees.

I returned home as a passenger on board a Royal Navy cruiser. It made me realize how lucky I had been to serve my sea-going days in a small ship among a compact band of brothers in arms.

Having joined the Royal Navy as a boy seaman I remained a lower deck rating until my demob in June 1946. Experience gained during the war, first as a civilian on the home front, then as a seaman in a fighting ship, served me well in the years that lay ahead. Recollections of those momentous days were of great value to me as an MP and eventually as a Minister at the Department of Defence.

JAMES DAVIDSON

Another very young wartime seaman was James Davidson, who served in the Royal Navy from 1944–1955. During his later political life he was Liberal MP for West Aberdeenshire from 1966–1970.

I was twelve years old when war was declared in September 1939. If I had been told that six years later I would be sailing into Tokyo harbour to celebrate the surrender of the Japanese, at the end of a war which had enveloped the whole world, I would have been lost between astonishment and disbelief.

My father, who was on the Royal Navy's retired list, working as personnel manager of an engineering firm, found himself recalled to command a flotilla of ancient sloops escorting convoys between the estuaries of the Thames and the Tyne. My mother, my sisters and I were invited to an aunt's house in the depths of rural Sussex –a house which was to be straddled more than once by incendiary and high explosive bombs over the next few years. Occasionally we saw my father between convoys.

From my grandmother's garden in Nairn I had watched the Royal Navy's graceful but doomed battlecruisers *Hood*, *Repulse* and *Renown* emerging from the Cromarty Firth; I had been taken to see one of the earliest colour films, *Sons of the Sea*, in which an heroic naval cadet tore around the Devon countryside in a red sports car with a beautiful long-haired blonde; I had met a naval cadet, in the flesh, who carried a service gasmask (not one of those silly little civilian ones like a Box Brownie camera) and a tin hat; my father was at sea; what else could I do but join the Royal Navy?

I passed the written and medical examinations, weathered the

41

fearsome interview before a tableful of admirals, and in September 1940 found myself, a small 13-year-old in naval cadet's uniform, en route to the Royal Naval College, Dartmouth. My mother took me to London. In the suburbs the air-raid sirens sounded, the train was emptied and the passengers trooped into an air-raid shelter. We heard bombs drop, one close enough to shake dust and crumbs of cement from the roof. In the silence which followed my mother made an announcement to the motley crowd packed into the dim shelter: 'My son's just joined the Navy!' Amid the embarrassed titters which accompanied a release from tension I wished the last bomb had scored a direct hit.

Three and a half years –eleven terms –at the Royal Naval College passed swiftly: two years at Dartmouth where we were formed into a Home Guard unit armed with grenades, rifles and bayonets –shades of that horrific scene in the film *Dr Zhivago* where a line of uniformed children from a military school is mown down by Bolshevik machine guns. Senior cadets manned anti-aircraft weapons, but in September 1942 the college was bombed just before we returned from summer leave. We spent two terms in Muller's Orphanage in a dingy part of Bristol; the final year at Eaton Hall, Chester, seat of the Duke of Westminster, the atmosphere enhanced by Wren stewardesses who had miraculously taken the place of hoary old pensioners.

Early in April 1944, aged seventeen and three months, I joined the battleship *Anson* at Scapa Flow. Patrols in the North Atlantic failed to draw any response from the German Navy. My action station was in the TS (Transmitting Station) where an elementary computer controlled the guns from deep in the bowels of the ship beneath three layers of armoured deck sealed by watertight doors. I wondered why, when a certain cruiser put to sea, sailors in other ships lined the guardrails and bleated like sheep. Later I learned that a desperate sailor from that ship had been court-martialled for bestiality: his defence –he thought the sheep was a Wren in a fur coat.

When the older ships went south to cover the D-Day landings, to our intense disappointment *Anson* and the more modern ships patrolled in the north to prevent enemy ships emerging from the Baltic or the Norwegian fjords. When the Army was well-established in France, *Anson* went into dock to re-fit for the Pacific. I and other midshipmen were transferred to the cruiser *Newfoundland* in the Clyde, about to sail east to join the British Pacific Fleet. On leave before we departed I watched buzz-bombs and V2s streaming towards London. The engine of one cut out overhead and I watched it dive onto a golf course a quarter of a mile away and explode – by evil chance in the middle of a camp of Canadian soldiers waiting to embark for France.

Newfoundland finished her 'work-up' off Alexandria after crossing the Mediterranean unescorted, at high speed to outstrip U-boats, in the second worst storm I was ever in at sea: welded ladders torn off, butterfly nuts on watertight hatches sheared, the anti-aircraft gun-deck slightly distorted. While the damage was being repaired I and another midshipman volunteered to replace two RNVR sub lieutenants, both overdue for leave, as first lieutenants of two 'special service' motor launches: an exciting voyage through the Aegean, landing mysterious officers with maps printed on finest silk screwed into their uniform buttons, in the dark on German-occupied islands.

Before we left Alexandria, Pacific bound, *Newfoundland* entered a team for the Sporting Club of Alexandria rugby seven-a-sides. The whole South African Army had remained in North Africa when the British, other Commonwealth and American Armies went into Europe by way of Sicily. In the semi-finals we drew with the South African Army 'A' side and were only beaten in extra time. Never, before or since, have I been subjected to such vicious barracking from the touch-line. I am (still) glad to report that the South African seven was beaten in the final by 'Sporting Club of Alexandria' – a hotch-potch of British internationals and top club players. Before we sailed I heard with great sadness that my first cousin Duncan, a Cameron Highlander, had been killed leading a patrol in Burma – shot in the back by a Japanese sniper.

Newfoundland arrived in Sydney harbour on the wettest day in forty years. Our commander (executive officer), who was later sent home from Manus, the forward base in the Admiralty Islands (we assumed for incompetence), kept the ship's company at attention on the upper deck as we entered harbour, blanco streaming from the sailors' caps down their faces, while khaki-clad ratings on board Australian ships stood under shelter and hooted with derision.

We went on to work with ships of the Australian and US navies, covering landings and bombarding Japanese bases in the Marianas, Carolines and other archipelagos. While covering an Australian landing at Wewak in New Guinea I suffered permanent damage to the hearing of my left ear when a gun was fired without warning, blasting me ten yards across the deck. Later we escorted the carriers while their aircraft attacked the Japanese mainland. We were off Okinawa when the first atomic bomb was dropped. I and all those I talked with were horrified. We were convinced at the time that we already had the Japs well beaten.

Then the glorious entry into Tokyo harbour on VJ Day: never in history had such a huge and powerful fleet been assembled as that combined fleet of the United States, Britain and the Commonwealth. The sky swarmed with Allied aircraft. We stared without pity at Japanese sailors, sitting hunched on the decks of their ships, heads between their knees, hands clasped behind their necks, the guns of the Allied armada trained contemptuously on them.

I returned home on a troopship to start my sub lieutenants' technical courses. More than half my fellow-passengers had spent their war in Japanese PoW camps –men and women, civilians and armed forces. The assorted sounds of protest and terror, at night in the vast dormitories of tiered bunks, were eerie. By day the ex-prisoners were cheerful. I learnt just a little of that side of war where horror, humiliation and deprivation take the place of excitement, expectation and revenge.

NORMAN WYLIE

Norman Wylie was the Conservative MP for the Pentlands Division of Edinburgh between 1964–1974. In 1941, while a member of the Glasgow University Air Squadron, he volunteered for air crew duties with the Fleet Air Arm, which held out the prospect of a commission, and: 'to be frank, with the reported casualties on the bombing raids on Germany, which were beginning to take shape, and for which we were obviously being trained, I had come to the conclusion that the RAF was a somewhat dangerous occupation.' In any event, after an interview in Edinburgh, he was duly accepted and accordingly entered the Royal Navy in April 1942. After numerous courses he was appointed midshipman on 3 September 1943 and on his 20th birthday, 26 October 1943, he was duly promoted to the acting rank of sub lieutenant RNVR.

It took a further period of six months or so to complete his training as an observer, finally passing out of an operational training unit along with his pilot on Swordfish aircraft, and together they were appointed to RN Air Squadron 811. Their first ship, the escort carrier HMS *Biter,* took them to sea on the Atlantic convoys and to Gibraltar.

It was early days and, apart from one aircraft which ditched and the crew rescued from life-rafts, we sustained no losses. *Biter* had to undergo a refit and we therefore went ashore to operate with RAF Coastal Command, hunting for U-boats off the Irish coast from bases in Maydown and RAF Limavady in Northern Ireland. It was at this point that our luck ran out. The squadron was sent to the carrier *Vindex* on a Russian convoy to replace 825 Squadron which required a rest from these arduous and undoubtedly dangerous duties.

The Squadron joined the ship from Hatston in the Orkney Islands and in the course of about a week proceeded to Kola Inlet, near Archangel. Much has been written about these convoys which travelled in almost constant darkness in winter and were subjected to attacks from U-boats and Ju 88 torpedo bombers operating out of bases in German-occupied Norway. The trouble usually began on the second day out from Scapa Flow when we would be picked up by a German Condor aircraft which in due course reported our position, course and speed: we could usually expect an air attack that night. There was one instance in which the senior officer of the escort flashed to the orbiting Condor that he was making him dizzy and received the humorous reply, in English, 'Sorry, anything to oblige', after which the Condor promptly turned around and proceeded to orbit in the opposite direction.

The carrier force was usually well protected in the centre of the convoy. My own experience was, I shall never forget, the ordeal of night flying: taking off from a small deck, doing a 'Cobra' patrol – going round and round the convoy at a range of some twenty miles for two to two and a half hours – and then finally returning to the ship, to face the final ordeal of 'landing on' the same small heaving deck and engaging the arrester wire. On our second trip we lost twenty per cent of our crews who failed to make the landing and went over the side of the ship and were lost. The squadron was somewhat demoralized after this trip and was disbanded.

I remained with my pilot, Sub Lieutenant Charlie Gough, for my next appointment with 835 Squadron to the carrier HMS *Nairana* in January 1945. We again picked up the ship at Hatston. In order to keep up morale, we were required to take part in a shipping strike as part of a naval task force of three carriers, a cruiser and numerous destroyers. We carried bombs on this occasion – heavier than our normal depth charges – and in order to get off the deck we made use of a new device known as 'rocket-assisted take-off gear' which gave us a four-second boost after which we then sank down over the bows of the ship. I remember looking back at the ship which seemed to tower above us and I wondered if we were going to make it. We did of course and then flew low towards the Norwegian coast to avoid radar detection and then climbed up to operational height and up the fjords in search of enemy shipping. I recall that the anti-aircraft fire which greeted us at the mouth of the fjord gave the impression of being like fairy lights at a Christmas party: I could hear the hisses as some of the fire came uncomfortably close. Fortunately on this occasion we sustained no casualties, but had to return to the task force using radar and land on *Nairana* again. We attacked a gun emplacement at the mouth of the fjord but I very much doubt if we did any damage. This time, on reaching Kola Inlet, we were informed that on no account were we to try our hands at skiing, since our past performances had been so bad that we had eroded Britain's standing among the local Russians!

The third Russian convoy was as usual. We were severely attacked by U-boats and Ju 88s. Several ships were sunk on the way back to Scapa Flow and we had to act like shepherd dogs bringing together the ships which had become split up in the appalling weather. I recall flashing a merchantman which had been attacked by torpedo bombers and was sinking that help was on its way, but whether it reached them in time I very much doubt. At what was to be the final squadron reunion recently, we had as our guest a German Luftwaffe officer who had taken part in one of these attacks. He gave an account of the attack in a most effective manner and was given a standing ovation.

Unfortunately I became ill on this occasion with rheumatic fever and on return to Scapa Flow was invalided off the ship and spent three exceedingly pleasant months at a naval hospital near Aberdeen. The end of the war in Europe occurred during this period.

I considered myself fortunate to have survived and I was fortunate to have had the skill of an exceptionally able pilot through the years of my active service. One slip on his part in the difficult task of 'landing on' would have been fatal for us both. We still keep in contact. There was no question of the carrier stopping to recover crews who had gone over the side, for obvious reasons, and rescue if possible was left to the attendant frigate or destroyer. I know of only one instance in which this happened, in the Bay of Biscay in daylight. Unfortunately the crew which was rescued on this occasion was lost on the Russian convoy that followed.

After his period in hospital, Norman Wylie was sent on leave until September 1945. He was then posted as an instructor with the rank

of lieutenant to the Observer Training School in Arbroath, and thereafter to the School of Naval Air Warfare at St Merryn in Cornwall
until April 1946, when he was finally demobilized. He was later
elevated to the peerage as Lord Wylie and served as Lord Advocate
between 1970–1974.

JOHN SMITH

Old Etonian John Smith was Conservative MP for the Cities of London and Westminster from 1965–1970 and was knighted in 1988. He also served with the Fleet Air Arm and had a somewhat varied and unusual war, perhaps the most significant aspect of which was his part in dive-bombing the German battleship *Tirpitz*.

I joined up on Hitler's birthday in 1942. My father and uncles had been regular soldiers, but I liked the idea of sea and air, so chose the Fleet Air Arm instead. Our training began at a big, handsome eighteenth century barracks in Gosport, now of course demolished, where we learnt about ropes, boats, field training, sea navigation, and other things considered useful in the air. Then we went on courses in gunnery, signals, and finally flying. It felt strange in the cockpit wearing bell-bottomed trousers and a square sailor's collar under one's flying overalls. After eleven educative, enjoyable and carefree months on the 'lower deck' I was commissioned as a midshipman and sent to Machrihanish at the end of the Kintyre peninsula in south-west Scotland. Here in beautiful surroundings but vile weather we learnt how to operate at night, dropping torpedoes or depth charges from very low level – an alarming business which killed several of us.

After that I joined a Swordfish squadron, based at first in Gibraltar and then in Algeria, where we escorted convoys. It was very pleasant flying, in the sunshine, in the open cockpit of these robust, dependable aircraft; and remarkable to see how much the French colonists had improved the country. Then, after a spell in Tunisia, I joined a squadron in Malta, just before the end of the

49

'siege' of the island. Flying in from the south for the first time, Malta, laid on the blue sea, looked like a piece of a jigsaw puzzle, as indeed strategically it was. One had a feeling of being at the centre of great events; but the damage done by air raids to Valletta's beautiful stone buildings was most distressing; they just fell to pieces in clouds of dust.

When the invasion of Sicily looked like succeeding I was sent off there in a landing craft to prepare a base for our aircraft at Castelvetrano in the west of the island. The poverty of the Sicilians was extraordinary; hardly a house in the countryside had glass in the windows and all transport was by those highly-painted carts which are now museum pieces. However, after the surrender of the Italians the Fleet Air Arm was no longer required in that part of the world and I was sent back to England in a Flower class corvette escorting a convoy from Gibraltar, an experience I am glad to have had. Our course lay far out into the Atlantic, where huge seas would sweep right over the hull of the ship so that the open bridge just felt like a small square platform stuck in the ocean. When we were in the trough of a wave even the closest ship was invisible. As soon as we came within their range, one of the big Focke-Wulf Condors from occupied France would always be circling the convoy, paying no attention to our four-inch gun and doubtless signalling our position to the submarines. However, all of us, even the laggards, got home safely.

I was next sent as a liaison officer to the Ninth US Air Force, based in England. Part of my job was to help their aircrews to distinguish Allied warships from German ones before releasing their bombs. At the age of 20 it was a real education to serve with the Americans. They were positive, open-minded and brave. Whatever was asked of them, they tried to find a way to do it. They were also ingenious. At the headquarters where I was based a member of the map-making unit used its sophisticated American equipment to print a supply of the black and white £5 notes then in circulation here.

In early 1944 I did a conversion course onto the Barracuda, a most unsatisfactory aircraft which had taken the place of the Fleet Air Arm's biplanes. Equipped with this treacherous and ungainly machine, we next rehearsed for some weeks an attack on the German battleship *Tirpitz,* at that time holed up in Alten Fjord, in the far north of Norway, beyond the Arctic Circle. A flat target, the full size of the ship, was built for us offshore in Loch Eriboll, on the north coast of Scotland, and this we dive-bombed almost daily, operating at first from an airfield in the Orkneys, and then from the big aircraft carriers based on Scapa Flow. Finally our fleet of three carriers, four cruisers, a battleship (*Duke of York*) and a destroyer screen, set off northwards at speed –a fine sight –for the operation itself.

We had to attack the ship in daylight –at that time of the year there was no darkness in those latitudes –and since she lay at the head of the fjord, forty miles inland, there was also no question of surprise. She was the most beautiful ship, like a castle of steel – and well defended; in the course of our approach my aircraft was hit three times by flak. Each Barracuda carried a single armour-piercing bomb, slung underneath, with a long shiny steel nose sharpened to a point, like a 3H pencil. Having released this at the bottom of our dive, with what effect I know not, we fled away at sea level along the fjord. Although it was two o'clock in the morning many Norwegians living on the edge of the water, and doubtless woken up by the explosions, had put out in small boats to wave to us, which was very heartening –for them too, I hope. When we had landed back on our aircraft carrier a jagged piece of anti-aircraft shell was found lodged in my seat; it must have run out of steam just before reaching my bottom. I kept it for a time, but it seemed to lack whatever quality souvenirs need, so in the end I threw it away.

I was next sent out to the Indian Ocean where, in Ceylon, we did a further conversion course, to American aircraft –Avengers, greatly superior to the British Barracudas –and then operated mostly off the coast of Malaya and Sumatra, flying from 'Woolworth' carriers provided by the Americans. These were built up on merchant ship hulls and seemed to be made of little more than silver paper. On one occasion our carrier broke down and we were towed off the scene by the cruiser *Cleopatra,* whose Marine band struck up with 'Wings over the Navy' as she did so. We were at sea, about to bomb Penang, to which we did not look forward, when the first atom bomb was dropped and our operation was cancelled –thus, I quite expect, saving my life, as well as the lives of many others, a thought which colours my view of that gruesome event. Our ship was returned almost at once to the Americans so, as I had a minor scholastic award, I was released, and became an undergraduate at Oxford, where, after these wartime experiences, we were not allowed out after dark unless we were wearing a gown, and could not 'visit licensed premises' unless we were also having a meal – nor 'take instruction in dancing except from teachers licensed by the Proctors'. So we realized that everything was back to normal.

Part Two

THE CAVALRY

By the start of the Second World War the role and make-up of the British cavalry had changed quite considerably. Seldom using horses, although in places like Palestine they were still in some evidence, most cavalry regiments had replaced their mounts with some form of armour. The section also includes the yeomanry regiments, who before the war were reservists, descended from local cavalry units which had also been converted into armoured regiments. Having said that, many yeomanry regiments also worked in other areas, notably as signallers and gunners, but these are noted elsewhere.

JOHN PEYTON

John Peyton was both a minister in Edward Heath's government and a member of Margaret Thatcher's shadow cabinet. He was born in 1919 and went up to Oxford, Trinity College, in 1937 to read law. In the summer of 1939 he applied for and received a commission in the supplementary reserve of the 15th/19th Hussars. He joined the regiment for a two months' attachment in York, where they had already been equipped with Mark VIB light tanks and carriers: the regiment had still employed horses up until a year before. However, his two months' attachment suddenly became full time as war was declared.

In due course he was sent to join 54 Armoured Training Regiment at Perham Down, near Tidworth in Hampshire. At the start, there was very little to do, in terms of organized training: there were no tanks to train with anyway. Eventually he attended a driving and maintenance course at Bovington, a gunnery course at Lulworth and an intelligence course at Aldershot. In March 1940 he was considered fit to join his regiment in France. After a week or so in tents at Pacy, he rejoined the regiment near Lille.

On 10 May 1940 the Germans began their attack and the regiment moved into Belgium, where they were met at the border by cheering crowds who draped their vehicles with lilac. However, as they moved forward to face the enemy, there was a sense of bewilderment among the troops: there had been no time to prepare for such an operation and they had no idea of what they were expected to achieve, or how they would go about achieving it.

As the Germans continued their advance and the British began to pull back, the regiment was transferred to the 4th Division to provide cover. Eventually, with the bridge over the River Dendre in German hands, they found themselves cut off. John Peyton was sent by his commanding officer to inform 'C' Squadron of the situation and to see if they could cross the river at Liederkirk. From there he went to look at the bridges in the area to see if any of them were not in enemy hands yet. On the way he met a troop leader in his regiment and took a ride on the back of his carrier. Suddenly, as they entered a small town, they came under fire and the officer was killed instantly. John Peyton returned to 'C' Squadron in haste, but found confusion all around him. Joining others, he took shelter in a cornfield, and then a pig-sty. Before long, swarms of Germans appeared and they were taken prisoner.

Initially he was taken to the Grenadier Barracks in Brussels. The prisoners were then marched eastwards through Tirlemont to Maastricht. They were then taken by train to Bocholt in Germany, where the school had been turned into a prison. Next they were taken south by train again to Laufen in Bavaria, close to the Austrian border, where they were given numbers, photographed and had their heads shaved. John Peyton was put into a room of 117, who slept on straw palliasses on top of wooden slats in three-layered bunks. In the opening months of his captivity rations were meagre, but after a while food parcels began to arrive. Later, letters, clothes, food, cigarettes and books were sent from home, via the Red Cross.

From the time of his arrival at Laufen he dreamed of escape, but his first real chance came towards the end of 1941 when he was moved to a camp at Warburg in Westphalia. The hut in which he lived was about thirty yards from the wire. There was a corridor down the middle of the hut with six rooms on either side, inhabited by twelve people in each. At either end of the corridor were rooms where the more senior officers slept: among them was Douglas Bader.

Although the hut was some distance from the wire and a tunnel had already been started from another hut closer to the perimeter, John Peyton, with a group of subalterns obtained permission from the necessary authorities in the camp to start digging. The colonel in charge of the first tunnel was hostile towards their plan: his own tunnel collapsed shortly afterwards because it was too near to the surface.

By the time they had finished it, the second tunnel was eighty-five yards long and just wide enough to crawl through. At intervals of about twenty yards, there were chambers where men hauled bags of earth piled on small home-made sledges. The chambers were lit using a current from a home-made cable of copper-coated wire, taken from Red Cross parcels, which had been covered with pitch. Air was pumped into the tunnel through a pipe made from empty tin cans, which had originally contained Canadian milk powder.

The tunnel was entered through a hatch in the corner of John Peyton's room, which was regularly inspected by the Germans. On one occasion they removed every piece of furniture from the room, but still found nothing. Luckily, the prisoners had taken the added precaution of screwing the hatch down, due to the fact that it was someone's birthday and they had taken a few days off from their digging.

As their hut was built on legs, the hatch in the room was only the start of a complicated series of openings. Having climbed through this hatch into the space beneath the hut, diggers would have to crawl over the soft earth to where another hatch concealed a twelve- to fifteen-foot shaft, which in turn descended to where the tunnel itself started. On occasion the Germans would themselves crawl beneath the huts prodding the earth with bayonets, looking for any signs of tunnelling.

All of their tunnelling equipment and escaping gear was stored in the roof of their hut. One day a similar store was discovered in another hut at the other end of the camp. Within two hours, John Peyton and his friends had moved everything into the tunnel itself, so that by the time the Germans arrived to inspect the roof of their hut all evidence had vanished.

Eventually their digging took them to about fifty yards beyond the wire, where they broke surface in a cornfield. As they planned their escape, by a cruel turn of luck, one of the Germans prodding about beneath the hut with his bayonet discovered the outlet of the air pipe.

It was a weekend and the Germans didn't want to waste a lot of time looking for the entrance to the tunnel. Instead, they dragged a few of the inhabitants of the hut, including Desmond Llewelyn, who later became famous as 'Q' in the James Bond movies, off to solitary confinement. Next, they dug a trench, intersecting the tunnel, and filled it with raw sewage from the nearby latrines.

The Germans had discovered the tunnel in the spring of 1942. In the late summer of 1942 they were moved to another camp at Eichstatt in Bavaria. Conditions at the camp were slightly better than at other locations, but, following the discovery by Hitler that German soldiers captured during a raid on Alderney and Sark had been temporarily handcuffed, it was decided that a number of British PoWs, which included John Peyton, would receive the same treatment. These prisoners were handcuffed all day long, and their bonds only removed at lights out. At the camp, John Peyton was able to continue his study of law, but his shackles made life somewhat uncomfortable. Several of his fellow prisoners had been highly qualified before the war, including an academic lawyer of distinction, from Trinity College, Cambridge. Through the help of the Red Cross, it was possible to obtain the examination papers for the Bar and other professions. It wasn't long, however, before the 100 prisoners who had been handcuffed had learnt how to remove their bonds and, without the Germans realizing it, other prisoners took turns at being handcuffed, which allowed students to carry on with their studies.

Early in the spring of 1945 the order came that all PoWs were to be moved, on foot, to somewhere south of the Danube. Tragedy marked the start of the march, as Allied fighter aircraft strafed the column shortly after leaving the camp, assuming it to be a German formation, and several prisoners were killed.

The march took about a week, moving mostly by night, until they eventually arrived at Moosburg, where there was a huge camp, containing prisoners from many Allied nations. Suddenly the Germans disappeared and the Americans –including General Patton –arrived at the camp.

John Peyton arrived back in England in a Lancaster bomber, just as the bonfires for VE Day were being lit, after five years as a prisoner of war.

Still in the Army, he became a staff captain in HQ Western Command, Chester. Then, in 1946, as the new Labour government set about the ending of British rule in India, he inquired after a position in the chambers of Walter Monckton, who was the Constitutional Advisor to His Exalted Highness the Nizam of Hyderabad and Berar. Monckton asked him to accompany him as his personal assistant and the Army allowed him to go to India, leaving his demob formalities for when he returned.

John Peyton was Conservative MP for Yeovil in Somerset, from 1951–1983, when he was made a Life Peer (Lord Peyton of Yeovil). He became Minister of Transport in 1970, and perhaps his most famous legacy to the nation was the instigation of the compulsory use of seat belts.

ANTHONY KERSHAW

In September 1939 Anthony Kershaw had just qualified as a barrister and got married. He immediately enlisted with the 16th/5th Lancers and was awarded the MC in 1943. He was Conservative MP for the Stroud Division of Gloucestershire from 1955–1987 and was made a Knight in 1981.

A few days before the outbreak of war I met General Sir Hubert de la Poer Gough. Our generals normally come in two sizes. One big and bluff and the other small and terrier-like. He was a terrier. He had commanded the Fifth Army in 1918 when it was overrun by Ludendorff's offensive. Goughie (as he was known in the Army) was sacked. It was in fact entirely Lloyd George's fault. He had disregarded Goughie's warnings about his too long front and lack of ammunition. But Lloyd George was not a man to take blame if he could find someone else to take it.

Goughie said to me when I met him, 'What are you going to do in the war?' I said that I would like to join the Army. 'Good,' he said. 'Join my regiment.' Shyly, I said 'What one is that?' as I had no military experience. '16th/5th Lancers, of course', he said. So obviously I said yes. In due course, in May 1940, I was commissioned into that regiment. I had a postcard from him the following day which read, 'Glad to hear you have joined the Regiment. Ride straight, ride hard, watch your flanks and you will be all right.' Six years later I met him again. He knew exactly who I was, what I had done in the war and what I was doing after the war. Perhaps I make him sound rather a Blimp; in fact, he was one of our best generals in the First World War and everybody who served with him admired him deeply.

So I joined the 16th/5th Lancers. In May 1940 they had just arrived back from India leaving their horses there. We were sent from Colchester to the South Downs to defend against invasion. Our equipment was some Austin 10 motor cars; all the officers had to drive because we did not have enough other ranks who knew how to. Our armaments were rifles and, for officers who wanted to buy one, a pistol. So we sat on top of the hills waiting for the invasion. Sitting there one evening as darkness fell, I heard one of Winston Churchill's unforgettable speeches, 'We shall fight on the beaches, we shall fight in the hills', etc., and there I was, sitting on one of the hills. I understand that when the microphone was switched off after that speech Winston was heard to mutter, 'I don't know what with. Beer bottles, I suppose.' I at least had a pistol.

After a time we were located near Cambridge and on 22 June 1941, just before lunch in the Officers' Mess, we listened to the 1 o'clock news. 'This is the BBC at 1 o'clock. This is the news and this is Stewart Hibbert reading it. Germany has invaded Russia'. My next door neighbour, an ex Foreign Office man, threw up his hands, upsetting my pink gin, and cried out, 'Thank God, we've won the war'.

In due course we received some tanks and moved away from the south to the Midlands to train. Later still we moved to Scotland, to Ayrshire, whence we were due to sail to North Africa. Ayrshire was a very bad training ground for tanks. The roads were narrow and the bogs were deep. We had an exercise shortly before we sailed. Our Army Commander, First Army, General Anderson, was coming to see us. My tank was on the road and a staff officer came and said, 'The Commander-in-Chief is coming. Get off the road.' I said, 'I will bog if I do.' 'Doesn't matter,' he said. So I got off the road –it was two days before we could get my tank out. The Army Commander was heard to mutter as he left our area, 'First Army; last bloody Army'.

We sailed for North Africa and landed at Algiers and other places along the coast to the east of Algiers. The 17th/21st Lancers, who were in our brigade, rushed off east to try to get to Tunis before the Germans, but the enemy were too quick for us and held us up about 25 miles short of Tunis. Before long the weather deteriorated and tank movements were very difficult. The hills were steep and the mud was deep. It was hard infantry fighting without much help from the tanks. As the weather improved we made several attacks, but without much effect. The terrain was difficult and the Germans well placed. They were basically in a defensive strategy; we did not have enough power to attack them effectively. Then, in the New Year, we heard we would be supplied with new American tanks and we went to Fez to receive them. Only one of our regiments had changed over to the new tanks when, that night, there arrived a super urgent message to go as fast as possible 100 miles south because the American 1st Armoured Division had been almost destroyed by a German attack. So we jumped back into our old tanks and went off as fast as we could.

I was sent on ahead in a scout car. I had no maps. I came across an American tank and stopped him and asked if he had any. 'Sure,' he said, 'I don't want them any more,' and threw a bundle down to me and motored off. I studied a map and decided which way the brigade following me should go. There was a sort of crossroads and I directed them down one of the roads. I was joined by the commander of the Rifle Brigade battalion in our brigade. He studied the map with me after two of our regiments had passed and then turned to me with a wan smile and said, 'Anthony, they have gone the wrong way'. It took me four hours to get to the head of the column and turn it right.

Next day two regiments and the brigade HQ advanced down the road to the south until we came to the edge of the hills. A plain lay before us. In that plain the German 10th Armoured Division was forming up, the guns at the back, the infantry and lorries in the middle, the anti-tank guns on the flank and the tanks in the middle and on the front. We had brigade HQ on the road, 17th/21st Lancers on the right and the Lothian and Border Horse on the left. In support, two troops of 25 pounders. We were about eighty tanks in all.

An American Grant tank, which had a 75 mm gun, came to brigade HQ on the road. We were watching the enemy without doing anything about it. Only the 25 pounders could reach them and we thought we would need the ammunition later. The enemy lined up and at 3 o'clock started to advance. The American tank fired off about twenty 75 mm shells as fast as they could and then turned round and disappeared to the north in a cloud of dust.

It was very like an exercise on Salisbury Plain. We fired away, hull down, until they got too close, then went to the next hill and did the same. We lost tanks all the time because of the heavy armament of the German tanks. We continued to retreat in copybook fashion, inflicting damage but suffering ourselves.

At one point my driver panicked because of the shellfire and he drove my tank as fast as he could out of the battle. Nothing I could say on the intercom would stop him but in the end I managed to do so. I turned him out of the driver's seat into the scrub desert. I never saw or heard of him again. I don't think it was cowardice. I came across other cases in the war. I think it was the concussion of the shells which upset his balance in some way. One of my friends who reacted in this way was a fearless steeplechase jockey.

When I got back to the battle I found the Brigadier's radio had broken, so I had to run between his tank and mine with messages. A bit dangerous but I think that was why they gave me an MC.

As darkness fell we got back to the little village of Thala where the hills narrowed to a pass. During the course of the day a British battalion which had landed only two days before at Algiers had been preparing a defensive position. When I got to them I said, 'I am the last tank. You are not to let anybody through. Put those mines across the road'. I then motored on into our defensive position. By this time it was dark.

Ten minutes after I had passed some more tanks appeared and the commander of the first tank shouted out in good English, 'Take those mines off the road,' and they did. He was a German and a brave one. He and eight or nine more tanks came straight into the position and shot up the trucks which were on the road. They were petrol and ammunition lorries which of course burst into flames. Our tanks – only about twenty of them were left –were in darkness off the road, but the Germans' were illuminated. We knocked them all out. Sitting ducks. Actually, the first tank, which had followed me in, was not particularly damaged, but they had evacuated and run away into the darkness. I climbed into their tank and found they had left the radio on. I was very relieved to hear the Germans' orders coming over the radio to retire and retire at once.

All this of course made a tremendous clamour. Everybody was shooting in every direction without really knowing which way to shoot. When in the end the firing died down we discovered that our infantry battalion had run away, shouting, I understand, 'We are surrounded on three sides,' pursued by their furious officers. They had landed only two days ago. About a company's worth of them returned the next morning commanded by a tremendously fierce officer of whom, I suppose, they were more frightened than they were of the Germans. Later, in Italy, this battalion did its duty well.

As the night went on a full moon rose over the German position to our south. It is always very difficult to be sure of what you see by the light of the moon but we thought we saw movement on the hill. If indeed it was guns or tanks tomorrow morning would be curtains for us. So it was decided that the Lothian and Border Horse, who I think had about twelve tanks left, should drive onto the hill to put pressure on the Germans. The Commanding Officer led. The track was very dusty and the drivers of the following tanks could not see. When the Colonel turned slightly left to get to the best position the others went straight on into the German position. They were all lost.

Next morning to our great relief and surprise there was no sign of the enemy. They had been called back by Rommel to confront the Eighth Army at Medenine. We stayed where we were. The only activity came from an American gunner, strangely uniformed, giving extraordinary curses, with a big cigar in his mouth who walked up and down the road having his guns fire from behind us, and big guns they were too. He told me he had been ordered to retire but he was not going to goddam do it until he had had the chance to shoot those goddam, lousy Krauts. He stayed all morning. I am sure he did not know what he was shooting at, nor did we, but it made a consoling sound. In the end he said he had better obey orders and went off.

Our next battle was near Kairouan. We tried to debouch out of the mountains on to the plain, but the position was well defended until the 16th/5th Lancers found a wadi down the left side and outflanked the guns, which retired. We then swept across the plain which was ablaze with red poppies and the evening sun illuminated the beautiful little city of Kairouan with its mosques and towers. Then we met hills again and stopped.

Our next battle was the last in Tunis. We attacked from due west, after the 6th Battalion Royal West Kents had cleared the start line for us. There was some difficulty with a Tiger Tank, the first we had ever seen. It came over the hill straight at us. My tank commander, the Brigadier, shouted, 'Driver Reverse Left!!' The 88mm gun fired but missed us. Our tanks on our right disabled the Tiger from the flank.

We passed through the south part of Tunis City and came to a little seaside village under a cliff. It was strongly held. The Welsh Guards attempted to scale the cliffs but when they got to the top met heavy machine-gun fire and had to retire. On the left, the 17th/21st Lancers, wading into the sea, managed to turn the position and the German guns retreated rapidly into the dusk. We passed through the village and then stopped as it was almost dark and tanks in the dark are no good.

I became conscious of someone standing on the back of my tank. It was a gentleman in French military uniform who said that he was the brother of the Bey of Tunis and that His Highness, who was in the village behind us, wished to pay his respects to our general. I told my Brigadier, who said, 'Why not? There is nothing happening here'. So we told the crew to brew up and have something ready for us when we returned and went back to the village. There we came to a villa, rather larger than the rest, which was apparently the Bey's summer palace. Outside there was a guard of honour, dressed in flamboyant uniforms. My Brigadier said that we must have a guard of honour too. A patrol of Grenadiers was passing, faces black, woollen head-gear, filthy. I said to the Sergeant, 'Sergeant, we need a guard of honour'. 'Sah!' he yelled, (that's the way Grenadiers talk). He formed them up, one on that side and one on the other, and in we went. There was a large room and a sort of throne upon which sat a gentleman who was obviously the Bey of Tunis. I explained in French who we were and the Bey, in faultless French, made, or rather started to make, an eloquent speech. It was interrupted, however, by a senior British officer of the Military Police who came stomping in and said, 'Is there anyone 'ere answering to the name Bey of Tunis?' (I wonder if he spelled it 'Bay'.) I indicated with my hand and the officer said, 'Sir, you are under arrest'.

So we returned to our tank and, as I sat beside it having supper, a man in French uniform with a colonel's insignia came out of the darkness. He said, 'I wish to be your prisoner'. I said, 'Well, who are you?' and he said, 'I am a colonel of the Milice', which were the French Military Police who were on the side of the Germans. I said, 'I have no facilities to take prisoners here. You must go back down the lines'. 'If I see the French they will shoot me,' he said. 'I can't help that,' I replied, 'you can't stay here.' So I gave him a glass of whisky and he went.

Next morning we reached the sea. The Germans were completely surrounded. During the course of the morning the New Zealand Division met us and General Freyberg, VC, their commander, came to see us. He was standing on a track with my Brigadier, his staff and me. Down the track came some German soldiers marching in step, four abreast and singing a military song. They were the remnants of the German 90th Light Division. As they approached, General Freyberg waved them off the track and they stepped straight into a minefield. Some were killed and more wounded. Of course we all flung ourselves on to our faces, except General Freyberg who took absolutely no notice at all and went on talking as if nothing had happened. We spent a week on the beach –wonderful bathing. Our HQ was a luxurious villa with a coloured photograph of King Edward VIII in the bathroom.

After the victory in Tunis, King George VI came to see us to congratulate us. The Divisional Commander formed up with his three brigadiers behind him. I noticed just in time that the Divisional Commander had his medals on the wrong way about; the King would not have liked that. The King greeted the Divisional Commander who then presented his three Brigadiers. The gunners' Brigadier was first, on the right of the line. The King said, 'Have we m-m-met before?' The Brigadier said, 'I don't think so, Sir.' The King said, 'You should bloody well know,' and passed on.

I was then sent back as a student to the Staff College at Camberley. The Division went on to Sicily, Italy and Vienna. After the course I was posted Brigade Major to the Armoured Brigade, 11th Armoured Division. We trained in Yorkshire and Norfolk and as D-Day, 6 June 1944, approached we went to Aldershot. The brigade consisted of two regiments which had not yet been in the fighting and one which had been in the Eighth Army and had fought all across North Africa, Sicily and a little in Italy. Even before the war, for two years, they had been stationed in Egypt so that some of the men had not been in the UK for six or seven years. We were dismayed, about a week before D-Day, to see graffiti painted on the walls of this regiment's barracks –slogans such as 'No Second Front'. When we got to France this same regiment, though skilful, was much slower than the others. I could not blame them. When you have been around a blind corner four or five times and have been brewed up, you go around the next one very slowly indeed. Once in Normandy one German tank in a hedge held up this regiment for a whole day. But the home regiments were, if anything, too bold. In particular, the reconnaissance element motored fast and furiously all over the place. They failed to notice whether there were any enemy about or not. They were going too fast for that. Later, they were much better.

We had one battle east of Caen and our next one, west of Caen, was known as 'Goodwood'. This was preceded by what I am told was the heaviest aerial bombardment used on a battlefield hitherto. It had hardly any effect. The Germans were well dug in, fairly difficult to see and as soon as the bombing stopped they popped up and started to shoot (cf Kosovo?). I was wounded there. We called in the Canadian Armoured Division to help us and broke through while I was away. I came back to duty and saw the Falaise Gap where the Germans had been surrounded. The main road was a nightmare: so many bodies −men, horses −so much destruction. It was impossible to avoid running over them with our tanks and the stink was terrible. I don't think any Army except the British and the German would have been able to survive such a heavy defeat.

One evening, as dusk was falling, our Corps Commander, General Horrocks, came to us and said that he had arranged special petrol and also searchlights to point to the clouds by which reflection we could see enough to drive. We did so and drove all that night. As dawn broke we reached Amiens. The German Army commander, Seventh Army, drove out to meet us, not realizing who we were. He looked very displeased. Then we started to race across France; faster and faster we went. Our reception in France itself was cool except from the teenagers, but in Belgium the population was ecstatic. It was difficult to get through the towns because of the crowds, the bottles of wine, the sausages, etc. being thrown up to us.

At one town in France we had to stop; one of our liaison officers was half French and had spent most of his life in France. He saw some men standing on the war memorial in the main square. He seemed to erupt in a fury. He seized his tommy gun and rushed towards them shouting that they were collaborators. How he knew I have no idea. I sent another liaison officer after him. He was a Master of Foxhounds and soon brought him to heel. Meanwhile the men on the memorial ran for their lives.

Finally we got to Antwerp on 3 September 1944, five years to the day from the outbreak of war. The Guards on our right went to Brussels. The same reception awaited us. There was little sign of German troops, only a few prisoners, and so I occupied my morning in firing my gun occasionally, to amuse the girls on my tank, through the front door of an American bank which had been the Gestapo HQ. I could have done better. What I could and should have done was to motor north through Antwerp to the Albert Canal which was unguarded at that moment. The Germans blew up the bridge across it that night. If we had stopped them doing that we would have been able to seize the right bank of the river. But we left them in control of the east bank and it was three months before our main base of supply could be transferred from the Normandy beaches to Antwerp. Our Corps Commander, General Horrocks, said it was the worst mistake he made in the war.

After Antwerp we pushed on to the north and crossed into Holland. At that time I was sent back to the UK to be an instructor at the Staff College at Camberley. I did not see the Division fight up to the Rhine and cross north Germany. They finished at Lübeck. In and around Lübeck the brigadiers, all of them keen horsemen, found some horses, race horses and others, and almost at once held a race meeting. This came to the ears of Field Marshal Montgomery. He sent a message that they should return the horses, come to their senses and have no more race meetings. The brigadiers considered this and decided to write a letter which read as follows: 'Dear Field Marshal, We have followed you from Alamein across the African desert to Sicily, Italy, Normandy, Belgium, Holland and Germany and we are now bound to say that we have lost all confidence in you.' The war was over. Even Monty saw the joke. I ended the war quietly at the Staff College.

FRANCIS PYM

Francis Pym was appointed Foreign Secretary after the shock resignation of Lord Carrington at the start of the Falklands War in 1982. During the Second World War he served with the 9th Lancers in North Africa and Italy, and was awarded the MC in 1945. He was Conservative MP for Cambridgeshire from 1961–1983, and Cambridgeshire South-East from 1983–1987, when he was created a life peer as Baron Pym of Sandy in the county of Bedfordshire.

During his political career, his numerous appointments included Parliamentary Secretary to the Treasury and Government Chief Whip 1970–1973; Secretary of State for Northern Ireland 1973–1974; Secretary of State for Defence 1979–1981; Chancellor of the Duchy of Lancaster and Paymaster General 1981; Lord President of the Council and Leader of the House of Commons 1981–1982; and Secretary of State for Foreign and Commonwealth Affairs 1982–1983.

When war was declared on 3 September 1939 I had just left Eton. Throughout the Munich crisis and all the arguments it caused it had seemed obvious to me and my contemporaries that war was inevitable. What is more we understood that it was we who would have to fight it.

I chose to fight in a tank and in due course was commissioned into the 9th Queen's Royal Lancers. As things turned out I proved to be lucky in combat. On the first afternoon of the Battle of Alamein my tank was hit head-on by an armour-piercing shell which mechanically disabled it but left me and my whole crew unscathed. The next-door tank but one to my left, commanded by Corporal Dickinson, an excellent soldier, also received a direct hit and immediately burst into flames with all hands lost.

In May 1943, on the advance to Tunis, my tank was blown up on a mine. In no way was that life-threatening, but it was a damned nuisance having to transfer into a replacement tank. Then in the Italian campaign, when I was Adjutant to the Regiment, I was working in a Scout car which was drawn up with its back facing the enemy. Stug Perry, the CO, told me to turn the car round so that the armour-plated bonnet faced the enemy. This saved my life. We received a direct hit from a mortar bomb on the bonnet. Most unhappily it wounded Stug Perry in the hand and he had to be evacuated. The regimental radio operator, Sergeant Jenner, and I were hurled to the floor as the vehicle overturned, but we were able to crawl out from under broken glass and debris and carry on the battle. Naturally I have always been grateful to Stug for perceiving the danger and ordering me to turn the Scout car round.

On leaving Eton I went up to Magdalene College, Cambridge, to read Economics. I had intended originally to read Agriculture, but my father's advice was that because of the war it did not matter what I read. In the end I chose Economics. This was particularly interesting because the LSE was evacuated to Cambridge at that time. There were many well-known left-wing voices there –Harold Laski and Maurice Dobbs among them –so there was lively debate and discussion. My most vivid memories of the year at Cambridge centre on military training which occupied a day a week. The most enjoyable aspect were the mobile military exercises in small armoured cars. This was my first introduction to the villages and countryside of Cambridgeshire. Little did I know that twenty years later I was to represent that county in Parliament for over twenty-five years.

From Cambridge I went straight to 103 Officer Cadet Training Unit at Perham Down near Tidworth in Hampshire. Having passed out I was sent on embarkation leave prior to sailing to North Africa. I was just one reinforcement to that campaign. A convoy of liners, each containing some 5000 troops, set off from Gourock in June for a six weeks' journey to the Suez Canal. I was in the *Duchess of Atholl*. After an immense detour in the North Atlantic, we called in at Sierra Leone and Cape Town. We went by train from Suez to Cairo and within a few days I was collected from Abassir Barracks by Stug Perry, then second-in-command 9th Lancers, who took me to the Regiment stationed close to the desert road. I was put in charge of No 3 Troop, B Squadron, armed with Sherman tanks. The adjustment to desert conditions happened quickly: there was no alternative.

The Regiment –indeed the whole army –was getting ready for the Battle of Alamein. My soldiers had had considerable experiences of battle while I was plain green. They were an excellent crew.

The battle began at 10 pm on 23 October with an artillery barrage from thousands of guns –a spectacular and encouraging sight. The Royal Engineers set to work at once to make three clearways through the minefields –those of the enemy and our own –so that our tanks could drive through and spread out to start fighting. This had been intended to happen throughout the night so that we could engage the enemy at first light on D+1. It did not happen that way: it took much longer to clear the mines than planned, so we were stuck all day in a long armoured traffic jam. Fortunately the enemy could not take advantage of this sitting target. We waited until about 4pm when the advance finally took place. As soon as we had spread out the battle hotted up. Several tanks were knocked out within minutes, including mine, and the enemy suffered too. My crew and I limped back as fast as we could, obtained a replacement tank and were back in the firing line 24 hours later on D+2.

For the next ten days there was a major shoot-out. The German 88mm gun was greatly superior to our 75mm, but we kept firing away every day all day: in the end we wore the enemy down. A real chase should then have followed but, as ill-luck would have it, there was a violent thunderstorm which made the sand so wet that our supply lorries got stuck and could not reach us. Without supplies of petrol and ammunition we could go no further. It was a frustrating moment, but the enemy had been overwhelmed and was in full retreat west-wards, as we could see.

We spent the winter months at a place called Tmimi between Tobruk and Derna. For a reason I cannot now recall I was despatched to 'A' Squadron, then stationed near Benghazi, where I celebrated my 21st birthday. Jack Price, the squadron leader, regarded it as an important occasion and arranged a special dinner for it which was typical of him. We all enjoyed a day off. In that spring of 1943 we began to prepare for another advance. This involved attacking the German-held Mareth Line, some 20 miles west of Tripoli. It was during this period that I had a great surprise. Rex Hitchcock, the

Adjutant, was taken ill and Gerald Grosvenor, the Commanding Officer, asked me to take on that job. I thought it rather extraordinary in view of my juniority and lack of battle experience, but I thought it would be exciting and certainly interesting, so I accepted gratefully.

When the Regiment was in battle one's concentration was engaged 24 hours a day. The principal tasks were to ensure that supplies of fuel, ammunition, food and water reached every squadron every day; to listen to the regimental radio network linking all parts of the regiment; to the Brigade network; to receive orders from Brigade HQ and report back to them. In the event I remained Adjutant until the end of the war, serving three Commanding Officers, each respected throughout the Regiment and more widely. In some ways the most exacting aspect of the job was keeping the war diary. A great many things happened every day and at the end of each day one had to make notes before these events became forgotten! When a battle was over I tried to put these notes into some sort of order. This was a great strain, but I realized the importance of the record for the Regimental history which I helped write some years later. Sergeant Major Maloney reminded me a few years ago that on one occasion he came over to see me and apparently I was very short with him: 'Bugger off,"I said, 'I'm trying to write the war diary'!

As we approached the start line for the attack on the Mareth Line we went through a plague of locusts and soft sand made the driving conditions perilous. We were then ordered to make a wide left-flanking movement, to disrupt the enemy forces from behind. Our objective was the village of El Hamma. Before we had made much progress the night was closing in on us, but we carried on the advance setting the countryside alight with high-explosive shells and machine-gun fire. This is the only case I know when tanks continued fighting at night.

Meanwhile the First Army, comprising British and US units, had invaded the North African coast from the Mediterranean at several points. The First and Eighth Armies combined together to advance upon Tunis where the entire German Afrika Corps and all Italian units surrendered in May 1943. There were tens of thousands of prisoners to cope with. This was a major Allied campaign victory and it was widely celebrated after the set-backs and defeats of the first years of the war.

The Regiment was not required to play any part in the next phase of the war – the attack on Sicily – nor in the initial landings in Southern Italy. We had spent the winter of 1943/4 some 20 miles south of Algiers. In May 1944 we sailed over to Italy, calling in briefly at Malta then enshrouded in lava dust from the erupting Vesuvius: Naples itself was also thick in lava dust.

Eventually the men of the regiment and their tanks were re-assembled together in south-east Italy, near Bari. We were destined to be a part of the attack on the Gothic Line in north-east Italy, but the initial attack did not go nearly as well as expected. The main reason for this was that the regiment was totally exhausted after a very long approach across country. We had driven continuously throughout several days and nights just before the battle began. I have always regretted that General Montgomery was no longer in command of Eighth Army (he was preparing for D-Day) because I feel quite sure he would not have allowed us to embark on a fresh attack when we were so exhausted. You need to be fresh for any new attack. However, not for us to reason why. As it was, we made little progress at the price of a number of casualties: shelling was more or less continuous. Thereafter we fought a series of battles in appalling conditions – notably mud, with casualties on each occasion. This continued throughout the winter.

It was in the spring of 1945 that we were enabled to change our tactics drastically for the better. The 2nd London Rifles were put to operate with 9th Lancers. A platoon of riflemen were put to work in close conjunction with each troop of tanks, so that opposition to our advance could be dealt with immediately by the appropriate arm. Colonel Bala Bredin commanded the battalion and he and Colonel Jack Price, CO 9th Lancers, worked especially well together. So we made big advances in the Po Valley with few casualties.

Eventually, one beautiful spring morning we reached the bank of the River Po. I well remember standing beside the Command Tank in the village street of Francolino with the radio headset dangling over the side of the turret, when the message came over 'Kesselring, Commander of all German forces in Italy had surrendered! The war is over'!

And I thought 'whatever do we do now?'

Two months later, Francis Pym's father died quite suddenly. He had been Member of Parliament for Monmouth since 1939 and was re-elected posthumously in the 1945 general election. His death came between the closing of the poll and the count —a rare but not unique Parliamentary happening.

His own political career began fourteen years later when he lost his deposit in the Rhondda Valley, before eventually succeeding to become the Member of Parliament for Cambridgeshire South-East in 1961.

ANTHONY ROYLE

Anthony Royle was Conservative MP for Richmond from 1959–1983, when he was made a life peer, as Lord Fanshawe of South Cerney in the county of Gloucestershire.

He joined The Life Guards at the age of 17 in 1945 and spent the rest of that year training to become an officer in the regiment. He spent eight weeks at the Guards Depot which was then at Lingfield, Sussex, and this was followed by two months training at the Guards Training Battalion at Pirbright prior to entering Sandhurst. He was commissioned in the regiment in December 1945 and was posted to Combermere Barracks Windsor, where he spent a few weeks prior to joining the regiment which was then part of the occupation forces in Kladow Barracks, Berlin. It will be apparent from these comments that, although he was in the Army during the Second World War, he was unable to see any active service as he was still training when the European War finished in May 1945. He would, however, serve in Palestine immediately after.

> After joining the Life Guards in Berlin I served in the squadron which was detached from the regiment guarding the war criminals who were incarcerated at Spandau Barracks. This was a detached squadron equipped with armoured cars. We rejoined the regiment in early August 1946 and were posted to Alexandria in Egypt. This was followed by a period in Kasr el Nil Barracks in Cairo, again as a squadron detached from the main regiment which was posted to Fayed in the Canal Zone. We trained in the desert near the Libyan frontier after arrival in Egypt and this was followed by training in the Sinai Desert until the regiment was posted to Khassa in Southern

Palestine where I commanded a troop of armoured cars. These cars were Daimlers equipped with two-pounder guns and light reconnaissance vehicles known as scout cars. I travelled widely in Palestine, spending two months on detachment with my troop with the Arab Legion in TransJordan. This covered a very difficult period, as we were constantly under attack by Jewish Terrorists. They formed the Jewish Army called Haganah who masterminded the constant stream of refugees who flooded out from Europe at the end of the War. We spent most of the time patrolling the Mediterranean coast from Gaza to north of Tel Aviv.

The regiment took several casualties, the most unpleasant being the one when a fellow officer, Victor Hoare, and the Squadron Corporal Major were both shot in the back whilst in Jerusalem.

I finished my time in Palestine as captain and signals officer being demobilized in January 1948.

My other military service was at the time of the Korean War. I had joined up as a territorial in the 21st SAS Regiment (Artists Rifles). Whilst being stationed with 'M' Squadron in Aldershot preparing to leave for Korea, I was invalided out of the Army having caught polio. This squadron did not go to Korea, it went to Malaya where it formed 22 SAS Regiment which is the regular SAS regiment today. In 1951 I returned to work at Lloyds in London.

THOMAS BOARDMAN

Tom Boardman was Conservative MP for Leicester South-West from 1967–1974, and Leicester South between February and September 1974: he was made a life peer in 1980, as Lord Boardman of Welford in the county of Northamptonshire. He was a Director of Allied Breweries and President of the British Chambers of Commerce from 1977–1999. During the war he served with the 1st Battalion Northamptonshire Yeomanry and was awarded the MC in 1944.

In the following narrative, Thomas Boardman concentrates on 'Operation Totalize' 7 August 1944, which was an Anglo-Canadian offensive launched from near Caen. In the preceding hours the Germans had made a determined counter-attack against the Americans in the west, which had taken them to within 9 miles of Avranches. At 11pm, 400 Allied tanks rolled forward in the wake of a terrible carpet bombing. Thomas Boardman found himself acting as one of the navigating officers during the advance, which meant that he was at the very head of the column. He would also become involved with some of the fiercest fighting, around the Falaise road, where SS Captain Michael Wittman, the victor of Villiers-Bocage, was to be killed. Although the thrust went well in the initial stages, it was eventually brought to a halt ten miles from Falaise.

The 1st Northamptonshire Yeomanry, in which I had served since 1939, landed in Normandy on D+5. I had gone over on D+2 as advance party with our Brigadier and one officer from each regiment in the brigade.

In Normandy we fought numerous relatively small battles, supporting infantry advances, to secure the bridgehead against an increasing German force that was determined to push us back into the sea.

We suffered a number of casualties, including those from German high explosive fire on woods where we were taking cover from aircraft. The Germans found that such fire could cause the shells to detonate in the trees and spread their deadly shrapnel over a wide area below. Apart from the casualties, this caused us, when going into harbour in a wood at night, to dig a trench and run the tank over it to give protection to the crew – and much discomfort – for the few hours of darkness when we hoped to sleep.

Our own gunners and the USA aircraft made their contribution to our casualties at this stage.

We took part in the battle for Caen and in the various actions, which we now know was General Montgomery's plan to draw the main force to the British front and make it possible for the Americans to break out of the bridgehead to the west. The strength of the opposition facing the British Army was shown in 'Operation Goodwood' where from 18–21 July, three British armoured divisions – The Guards, the 7th and the 11th Armoured Divisions – unsuccessfully tried to reach the Bourgebus ridge with the loss of a very large number of men and many hundreds of tanks. It was a sad sight when our forces were withdrawn.

Clearly, as we can now see, it was Monty's policy to break through the hinge south of Caen and then entrap the Germans as the Americans broke through on the west. The achievement of what became known as the 'Falaise Gap' depended on this.

On 3 August I was sent for by our Brigadier (Harry Scott). In his caravan he outlined to me the strategy and the proposal to break out where 'Goodwood' had failed, by our making an armoured attack at night. He told me that on the night of the attack we would be leading the Canadian Army in the assault and I had to lead the left hand-column and navigate to reach St Aignan de Cramesnil before first light.

The plan was for me to lead in my tank, followed by another officer – as a reserve – then two troops of tanks from my squadron, followed by 'Flail' mine-clearing tanks, then more of my regiment and backed by the Black Watch from the 51st Highland Division mounted in self-propelled artillery vehicles with their guns removed to provide space for the infantry, and armoured carriers. The tanks were to be in columns of four with 10 yards between each column –moving closely together, following the tail light of the tank in front.

My tank was fitted with a special compass on the commander's hatch which I was warned would be useless if I traversed my turret – not very comforting. They also fitted a special radio which was a RAF means of indicating the direction in which I was travelling.

The Brigadier had told me that there would be Bofors guns firing tracer rounds over my line of advance to assist in giving the direction I hoped to travel. He also told me that there would be very heavy shelling and bombing on our left flank and it was essential that I kept clear of that. He told me that artillery of nine Field and nine Medium regiments would provide a barrage from 15 minutes after I had crossed the start line –moving forward at 100 yards per minute.

The attack was to be on the night of 7 August, but on the previous day infantry patrols reported that they had seen a track with steep banks at the beginning of the route we hoped to cross. I was therefore asked to make a 'recce' with infantry cover to inspect this. With a RE captain, we crawled some way to inspect the track. It was very close to German positions, as they could be heard talking. I decided the bank could cause problems and it was agreed that Sappers would blow gaps and light places where the columns could cross. This was to be done immediately before we were due to cross.

The 'recce' was not a happy time for me. I had not been trained at infantry tactics of crawling on one's belly in earshot of the enemy and I was very glad to return to my squadron. My scout car driver, whom I see at our annual reunions, reminds me that I told him, when setting out from cover to view the track, that if I was not back in 30 minutes he was to return and report to my squadron leader; he tells me that he waited 40 minutes and I was very glad that he did.

During 4 and 5 August we had rehearsals of the assault well behind our lines, first by day and then at night, and it was obvious that it would be difficult to keep in order during a night advance, even if we could move in the right direction.

At 2215 on 7 August the column was lined up to move to the start line –200 armoured vehicles including the infantry mounted in the gun carriers with the guns removed. The colonel from the Military Police who was assisting in the marking greeted me to wish me luck. He was the former chief constable of Northamptonshire, whom I well knew, and it was encouraging to be sent on our way with such friendly police support.

As our advance started a massive bombing attack commenced, their target being the area around the village of Bourgebus, on our left flank and very heavily defended by Germans; we had to leave this to our left but also miss the area around Tilly la Campagne which was on our right and held by Germans in considerable strength. The gap between Bourgebus and Tilly was only about 1000 yards –not very wide to navigate in pitch darkness.

Of the navigation aids with which I was supplied, only the compass was of any real help. The radio giving 'pips' if I went off line one way and 'bleeps' if I varied the other way may have been invaluable in aircraft travelling at several hundred miles per hour, but it was useless in a tank moving at under a tenth of that pace. The tracer bullets fired by the Bofors guns were impossible to follow amongst all the smoke and dust created by the artillery barrage and the bombing. But luckily the compass must have remained accurate and, despite small arms fire, we avoided any demand to traverse our turret.

When we had gone some miles through the German lines I received a message that 'the Supreme Commander is most anxious you do your best to push on at all speed'. As I learnt later, the other column to our right –144 RAC –had struck severe problems and both their navigating officers had been killed. As the whole of the Canadian Army, under General Simonds, was poised to follow our advance by dawn to break out from the bridgehead, the urgency of our successfully arriving at St Aignan was great.

Clearly there had been a lot of difficulty in crossing the track that had been blown and tanks were unable to follow the tail light ahead. The dust and smoke made visibility almost impossible.

On the radio I asked my Colonel if I could use Very lights to show the column where I was. He agreed and I fired some –stating on the radio which colours I was sending up – as I advanced. These, I gathered later, were very helpful in getting the column collected. Soon I had used all my Very lights so I asked my reserve navigator, Captain Todd, to get his ready and I would collect them. I got out of my tank to run back to his and collect his Very lights, but on the way back I almost fell into a large slit trench which, by the sound of them, was occupied by several Germans. They must have been even more frightened than me because I rapidly escaped back to my tank and continued the advance. At 0238 I was able to report that I believed I had arrived at the outskirts of St Aignan de Cramesnil where the Infantry were to debus and clear the village. My Colonel and the Colonel of the Black Watch joined me and, to the relief of all of us, agreed we were at the right place –over 4 miles behind the German lines and with relatively light casualties.

The Black Watch quickly assembled and then, with our tank support, made an attack on the village of St Aignan, capturing a large number of Germans. When the village had been cleared and it was getting lighter the Northamptonshire Yeomanry moved through the village to the orchards on the north and took up positions to protect the area from anticipated counter-attacks from any quarter. As we had, during the night, moved through the German lines there were many thousands of Germans behind us.

During the morning we suffered shelling from the Germans and, I regret to say, from our own medium guns until they were contacted, but no German ground counter-attack until about 1230.

At that time No 3 Troop, covering the south-west and the vital Caen-Falaise highway, reported three Tiger tanks moving across the front, parallel to the main road and at about 1200 yards distance. I told the troop leader, on the radio, to hold his fire and I would come over to them. The troop were well concealed in a hedgerow and, when I reached them in my tank, the Tigers appeared unaware of our presence, as all their guns were traversed north-west, apparently expecting trouble from that direction. They were using 'dead ground' concealed from the other side of the main Caen highway.

When the Tigers were what I estimated to be about 800 yards away I told the Troop to open fire on them. The Troop had one tank with a 17 pounder gun (known as a 'Firefly') which should, I thought, be capable of knocking out a Tiger at 800 yards. The remainder of the troop and my tank had only 75 mm guns, no match for a Tiger. The 17 pounder knocked out one Tiger when the commander of the 'Firefly' was wounded and the troop leader took over his tank and knocked out a second Tiger. The other tanks and mine were firing our guns and appeared to cause some damage –possibly to the tracks of the third Tiger which went round in circles until the Firefly finished it off. It was not until 37 years later that the bodies buried where one of the Tigers had been knocked out –and the dentures and effects found with it –proved that the Tigers were under the command of

SS-Haupsturmfuhrer Michael Wittman, the ace German tank commander who had 138 tanks to his credit in battles in Russia and then Normandy.

There followed some hours of intensive fighting in the orchards south of St Aignan. There was a deep defile to the south of our position and German tanks could reach this under cover and then crawl up and from a 'hull down' position pick off our tanks that were stationary in defensive positions. One example was when I suddenly saw one Mk IV German tank about 200 yards away moving up from the defile, traversing his guns onto my tank. I told my gunner 'Traverse left –on –fire' and he did so just before the German tank got on to me. He 'brewed' straight away –but it was a near thing.

We then had large infantry attacks from the woods ahead of us, but, with the Black Watch, managed to repel them. Repeated attacks by German tanks were made during the day to try to remove us from our key positions, which were essential for the Canadian and then the Polish to advance to try to close the Falaise Gap. The Northamptonshire Yeomanry suffered many losses, but we held the ground.

At the end of an interesting 24 hours we withdrew to harbour, the Northamptonshire Yeomanry having knocked out over twenty German tanks, though sadly we had lost many of ours and some fine men.

Part Three

THE ROYAL ARTILLERY

By 1945 one in every four soldiers in the British Army was serving as a 'gunner' in one of the many artillery regiments. Employing such a high proportion of young men, inevitably, a high proportion of MPs also served in the RA.

EDWARD HEATH

Undoubtedly the most famous gunner has to be the ex-Conservative Prime Minister Edward Heath.

Edward Heath left Oxford at the end of the 1939 summer term and spent the vacation touring Europe, mostly by hitchhiking. He visited France, Belgium, Germany and Poland, returning to Dover a week before war was declared. Immediately war was declared, he returned to his former college, Balliol, asking for his name to be placed on the list of volunteers, which it was.

He had planned to visit the United States of America with another colleague from Balliol, on a debating tour of some twenty-five universities, as he now explains:

> I naturally assumed that this would be cancelled but shortly afterwards I received a proposal from the Foreign Office that, as they understood I was unlikely to be called up until 1940, I should continue with the debating programme. My colleague, Hugh Fraser, had been carrying out his summer Territorial training when war broke out so he was no longer available and Peter Street from Exeter College, a prominent Liberal leader in the university, joined me instead.
>
> I returned to England from this tour in February 1940 by sea on a somewhat lengthy voyage and waited to be called up. In the meantime, as my home was on the coast not far from Dover, I saw a lot of the activities surrounding the evacuation from the continent.
>
> I was called up in early August for the Royal Artillery training camp in Sussex and then moved to the officer cadet training unit at Shrivenham, from where I was commissioned.

My first posting was to 335 Battery of the 107th Regiment Heavy Anti-Aircraft Royal Artillery, at Warrington, where we were fully engaged for a month during the major German attack on Liverpool.

After being appointed Adjutant to the Regiment, I moved with the headquarters further north near Preston, then to the outskirts of Birmingham, and thereafter down to the south of England. My regiment became a mobile 3.7 inch HAA Royal Artillery regiment, and we went north again for mobility training to the outside of Newcastle. After this the regiment was trained in anti-shipping work on the east coast and then returned to the south. It continued training until it prepared to move into positions for moving across the Channel on D-Day.

My regiment landed in France early in July and was moved into position to provide ground fire for the protection of the 6th Airborne Division forces still deployed there. We then deployed for the bombardment of Caen, said to be the heaviest bombardment ever known at that time. Following that we moved through Caen and across France, through Belgium up to Antwerp, where our recce party was one of the first in to the docks. Its capture of some of the barges containing vast quantities of liquid refreshment was very satisfactory. We then moved across Holland to Nijmegen and over the estuary in an attempt to reach the airborne forces at Arnhem on the other side –an attempt which failed.

We then moved south-east where we deployed along the Maas. Having taken part in the battle there we moved up to the Rhine and, after celebrating VE Day, went right up into Germany where we established a permanent base at Hanover. I was given the job of organizing the rebuilding of Hanover with two divisions of prisoners of war. Many political candidates then left their regiments to take part in the general election, but I decided that, as the rest of my regiment was holding together, the least I could do was to stay with them rather than try for an easy way home.

Shortly after this I was posted as second in command of 86 Regiment Honourable Artillery Company, another mobile anti-aircraft regiment. Due to rapid changes in command, I then became acting commanding officer for some four months, part of which was spent outside of Germany. The main achievement of that time was that I organized the regimental soccer team –composed entirely of professionals – to become winners of the Rhine Army Football Championship.

In June 1946 I was called home, although not without having the opportunity of visiting the universities in southern Germany and attending the trial of the Nazi war criminals in Nuremberg, the city where I had watched them organize their Nazi activities ten years earlier. On my return to England, I was discharged from the Army and then took up command of the 2nd Regiment HAC when the company's regiments were reformed in 1947.

By the end of the war Edward Heath had risen to the rank of lieutenant colonel, won an MBE, and was mentioned in dispatches. He entered the House of Commons in 1950 as the MP for Bexley, which became Old Bexley and Sidcup in 1974. He became the first elected leader of the Conservative Party while in opposition in 1965, and was Prime Minister from 1971–1974. His major success was to bring the United Kingdon into the European Community. Later appointed a Knight of the Garter, he finally retired from the House of Commons at the 2001 general election.

ROY JENKINS

Former Home Secretary and Chancellor of the Exchequer, Roy Jenkins was born on Armistice Day, 11 November 1920, and lived in Pontypool before going up to Balliol College, Oxford, in October 1938 and graduating in 1941. His entry into the Army was somewhat unusual, in that he was requested to join the Oxford University Senior Training Corps. Here he would be able to take the necessary tests, which would enable him to go straight to an Officer Cadet Training Unit. What was unusual about this was that he had already finished at the university and was working in London at the American Embassy. Therefore he was required to travel to Oxford twice a week to undergo two half-days of military training.

In February 1942 Roy Jenkins attended an artillery OCTU at Alton Towers in north Staffordshire, and after six months was posted to 55 Field Regiment, Royal Artillery, which had previously been the West Somerset Yeomanry and still bore that subsidiary title. Together with the Leicestershire Yeomanry, they provided the artillery support for the Guards Armoured Division. The regiment was under canvas on the northern edge of Salisbury Plain, just above West Lavington.

Shortly after arriving, the Dieppe raid took place on 19 August 1942, and the regiment was put on a state of readiness. It was widely believed that Dieppe was the precursor to a much wider assault on the coast of occupied France. By late autumn they had been taken off a state of readiness and moved off Salisbury Plain to a hutted camp at Upton Lovell in the Wylye Valley. In December a new field artillery regiment was formed –192 Field Regiment, RA –by taking a battery from the West Somerset Yeomanry, and another from the Leicestershire Yeomanry. Roy Jenkins was serving with C Battery of the former, which was sent to Clevedon near Bristol, to become part of the new regiment. By the spring of 1943 they were ready to be integrated into a division and were deployed on coastal defence. At the end of April they were moved to Sussex, first to a tennis club in Brighton, then to a pub in Bramber. From here Roy Jenkins was transferred to the Leicestershire Yeomanry battery, in a housing estate near the golf course at Angmering-on-Sea.

Starting in September 1943, he spent six weeks as temporary ADC to the general commanding the Division, at Staplefield, near Hayward's Heath. Then, just before Christmas, he was instructed by the War Office to go to Bedford for training for special intelligence work at Bletchley Park, one of Britain's most top secret establishments, where academics, mathematicians, linguists, and even chess players struggled to interpret complicated coded messages, which the Germans sent using their Enigma cipher machine, which they believed was unbreakable.

Once in Bedford, Roy Jenkins joined a twelve-week course in which he was given a basic understanding of the different types of codes and ciphers, and possible ways to break them. In April he was ready to join the staff at Bletchley, a period he recalls in his autobiography *A Life at the Centre.*

> Bletchley was shrouded in secrecy at the time and remained so for thirty or so years subsequently. It constructed vast calculating machines out of which by a great but miniaturizing leap from valve to solid-state technology the whole computer dynasty has developed.
>
> There were two sections which worked on the German military cipher known as Fish. One was called Dr Newman's Section and consisted mainly of civilian mathematicians assisted by Wrens and by the embryonic computers. Their task was to strip the first layer of disguise off the intercepted messages. This they did purely by the techniques of probability mathematics, for their product had no more obvious meaning than their raw material. Both were a stream of five rows of noughts and crosses (or positives and negatives). Each vertical row of five represented a letter of the alphabet or a figure or a conventional sign.
>
> Having got this far they sent the half-deciphered messages over to us in Major Tester's Section. We were a more mixed bag, Army officers if we were already so, RSMs (Warrant Officer Class I) if not

(this saved time; the rank, at least equally well paid, could be conferred without officer training), one American lieutenant, and a few civilians who were nominally on the strength of some section of the Foreign Office. We were assisted by ATS girls, but by no machines, for our task was the more intuitive one of seeing the clear German (or at least German obscured only by Wehrmacht jargon) under the second layer of cipher, and this was thought to be beyond the help of machines. I would guess, however, that what we did could now be easily computerized.

Tester's section was divided into two parts. There were the 'breakers' and the 'setters'. The breakers were obviously the elite. Setting was relatively routine. You had to know all the properties of the cipher which had been discovered during the past three years or so, and work with logic and precision. But, if you did this, output for any individual was more or less predictable.

After about six weeks as a setter I was allowed to become a breaker, or at least a would-be breaker. Sometimes nothing would happen at all. It is the night shifts which remain engraved on my mind. We worked three shifts, for there was great urgency about the need to get the intelligence, and changed shifts within a compass of three weeks, one week of days, one of evenings and one of nights. The night shift for some strange reason was the longest –nine hours –and it was certainly the bleakest. I remember quite a few absolutely blank nights, when nothing gave and I went to a dismal breakfast having played with a dozen or more messages and completely failed with all of them. It was the most frustrating mental experience I have ever had, particularly as the act of trying almost physically hurt one's brain, which became distinctly raw if it was not relieved by the catharsis of achievement.

On the other hand there could be nights when a cornucopia of success was upended on one's head. I remember one shift when I made thirteen separate breaks. They just fell into my lap like ripe apples. I thought it was too good to be true, and grew rather super-stitious towards morning, particularly when it became clear what the exact score was going to be. I was going to London immediately I came off duty, a journey which at the time was accomplished by walking down to Bletchley Junction and getting on the first night train from Scotland which heaved into the station. They were often two or three hours late and contained some fairly exhausted passengers. There were then a lot of flying bombs arriving in London by day as well as by night, and the thought crossed my mind that the unnatural success of the night might be a fine apotheosis before being caught by one.

Our ability to break depended crucially on the quality of the work sent over by the probability mathematicians. No one could break a transcript if the first process was wrongly done.

In September (1944) I went seriously off form for several weeks and was rightly returned to the setting room. It was a considerable blow, which ironically coincided with my being promoted to captain, a good indication of how indifferent the whole operation was to rank. Fortunately, I was judged to have recovered form after a couple of months, and was allowed back.

Throughout his Army career, Roy Jenkins maintained an interest in politics, and he was able to attend two wartime Labour Party conferences in Central Hall, Westminster, as a visitor, not a delegate. By December 1944 he was already keen to be selected as a Parliamentary candidate. He tried for the Aston Division of Birmingham, but was unsuccessful. At Sparkbrook in February 1945 he was beaten by one vote. Eventually, in April, he succeeded in Solihull: he was twenty-four years old. Solihull was a staunch Tory seat, and although there was a Labour landslide on 26 July 1945, Roy Jenkins was unable to share in the celebrations: beaten 26,000 to 21,000.

So it was back to Bletchley Park, and although the war in Europe was over, the Russians had taken over the German Fish machines after their entry to Berlin. They began to send their own coded messages between the capitals of their vast empire. The staff at Bletchley intercepted and tried to decipher these messages, but were never able to succeed.

Roy Jenkins left the Army in January 1946. He took a job as a junior banker in the City of London, while waiting for a political opportunity to arise. He was eventually elected to the House of Commons in April 1948 as MP for Southwark.

His political career culminated as Home Secretary, and then Chancellor of the Exchequer. He was regarded as Harold Wilson's heir. However, as Labour drifted further to the left, he resigned its deputy leadership, and later resigned from Parliament in 1977 to become President of the European Commission. On his return to

British politics he co-founded the Social Democratic Party and, after victory in the Glasgow Hillhead by-election, went on to lead it. He was made a life peer, Lord Jenkins of Hillhead, in 1987, and later became leader of the Liberal Democrats in the House of Lords and Chancellor of Oxford University.

GORDON CAMPBELL

Gordon Campbell, whose political career culminated as Secretary of State for Scotland, was still at school in 1939. As war seemed inevitable, he switched from preparing to sit for a university history scholarship to being commissioned as a regular gunner. War broke out shortly after his 18th birthday, by which time he was already in uniform. On VE Day, over five years later, having already won an MC and Bar, he was semi-conscious because he had just been severely wounded, and was to spend 14 months in hospital being skilfully repaired by Bart's. He now recalls a few of his experiences during the intervening years, which he describes as 'intensely occupied.'

After a concentrated course at Larkhill I was retained there as an instructor, lecturing in mathematics and gunnery to officer cadets all older than me. Surprisingly I was made a captain soon after my 19th birthday.

When my year of teaching (and prior swotting) was over, I joined the 15th Scottish Division, in which friends were serving, and soon became a major at 21, commanding a field battery. This was 1942 and one was expected to mature rapidly.

The most demanding period was the campaign from Normandy to the Elbe, when our Division was constantly in action and suffered crippling casualties in the first two months. I lost many friends, then and later, in Belgium, Holland and in the offensives to break through the Siegfried Line and other defended barriers. I seemed myself to have a strange immunity, especially when members of my personal forward observation teams were being hit beside me. In one battle all four of my team were killed by a salvo of shells which buried me, dazed but unscathed, under earth and rubble.

The field gunners were constantly in action during the North-West Europe campaign. If our guns could be within range of the enemy they were deployed and ready to fire, whether our Division's infantry were involved or not. Our standard weapon, the 25 pounder, was a versatile, well-designed and accurate gun that could be handled easily. Like the Spitfire it came into production at the crucial time in the early days of the war. I compared notes at the time with my brother, Ian, who was a Spitfire pilot, but who lost his life in action in 1943.

It was a field battery commander's job to give close support to his infantry and tanks. This usually meant being with the leading troops, if necessary on foot, to be able to bring down shells quickly in the right places, just in front of us. Powerful radios were essential and good fire control order systems.

The flexibility of the British artillery was envied by others, both allies and enemy. For example I could be lying on the ground beside a company commander, perhaps a junior officer because of recent casualties, and arranging over my portable radio for shells from twenty-four guns to fall on the enemy's positions in front of us at the moment when we were going to attack them.

It was a matter of pride in achievement for field gunners to be able to bring onto the local battlefield the extra fire of our powerful weapons, invisible and perhaps two or more miles away. It could intimidate the enemy and prove to be the deciding factor in attack or defence.

The 15th Division specialized in river-crossing battles and we took part, with assault boats, in the battles to win crossings over the Seine, the Rhine and the Elbe. In Normandy, in the first major battle to break out of the beachhead, Operation 'Epsom', in June 1944, we captured two bridges over the Odon intact and then had to hold the bridgehead for five gruelling nights and days, losing half of our infantry and forward troops.

In the low countries we fought from canal to canal and followed up the airborne operations at the time of Arnhem in September. We endured muddy and wintry woods and trenches through the winter, until the fierce fighting after we entered Germany early in February, around Cleve and in the Reichswald forest, which continued until late March.

The Elbe was a wide obstacle with steep wooded slopes on the other side. We could not bring tanks with us, so our artillery had a crucial role in which my part was, as usual, to direct the fire of many guns through my walkie-talkie radios. Even at this stage of the war (the day before Hitler committed suicide) the German defence was well organized. Heavy shelling and other fire opened up on us as soon as our assault boats started off in the early hours.

After we landed there was prolonged fighting at close quarters during which a bullet went through my middle. I heard later that soldiers of the Gordon Highlanders (who knew me well) had made a special effort to get me back to the river to be taken across for medical aid. Later I learnt also that the reason for this last battle was to prevent Soviet troops occupying Denmark by reaching Lübeck before them. My Danish friends are grateful.

Two weeks before I was wounded we had discovered Belsen, which lay on our route and was the first concentration camp to be found on our front. Its horrors were final proof, if it were needed, that war had been unavoidable.

During the campaign our guns continued to support other infantry when our Division was no longer in the line. So our gunner forward teams were in action for long periods and sustained many casualties at an even higher rate than those of our infantry. This was very worrying as we could not afford to lose so many skilled officers and men. Although we had reserves and rotated the teams, finding suitable replacements became difficult from reinforcements arriving from elsewhere.

Before I was wounded, in our last battle, I was the only field battery commander left in our Scottish Division of the nine who had started in Normandy. Seven had been killed or wounded. I must have taken part in over a dozen major battles and many more smaller operations.

Particularly hair-raising situations that I am unlikely to forget were two occasions when my forward teams, with our infantry in makeshift trenches, were overrun by enemy tanks. Despite many casualties from their sweeping fire, we succeeded in holding our ground and knocking out some of the tanks.

Immodestly I record that I received two immediate awards, of the MC in Normandy, and of a Bar to it in the Reichswald.

When I became conscious after being evacuated back across the Elbe, before a first surgical operation in a field hospital, I seemed to be paralysed below the waist. In fact it proved to be only my left leg, although movement in the right leg was limited. When I started to walk again, nearly two years later, I had a caliper on one leg and have had one ever since.

Penicillin, which had just started in use, was a boon for me and others in preventing and reducing infection.

I used my time in hospital to work for the Foreign Office exam in which I was then successful. I also passed the medical exam, although I still could not walk. The medical tribunal commented that, as a diplomat, I would not need to walk or stand! True then, but not later.

Gordon Campbell worked in the Diplomatic Service for the next twelve years and was given what he describes as 'sedentary jobs in salubrious places, where required medical treatment was available.' Among other things he went to New York as part of the United Kingdom Delegation to the United Nations. For two years, he was assigned to work for the Prime Minister, then Winston Churchill.

He entered the House of Commons in 1959 as Conservative MP for Moray and Nairn, representing the same constituency until 1974. While in opposition, he was the Conservative spokesman on Defence and notes: 'It was very helpful that some of the generals in the Ministry of Defence and Commands abroad had served with me in the war as friends and military colleagues. I was not regarded simply as a politician.' During Edward Heath's government he served as Secretary of State for Scotland and was later elevated to the peerage as Lord Campbell of Croy.

EDWIN LEATHER

Like Gordon Campbell, Edwin Leather mixed a career in politics with being a diplomat, only he did it the other way round. Whereas Gordon Campbell worked in the Diplomatic Service before being an MP, Edwin Leather departed from the House of Commons in 1964 to follow a course that would eventually see him appointed as the Governor of Bermuda.

On the day war was declared he had just turned 20 and was about to enter his third year at the Royal Military College of Canada. His intention was to go on to Cambridge. On 19 December 1939 he was commissioned into the Canadian Army; in March he married his 20-year-old bride; and in June 1940, along with 25,000 other Canadian troops, he was shipped to Britain. He remembers arriving while Dunkirk was still taking place, so all hopes were dashed of the Canadian Army being sent to join their British cousins on the continent.

We landed while the Dunkirk evacuation was still going on. Those of my class who had joined the Air Force or the Navy, were taking part in the continuous battles of the North Atlantic, and all of those who had joined the Army settled down to a long operation of training, and training others, which lasted for three whole years. Shortly after D-Day, June 1944, I finally managed to end this extraordinary interlude and was shipped as a reinforcement officer, a few days after the break out from the Normandy beachhead.

We were immediately moved as close behind the fighting troops as possible. I was promoted to the rank of captain and saw service as a staff officer until the end of the war, most of which time I was in charge of the 'map room' at 2nd Canadian Corp Headquarters.

The Canadian government, with the full approval, I think, of most Canadians, insisted that the Canadian Army was on the extreme left of the 21st Army Group and as they gradually moved further north we moved with them. By 3 May we were well across the Rhine and fighting in our sector came to an end, and although we were frequently bombed or shelled, our war was over. So, I have frequently been involved in air raids, bombed and shot at, but I never actually fired a shot myself from beginning to end.

On 6 May 1945 Edwin Leather was recalled to London to present himself to the chief of the Canadian general staff. The result of this was that he was discharged within a week and some three weeks later became the Conservative candidate in South Bristol, a safe Labour seat. He subsequently became MP for North Somerset from 1950–1964; and was Governor and Commander-in-Chief of Bermuda between 1973–1977. Knighted in 1962, he was later made a Knight Commander of the Order of St Michael and St George and a Knight Commander of the Royal Victorian Order.

JOHN HILL

John Hill, who was Conservative MP for South Norfolk from 1955–1974, was an undergraduate at Merton College, Oxford, when a Union debate passed the sensational motion that 'the members of this house will never under any circumstances in the future agree to fight for King and Country'. Nevertheless, when the danger posed by the international situation became clear, many of these same undergraduates had the incentive to join one of the volunteer units of the university OTC. John Hill opted for the Royal Artillery and the experience of going on camp to Larkhill and learning to fire field guns put him in good stead when he applied to join the Territorials in 1938. His certificate qualified him for a commission in 64 Field Regiment RATA, at Putney. However, unlike other, more conventional, gunners, his career would take a slightly different, and more uplifting course, as he now describes.

When the war started I was completely untrained in artillery, except for a few lectures and the experience of the camp at Larkhill, but with four years' experience in school OTC I had the benefit of being able to march and salute on the parade ground!

Shortly before the outbreak of war we were mobilized and were posted to Golders Green. By a strange coincidence we were posted to within a few hundred yards of the little house that my mother had bought there after my father was killed at Ypres in 1917. There we were somewhat amazed to find that public notices at the Police Station were put up in German as well as English, and our role was not, as the Germans thought, to commit a 'Pogrom', but rather to reassure them against the danger of air raids. We were soon moved out to Kent and spent a month in training, with a defensive role always in the foreground.

So through the first winter of the war I was a junior gun position officer, until I unfortunately was appointed assistant adjutant. I escaped from that very dull job by volunteering for the short-lived skiing battalion (5th Scots Guards) raised to support Mannerheim of Finland in his brave defence against Russian invasion. That lasted just over a month, then Mannerheim made peace when we were already loaded up on a Polish liner ready to sail from Glasgow to Finland. Being disbanded and sent back to units was a great anti-climax.

Back in Kent by way of a polite punishment I was sent on an anti-gas course at Tregantle, Cornwall. Knowing nothing about gas or chemistry in general, I was surprised when I was awarded a D, which apparently was for distinction rather than dunce! In September, much to my disappointment, I was then posted as a gas instructor back to Tregantle, leaving Kent and my unit, which was involved in an anti-invasion role, mainly defending the RAF fighter airfield at Hawkinge, at the height of the Battle of Britain. My short experience of moving artillery in the Kent countryside convinced me that it was futile to be able to observe from the ground alone, since only about 25% of the area into which the guns could shoot was visible. I had heard that some experiments were going on in the use of light aircraft for observation and so I concentrated all my energy and study into joining these experiments. Thanks to Geoffrey Mure at the War Office (one of my tutors and later Warden of Merton College) I found out what was going on and so applied to join the Air Observation Post course. I was initially attached to the RAF for elementary flying at RAF Peterborough in September 1941, which simply taught us to fly Tiger Moths. We were then transferred to the Air OP Course at 1242 flight RAF Larkhill on Salisbury Plain. Although I was an Army officer flying light aircraft, the RAF insisted on owning all the aircraft. In addition to flying we experienced at first hand most of the difficulties of using Army tactics on the ground hampered by RAF bureaucracy, which insisted on tying aircraft to aerodromes, thus considerably limiting our movements.

I was fortunate to be posted to the first Air OP Squadron (651) which was formed on 23 January 1942 at Old Sarum just outside Salisbury. It was labelled an RAF Squadron but with all Royal

Artillery pilots, and although there were no RAF pilots the personnel was both Army and RAF, the latter to service the aircraft.

The difficulty then was that there were more pilots than usable aircraft. The main problem was that only the RAF could own and order aircraft. The Air OP Squadron needed new aircraft designed for its purpose but it was stalled in the general disagreement between Air Ministry and War Office on what was needed and who should fund it. In the spring of 1942 the Air OP was a victim of the national inter-service disagreement as to whether the war could be won by bombing from the air. The Artillery were convinced that it could not be as effective and accurate in the existing technology of the time. The Air OP became stranded by lack of attention and agreement from above. So much so that the Squadron CO, Lieutenant Colonel Charles Bazeley, whose patience was exhausted, asked me as a fledgling barrister of two years' standing, to go through the office files and prepare a statement showing the shortages and disappointments which beset the squadron. This was at a time when the evidence from manoeuvres with the only civilian small aircraft available (the Taylorcraft made under licence at Leicester and later christened the Auster) seemed to confirm the belief that this type of aircraft could see and survive in the heat of battle, subject to strict flight discipline and training.

I was given an office typist and we worked flat out for about three weeks and produced a draft, an accurate but damning report supported by appendices of detailed evidence. The CO presented it to the Divisional Commandant Royal Artillery and it went up to the GHQ Home Forces forthwith. I was detailed to introduce it to the High Command, Major General Otto Lund, OC Royal Artillery Home Forces, who asked me to produce a condensed report for further transmission upwards and sideways. So a new section of the War Office was established, the Directorate of Air, which included parachutists and gliders. By this time I had resumed flying with my section on a glorious exercise from Bournemouth to Norfolk when I was ordered to report to the new department of the War Office forthwith.

I was there for six months from April to September 1942, during which time more Austers were ordered, there being no agreed prototype for a more suitable aircraft. The establishment of the Air OP was finally negotiated and agreed. Many other air matters with a military element flooded in to Air One, under the directorate of Sir Richard Gale, later to command the 6th Airborne Division. I had done my best to concentrate on the Air OP's development but inevitably got entangled in minor issues besides the central issue of Army air requirements. I did not wish to stay in the War Office as I wanted particularly to see active service and luckily was relieved just in time to rejoin 651 Squadron in Scotland ten days before they set sail for Algiers.

As an Air OP pilot I was attached to a division and therefore in a position to speak to both the top brass in artillery as well as to all other ranks, which gave me a wide overview as well as being a very interesting social experience.

I also acted as an unofficial liaison officer between the Army units on the one hand and the RAF on the other whenever a gap in communications between them occurred.

It was found in the first thrust for Tunis that bomber assistance was needed. Knowing that there was an American bomber force near Tebessa, only two hours flying time away but with no means of communication, I managed to find them and to convince them to come and join in. I was able to persuade the commander of the importance of it and he agreed, subject to various options of a technical nature relating to the fuses for the bombs. I had then to fly back to Divisional HQ to let our commander know of these options. After reading them, he decided on yet another visit next day and using my Auster he sent his RAF liaison officer, Wing Commander Mathias, back to Tebessa to confirm the details. The end result was that the American Squadron joined in as bomber support. This could only have happened once the initial contact was made, so it showed the value of that first liaison flight. The report confirming this joint venture was handed in to become an appendix to the official war diary. Three weeks later on the afternoon of 22 April 1943 I was to join No 1 Division which had come across from the Eighth Army to strengthen our final thrust for Tunis itself. I went up on a motor cycle with my batman to introduce myself and the Air OP to a regiment with no previous knowledge of our operation. While negotiating to borrow a truck to collect camouflage nets and stores to hide the aircraft on arrival at dawn, the regiment were provoked, by casual but accurate German fire, to reveal their position. This further provoked bursts of counter-battery fire by the German artillery which struck both me and the command post officer and thus ended my fighting career.

It was the very eve of the final push to Tunis and I had been badly hurt with flesh wounds and a small hole in the head which was not considered to be very significant at the time. I was evacuated in the normal way, down the line to hospital, and so missed by a day a new scheme whereby those with brain injuries were being flown directly to St Hugh's Hospital at Oxford, so it actually took me a full ten weeks or seventy days to make my own way there, having been told of its existence by a surgeon on the way to Algiers.

All my papers were lost on board the hospital ship the *Newfoundland,* and so with no papers I was powerless against the authorities' decision whereby we were entrained at Avonmouth (Bristol) and bound for a civilian hospital at Bishop Auckland. Eventually back in London, I was able to persuade former colleagues to arrange a medical board for me which was planned for the following Monday. However, I never got that far as on the Saturday preceding it I began to shiver and found that I was running a temperature of 103 degrees F at which point I was taken by ambulance from the Guards Barracks to the Royal Masonic Hospital from where, after another fortnight, I was finally transferred to St Hugh's in Oxford.

After a long period of recuperation following surgery John Hill was discharged from St Hugh's, but instead of going to an Army convalescent home, Merton College very kindly made him a temporary member of the Senior Common Room, until a month or so later when he was finally passed as fit for light duties again. His former examiner, Sir J C Masterman, had found Hill some agreeable security work in a branch of the War Office amid the art galleries of St James Street where he both broadened his knowledge and made several worthwhile purchases 'during many an enjoyable lunch hour'. The only fearsome threat at that time he concludes, 'being too near the landing of a Doodlebug!'

JOHN PAGE

Another former gunner John Page, was Conservative MP for Harrow West from 1960–1987, and was made a Knight in 1984. He spent some of his childhood in India where his father was a judge and later Chief Justice of Burma. He was educated at Harrow and Cambridge.

In September 1939 it took him two attempts to join the Army. On the first attempt he was rejected due to bad eyesight at the HAC recruiting office in the City. At the second attempt, at the Inns of Court recruiting office, he was passed fit and recruited into the Royal Artillery.

He reported to Fort Gomer, near Gosport, on 15 December 1939. After three months recruit training he was posted to 122 OCTU at Larkhill. After commissioning he was posted to 73 Medium Regiment RA, which was at Tarporley in Cheshire. By the time the regiment sailed to the Middle East in early 1941 he had risen to become the assistant adjutant.

After arriving in Egypt, the regiment was converted to an anti-tank regiment, having trained previously on 50 pounder medium guns. Eventually the regiment was completely split up, with each battery being put under the command of an infantry battalion and each troop with a company. John Page was attached to the Rifle Brigade and recalls:

> We were taking part in what was called the 'June Show', rather a disastrous movement towards Tobruk where the British and our regiment got badly mauled. It was my first experience of action.
>
> In the desert you never quite knew where you were. On that first memorable occasion I was standing up in my jeep looking for a Rifle Brigade platoon, being driven by Gunner Owen, who had been a

professional ballroom dancer in Liverpool. I saw him ducking a bit over the wheel and said to him, 'What's that funny whistling noise, Owen?' and he replied, 'Bullets, I think, Sir.' 'OK,' I said. 'Perhaps we'd better go back but don't seem to be in a hurry.'

About an hour later we were properly in a hull-down position with the guns facing the enemy. One of our guns was hit and one of the chaps killed –the first dead person I'd ever seen in my life. A super chap, Windsor, an ex-boxer, said, 'Leave it to me, Sir,' but determinedly he and I wrapped the body in blankets and soon a first aid vehicle from the RB appeared. It was a nasty time, but I felt glad that I could cope.

The desert war, under Wavell and Auchinleck, was a matter of each side going forward and then retreating. Our regiment had had a lot of casualties, and our battery was reformed under Tony Hinde. To start with my troop was attached to a Scots Guards battalion.

There was a very wet winter in 1941 when neither side could move –but early in 1942 we made progress towards relieving Tobruk. At a place called El Adem we were surrounded by Germans and Gunner Windsor and I, on one of the guns, took pot shots at the German tanks. We were hit and my face became warm and wet, which I thought was blood from the top of my scalp, but luckily it was only warm water from a holed jerrican! We had a couple more shots and then decided it was time to go. I reported the action and Windsor got an immediate DCM.

So, back to regroup near Garawla –and this is the very saddest part of my story. I was told to go to a map reference along a telephone line 2 or 3 miles into the desert from the coast road. The movement of our troops and the enemy was very fluid and, at about the right spot, I saw a group of British vehicles – later I realized they had been captured. My driver was a young chap (the same age as me) called Wyn Thomas. We were just leaving the telephone line when there was a crack. I felt a sharp pain just above the left knee and the car started to move jerkily. I looked at Thomas, who was slumped over the wheel. The truck stalled and I realized that a single round, probably armour-piercing, as it did not explode, had gone right through poor Thomas, hit me and then gone through the passenger's door. I pulled him out of the truck and realized without going into details, that it was all over for him and said a prayer for us both as we were then being sniped at. There was nothing I could do. I was bleeding rather a lot, but put on some kind of dressing and crawled, still being sniped at, away from where the fire was coming. After a couple of hundred yards I heard a shout 'over here' and a hand waving from a slit trench –some of our infantry. I crawled across, got in and, at some stage, was taken away on a stretcher, then to a casualty station and, I think, two days, in an old Austin ambulance, exactly like 'Ice Cold in Alex,' then on to a hospital in the Delta.

After five or six weeks in hospital John Page went to a comfortable convalescent home in Jerusalem and took advantage of the situation by visiting all the holy places.

After his period of convalescence was over, he went on sick leave to Cairo, where he took a room in Shepheard's Hotel. On the Saturday he and a friend collected all the money they could raise and went to Gezira Races. They put all their money on a single horse, which won. They collected £200, which was a small fortune at the time, and set about living in style for the next two weeks.

After his leave was over John Page was summoned to GHQ and was appointed Intelligence Officer, Royal Artillery (IORA) to 4th Indian Division. He joined them immediately at Alamein, where the Eighth Army had dug in; it was now September 1942. Brigadier Ken Dimoline and his chief of staff, John Wyld, had three field regiments and an anti-aircraft regiment under their command. John Wyld co-ordinated much of the targeting before the Battle of Alamein. John Page attended various meetings with the 4th Indian Division Commander, General Tucker, and the XXX Corps Commander, General Horrocks, and recalls:

Everyone was completely inspired by Monty (Tucker less than most) and there was a confident atmosphere of victory. At the battle our infantry were in reserve, but our gunners and Sappers were flat out. The noise and the excitement were intense and when we had Rommel on the run there was great rejoicing.

At some stage during the advance towards Tunis a small group of us went to meet the Free French General Leclerc. We had to stop at dusk, in the middle of nowhere, our Mess truck had mislaid itself, but we had a few meagre rations on our vehicles. Just before final darkness we heard a very low-flying aircraft, which crashed and then burst into flames about a mile away. It was, of all things, an American aircraft and the two pilots and four officers on some highly secret mission all escaped. As they came back with us, miraculously out of nowhere the Mess truck suddenly found us and not only started to produce a meal for everyone but even gave out some mail.

We successfully met General Leclerc, a strange figure in shorts, kepi and polished riding boots. Then on to Tunis where we were being stubbornly held up at Wadi Akarit. It was a feverish battle, with our Division attacking an impregnable mountain pass. I was sent by jeep to General Tucker with some bad intelligence news and ran breathlessly to his open staff car where he was reading. He gave me time to collect my breath, half-closed the book he was reading, said, 'Thank you, Jack' and turned back to his book. On the following night our Gurkhas climbed a sheer precipice and, kukri in hand, took the Italians from the rear. A great feat of arms and there were few, if any, prisoners.

Then a left hook to make the final assault, together with the First Army, conventionally turned out, having recently arrived from England. They were astounded to see us unshaven in our white sheepskin coats, yellow cords and spotted scarves, but in a few days Tunis was ours and the desert battle won.

After the fall of Tunis John Page was sent on a staff course in Palestine and was then posted to Combined Operations Beach Group called a 'Brick'. He flew to England to join the forces preparing for the invasion of Europe, and was given a week's leave at home with his parents in Kent. His tiny unit, 23 Brick, which consisted of about forty officers and men, was stationed in the docks in the East End of London. It was supposed to be very secret and their job was to arrive on the beaches at H+6 (H-hour being the moment of first contact with the enemy). There would be three teams –travelling separately –so at least one should arrive. Their object was to protect an RAF signals team of one officer and two signallers, who would call up air support for the landing.

The day before embarkation, John Page was sent to pick up sealed orders for the invasion from Combined Ops HQ in Ashley Gardens, Westminster, and bring them back to his Colonel.

Next day we boarded SS *Neuralia,* an ancient small liner, with normal civilian crew and management. It seemed extraordinary to be going into the invasion in such comfort –printed menus for each meal –that for breakfast covering about 15 lines of options –I wish I had kept a copy. We had just one section of our Brick on board – the other passengers included my cousin Cholmeley Lewis and his anti-aircraft unit.

Quite soon we left Tilbury for Southampton Water, where the invasion fleet was being assembled, and we remained there for a few days waiting for the green light. One morning at 7.30 Foster, my very slack batman, called me with a mug of tea. 'It's started yer know' he said. 'What's started,' from me. 'The invasion.' 'But it can't start without us.' 'Well, the BBC says it has –at 6 o'clock this morning.'

Before breakfast we went to see the ancient, grumpy captain, who was actually very pleased that it appeared that he and his ship were not to be endangered and he utterly refused to ask for orders. After two days we persuaded him to allow Cholm (Cholmeley Lewis) to go ashore and by waving and shouting we stopped a small naval craft going to Southampton and he climbed down a rope ladder and left. He took a taxi to a headquarters on a hill above Southampton, demanded to see the senior Army officer, walked into a room in which were a brigadier, a naval captain and a group captain, saluted and announced, 'Sir, I've come from the *Neuralia.*' There was dead silence, then the captain shouted into a telephone, 'George, I've found the *Neuralia* –send her off at once.' It appears that we had been checked out of Tilbury but never into Southampton, so the Navy got a black mark.

Cholm insisted that he be taken out, as *Neuralia* was already on the move. We saw him appear, in choppy seas, and make a daredevil jump on to a scrambling net. In every way he was a hero except to the ship's captain.

So we arrived at Arromanches alongside one of the Mulberry piers which were already in place. I saw one of our jeeps and was taken to Brick HQ in a small house, undamaged, with a garden path lined with flowers. By then I had been reported missing. As I walked towards the door Colonel Ralston came out and theatrically threw his arms across his eyes. 'Jack,' he said: 'We thought you were dead' –pause – 'I think this calls for a little celebration' – which went on until lunchtime. Thus ended, very comfortably and safely, my life at the sharp end of Combined Ops. I am happy to say that our other two teams arrived on time and did their job well.

John Page spent the next few weeks helping to organize the huge amounts of ammunition and supplies going to 21 Army Group, and was then posted as battery captain to 258 Battery of the Norfolk Yeomanry, who were the anti-tank regiment of the 7th Armoured Division. His job was to see to all the administration and supplies for their four troops. Each troop consisted of four M 10s with 16 pounder anti-tank guns mounted on tanks. Each troop was attached to a different infantry battalion, so it was an extremely difficult task. From then to the end of the war he accompanied the battery through France, Belgium and Holland, including the attempted relief of Arnhem, and finally into Germany itself.

CHARLES SIMEONS

Charles Simeons was Conservative MP for Luton between 1970–1974. He was in his final year at school when war broke out and enlisted through a system which enabled people to join an arm of their choice and then await call up when their studies were finished. After school he went on to Cambridge, where he obtained a certificate B in the STC (Senior Training Corps), Royal Artillery section, and remained there until his call up in February 1942, when he was posted to 123 OCTU RA at Catterick, Yorkshire.

He was commissioned in August 1942 and posted to 52 Manchester Regiment RA, stationed at Holt in Norfolk. Upon arrival he was told to go on immediate embarkation leave as the regiment was under orders to go overseas. The guns had already been despatched. The regiment finally left Holt for Liverpool on 23 September 1942, to embark on the *Highland Monarch*, one of over twenty ships, including cargo vessels, that set sail via the Cape to Egypt.

Happily we experienced a relatively uneventful voyage, the only real sign of hostilities being when I was matched against a fellow officer in the inevitable boxing show. We were both heavyweights, having been members of our respective university boxing teams. Fortunately for me, I won the bout.

On arrival at Port Tewfik, at the southern end of the Suez Canal, we went to a very large camp about 40 miles east of Cairo, where we trained, while awaiting our guns. We remained there until the New Year, when we moved up to Kiffri, about 150 miles from Baghdad, where the 8th Indian Division was formed. One of the other two regiments of artillery was 53 Field Regiment RA, which came from Bolton

110

and which the First Division Bolton Wanderers Football Team had joined en masse.

In the spring of 1943 we moved to the Lebanon, and then Syria, where we engaged in dry-shod training, practicing seaborne landings. At the end of July 1943 the Division, recognizable from its Divisional sign of yellow clover leaves on a red background, moved to Suez. After a short while we embarked on liners, the rumour being that we were due to land on Rhodes. In the event this expedition did not take place because the large contingent of Italians which had occupied Rhodes were overcome by a handful of Germans. Instead, we carried out an exercise, landing from the Red Sea. We then returned to Damascus.

However, as the last trains were arriving at Damascus, the first were on their way back to Alexandria, where we were confined to camp for three weeks until on 23 September 1943 six liners carried the 8th Indian Division to Italy. After a brief stay at Taranto, we joined the line near Foggia. It was at this point that the mountain chain created watersheds which directed the Italian rivers to the east and to the west into the Adriatic and Tyrrhenian seas. Scores of such rivers on each coast lay across the path of any invader from the south, each offering an obstacle to mechanized forces. The enemy exploited the terrain to the full, with enemy forces committed to decisive battle only in key positions. The German plan required a great many troops, including high-class shock troops, paratroops, Panzer Grenadier divisions and other specialist formations. When the weather broke, rains filled valleys and softened hillsides. Roads softened under excessive traffic and retaining walls slid from the hillside. Lorries skated on their way or skidded into ditches. All bridges had been systematically blown.

Among the many devices especially built for the campaign the bull-dozer to deal with solid earth and the meccano-like frames and sections of the Bailey bridge to deal with unstable water stood out. A bridge of any length and height, tensile strength or carrying power would be built in a matter of hours. It was these devices that made our advance possible at river crossings such as the Sangro and later the Senio near Ferrara, both scenes of considerable fighting and bravery, where two Indian soldiers were awarded the VC.

During a period of bad weather and relative stalemate the Divisional Commander, General Russell, decided that he would build a bridge over the Moro, on his front, at such a place that the Germans would be sure that it was meant to be used. The point chosen, at a right-angle bend in the road, made it an impossible site from which to build a bridge from the south bank. The commander of the Divisional Sapper's, Lieutenant Colonel C M MacLachlan, decided to build the bridge from the enemy side. It became known as the Impossible Bridge.

On the last day of the year a blizzard swept in from the Adriatic with biting winds, drifting snow and driving sleet. Long lines of frost-bound vehicles stood starkly by the roadside. The offensive slowed to a standstill. It was then that General Montgomery left Italy and the landing at Anzio began.

Up to this point I had been a gun position officer, responsible for providing data for the guns and responding to fire orders from our forward observation posts. However, shortly after the third battle at Cassino I became regimental survey officer.

During the period from Christmas to the spring I spent periods in forward positions with the infantry, the 1/5 Royal West Kents and the Argyll and Sutherland Highlanders, providing artillery cover. The most memorable was when I spent two weeks in the station at Cassino, where apparently so important was possession of the town that I could have called upon the whole Corps artillery fire power had there been a full-scale attack envisaged. I have often wondered what would have been the response had we done so, but then I would not have been here today to tell the tale.

Happily the third Battle of Cassino was successful and in due course we were moving forward at a very fast rate. As survey officer I was given areas for the 25-pounder guns which at times were behind enemy forward defensive lines. On some occasions the guns never actually occupied the positions chosen, so fast was the advance, moving on to the next area. In this manner, with occasional and fierce resistance, we bypassed Rome and stopped at Florence. Winter caused us to halt in the mountains just short of Bologna, when I was posted back to the UK to train as an Air OP Pilot. We had been in action for eighteen months apart from a fortnight's rest outside Pisa.

After an observation of fire course, which surprisingly, only half the squad passed, Charles Simeons went to Cambridge for flying instruction on Tiger Moths. However, with the war in Europe ending, only the best three were accepted and the rest returned to Woolwich, the Royal Artillery depot. From there he was posted to Kenya, where he was given a staff captain's job at HQRA, where he remained for a year, until his four years overseas expired. Upon return to UK he was posted to Northern Command Headquarters in York, as a staff major where he remained until being demobbed prior to returning to Cambridge.

At the time of writing, Charles Simeons was Honorary Secretary of the Clover Club, 8th Indian Division Officers Association, and the 52nd Field Regiment RA, organizing their annual reunions. He has also been involved in fund raising for the Royal Artillery Museum project at the Woolwich Arsenal site.

DAVID RENTON

David Renton was elected as National Liberal MP for Huntingdonshire in 1945: while at Oxford University he had been President of the Liberal Club. He represented the same seat until 1979, but in 1968 became a Conservative. His appointments during that time included being Parliamentary Secretary for the Ministry of Fuel and Power and Under Secretary of State, and then Minister of State, for the Home Office. He was created a life peer, as Lord Renton of Huntingdon, in 1979, and was Deputy Chairman of the House of Lords from 1982–1988.

David Renton was born in 1908 and, while at school, was in the Junior Division of the OTC, where he trained for the infantry. At University College, Oxford, he was in the Senior Division of the OTC and trained for the horse cavalry. After graduating in Jurisprudence, he was called to the Bar in 1933 and was elected to the General Council of the Bar in 1939. Although first a Sapper, he was later transferred to the RA, attaining the rank of Major.

> In June 1938 I was commissioned as a Territorial Officer in the Royal Engineers in north Kent, because by this time it was obvious that the Germans were going to start a war. When the war began in September 1939 we were doing our annual training on top of a hill on the North Downs in Kent and from there we moved to our war stations. I found myself responsible with another officer for six searchlight sites in and around Gravesend.
>
> The Battle of Britain started in June 1940 and I was by then made Staff Lieutenant of an anti-aircraft brigade, which covered Essex and Suffolk. In August 1940 those of us who were Sappers were transferred to the Royal Artillery.

Seeing hundreds of German bombers flying overhead at a range higher than 20,000 feet, which was the maximum range of our heavy anti-aircraft guns, was a formidable sight. One greatly admired the fighter pilots of the RAF, who rapidly climbed above the height of German bombers and brought many of them down.

It was a horrible experience, especially as so many civilians were killed, not only in London but out in the country too. In September 1940, when our Brigade headquarters had moved to Boxted just north of Colchester, we heard at midnight a colossal explosion in the nearby village and we got out of bed, got into our jeeps and found that a 600-year-old church had been destroyed by the first parachute bomb to be dropped by the Germans in the UK.

In October 1940 I managed to get 48 hours' leave and went home to my parents at Dartford. My mother and I decided to have a game of golf on Dartford Heath golf course and my father, who could no longer play, walked around part of the course with us. Some German bombers flew over, having bombed London and got rid of several more bombs, one of which exploded near us and knocked my father over, although he was a tall and heavily built man. The bomb made a hole in the middle of the fairway of the eighteenth hole, which was later turned into a bunker and they called it 'Renton's Bunker'. On two other occasions German bombs just missed me and other gunners.

In early 1941 I was sent on a Command Staff Course for two months and then was made Staff Captain of the anti-aircraft brigade which covered the whole of Devon (except Plymouth), West Somerset and West Dorset. It was a lovely area and we did not have much enemy activity, but we had to train quite a large group of conscripts.

In March 1942 I was sent by the War Office to the RA HQ at Woolwich, where I found that I was to be made Staff Captain of another artillery brigade for service overseas and had to ensure that 102 items were fulfilled, among the last of which was the appointment of a Brigadier.

The Brigadier sent to us by the War Office was known in the regular Army as 'Barmy' Morton, who seemed more interested in religion than in the war. The Brigade Major was John Brocklebank, a splendid man, who in the 1960s became chairman of Cunard. In April 1942 we sailed from Liverpool in the large convoy which was the build-up before the Battle of Alamein.

When we arrived in Egypt we found that we were to be responsible for anti-aircraft defence throughout the Delta of Egypt and in the Western Desert. Until the battle started in September 1942 we had a busy time because of the vast area we had to cover, but we were only slightly troubled by German aircraft.

At the Battle of Alamein some of our heavy anti-aircraft guns were used in the artillery barrage. During the advance after the Germans had started to retreat it was a thrilling time and a rather wonderful journey along the Mediterranean coast of the Western Desert. Our light anti-aircraft Bofors guns played a useful part as ground attack weapons and managed to keep moving quickly. When we got to Mersa Matruh, where we were ordered to stop, we found that the buildings had all been damaged. But in the remains of a small hotel we managed to find accommodation for the Brigadier and several others. The rest of us found that the small desert tents were all that we needed. However, the worst part about Mersa Matruh was that, before retreating, the German and Italian soldiers had been told to use the whole place as an outdoor lavatory and they did not use toilet paper in doing so. The enemy hoped that this would spread disease among us and within a few days I found that I had lost my voice, had a high temperature and a fever and the medical officer said that I had diphtheria and would have to go back to Alexandria and go to hospital. However, before I got there our brigade headquarters was ordered back to create an assault group on the Dodocanese Islands. When I was in hospital, the Brigade Major and my successor as Staff Captain were made to go in a submarine to the island of Leros, where the Greeks, instead of showing them the best places for the group to land, took them straight to the German garrison and they spent the rest of the war as PoWs. This would have happened to me if the enemy had not turned Mersa Matruh into a lavatory!

I was kept on my back in hospital for a month and successfully recovered from diphtheria. Having become very weak, I was sent on sick leave for six weeks and went up the Nile Valley to Cairo, Thebes and Assuan, after which I had to report to the Legal Department of GHQ Cairo, where I was told I was to be trained in Italian Law and become President of the Courts of Tripolitana, at which I protested as I wanted to follow the Eighth Army into Italy and pointed out that I was only 34 and had not tried a case in my life. The legal officer directing me then said, 'Can't help that. There's no one else, so you'll have to do it.'

So, after six months preparation in GHQ Cairo, I went to Tripoli, having learned some Italian and Italian Law and I spent the rest of the war there. It was a very interesting experience, but I felt frustrated at being kept away from the Eighth Army. Besides having a wide jurisdiction to try cases of first instance, I had to try appeals from grey-bearded Italian judges who wore scarlet silk robes!

FREDERIC BENNETT

A gunner with a very different story to tell is Frederic Bennett, who was Conservative MP for Reading North from 1951–1955, Torquay from 1955–1974 and finally Torbay from 1974–1987: he was knighted in 1964. Although he was eventually commissioned into the Royal Artillery, he began his military life with the Middlesex Yeomanry and ended it with the Petroleum War Department, where he experimented with new and awesome weaponry.

At the age of 19 I joined the Middlesex Yeomanry, via their head-quarters in Lincoln's Inn as a 'trooper'. For in theory although by then a signals regiment and a mounted one at that, but with no horses, because of a chronic heart condition of one and later two leaking valves following on rheumatic fever at the age of 12, I only narrowly escaped being classified C3 and discharged from the Army shortly after the war broke out. In the end (which is another story) I managed to get up graded to B1, which enabled me to stay in the forces, but with certain restrictions on what I was permitted to do.

When the phoney war ended my unit was transferred to go to France from our training base in Eastbourne, to join our forces on the continent. However, by the time we got there, Dunkirk had occurred and one's priority task was not to cross the Channel going eastwards but to help our defeated Army, and many of the French too, to be landed at Dover.

Very shortly afterwards I was offered a commission in the Royal Artillery (Coastal Defences) and stayed there, serving in various places in England and Wales in the course of which period I was highly commended, officially, for gallantry and initiative – but that too is another story.

I was then seconded, at my own request, to the Petroleum War Department, PWD, which was formed under the political leadership of the late Geoffrey Lloyd, with Brigadier Sir Donald Banks as its military chief, specifically to explore and develop the best possible uses for large petrol stocks, including flame throwers, incendiary mortar bombs and shells, FIDO (fog intensive disposal operation), to help our aircraft to land more safely after their bombing forays across the Channel. It was this same department that invented the terrible weapon of war, Napalm, as it is now called, and Pluto (pipe line under the ocean) to supply our forces with fuel after D-Day.

While serving in that particular context, as an experimental officer, I was very severely burned when one of the first mortar bombs, with its contents, prematurely exploded.

These episodes are all recorded in a book, now I imagine out of print, by Sir Donald Banks called *Flame over Britain*.

As the war drew to its close, the tasks allotted to me were to travel to Western Europe primarily to bring back all the technology in this field which the Germans possessed, presumably to stop it falling into the hands of the Soviets.

In the spring of 1946 Frederic Bennett was given the opportunity of going on the reserve of officers and did so with the permanent substantive rank of major.

1. James Callaghan in the uniform of an Ordinary Seaman, Royal Navy. The picture was taken in the early 1940s in Llandudno, where his wife spent the war years with their young family.
(Photo courtesy of The Rt Hon Lord Callaghan of Cardiff)

2. Passing Out photograph, March 1944. James Davidson is pictured in front row extreme left. *(Photo courtesy of James Davidson)*

3. HMS *Anson* at sea in May 1944, the ship which James Davidson joined immediately after Passing Out. *(Photo courtesy of James Davidson)*

4. 'Abandon Ship at Dawn' painted by Reginald Bennett in 1940. *(Photo courtesy of Sir Reginald Bennett)*

5. Wartime photograph of the former
   Prime Minister Sir Edward Heath,
   who served throughout the campaign
   in North-West Europe with the
   Royal Artillery.
   (Photo courtesy of Sir Edward Heath)

6. Gordon Campbell in October 1946,
   shortly after his release from hospital.
   (Photo courtesy of Lord Campbell of Croy)

7. Local dignitaries assembled outside the Pontypool house of Roy Jenkins (far right) to
   meet the Deputy Prime Minister, June 1941. His mother is pictured 2nd from left, his
   father, who was the MP for Pontypool, is 3rd from right.

   (Photo courtesy of Lord Jenkins of Hillhead)

8. Roy Jenkins on his wedding day at the Savoy Chapel, 20 January 1945.
(Photo courtesy of Lord Jenkins of Hillhead)

9. John Page surveys the ruined buildings of Berlin in 1945.
(Photo courtesy of Sir John Page)

10. John Hill wears the wings of a pilot with the Royal Artillery.
(Photo courtesy of John Hill)

11. Denis Healey as a Captain in the Royal Engineers in 1944.
(Photo courtesy of Lord Healey of Riddlesden)

12. Denis Healey in his jeep.

(Photo courtesy of Lord Healey of Riddlesden)

13. Ivan Neill, who was later the Speaker of the House of Commons, served with the Royal Engineers.

(Photo courtesy of Sir Ivan Neill)

14. Labour politician Ronald Murray, who was later Lord Advocate, served with REME in Asia.

(Photo courtesy of Lord Murray)

15. John Osborn, later the MP for the Hallam Division of Sheffield, as a 2nd Lieutenant in the Royal Corps of Signals in 1944.

(Photo courtesy of Sir John Osborn)

16. John Osborn at the Royal Signals Camp, Lagos, Nigeria, in 1945.

(Photo courtesy of Sir John Osborn)

17. Drawing of Robert Redmond made by a fellow officer in SOE on the shores of the Adriatic Sea.
(Photo courtesy of Robert Redmond)

18. Paul Bryan in 1943. He joined the Queen's Own Royal West Kent Regiment in July 1939 as a private soldier and rose to the rank of lieutenant colonel in the same battalion, without ever having left it.
(Photo courtesy of Sir Paul Bryan)

19. Paul Bryan (right) and soldiers of the 6th Battalion, Royal West Kents, look down on Centuripe in Sicily.
(Photo courtesy of Sir Paul Bryan)

20. Paul Bryan (left) at OCTU Barmouth in 1944, with Denis Forman (2nd left) who was his 2IC in Italy. Later, they were both directors of Granada Television.

(Photo courtesy of Sir Paul Bryan)

21. Clive Bossom, who served in The Buffs with his younger brother Captain Doric Bossom of the Coldstream Guards *(Photo courtesy of Sir Clive Bossom)*

22. James Spicer, later the MP for Dorset West.
(Photo courtesy of Sir James Spicer)

23. James Spicer (centre) and other candidates relax on The Isle of Man. Spicer attended the OCTU on the island from September to December 1943, from where he was commissioned into the Royal Fusiliers. *(Photo courtesy of Sir James Spicer)*

24. David Stuart, James Spicer, Tony Paget DSO and David Taylor MC, at the start of the attack on the Reichswald. Within a week of the photo being taken Paget was killed and Taylor wounded and evacuated. *(Photo courtesy of Sir James Spicer)*

25. Members of 18 Platoon the Ox & Bucks Light Infantry make their preparations for entry into Hamburg. *(Photo courtesy of Sir James Spicer)*

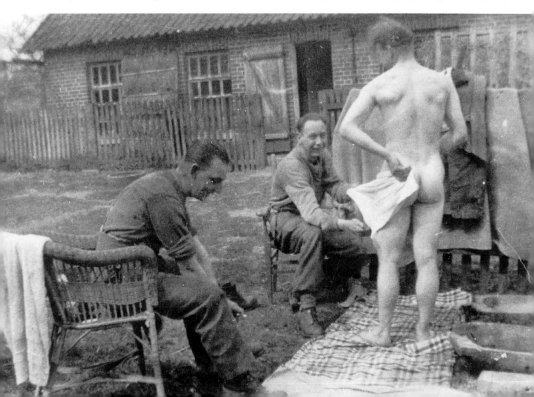

26. Marcus Worsley, who was a Conservative Member of Parliament between 1959-74, and later Lord-Lieutenant of North Yorkshire, served during the war with The Green Howards. *(Photo courtesy of Sir Marcus Worsley)*

27. Stephen Hastings (in beret) with Partisan escort in the Italian mountains. *(Photo courtesy of Sir Stephen Hastings)*

28. Stephen Hastings, Cairo, 1942.
(Photo courtesy of Sir Stephen Hastings)

29. Victory parade through Piacenza after the Partisans had taken it from the Germans.
(Photo courtesy of Sir Stephen Hastings)

30. Jeep mounted with a Browning machine gun. It was from such vehicles that future parliamentarians Fitzroy Maclean, Carol Mather and Stephen Hastings operated behind enemy lines in North Africa with L Detachment of the SAS under David Stirling. *(Photo courtesy of Sir Stephen Hastings)*

31. Near Goch, waiting to join battle to clear the Germans from the west bank of the Rhine. Robert Boscawen is on the right. *(Photo courtesy of Robert Boscawen)*

32. Robert Boscawen (far right) and a party of ex 1st Coldstream Guards and 3rd Irish Guards visit Sourdeval in 1994, where they fought a fierce action fifty years earlier. *(Photo courtesy of Robert Boscawen)*

33. Tony Benn, who did much of his pilot training in the RAF in Rhodesia. *(Photo courtesy of Tony Benn)*

34. Jim Molyneaux's only photo of himself in uniform, taken at a captured German air base in 1945.
(Photo courtesy of Lord Molyneaux of Killead)

35. Peter Shore in 1946, pictured on his way back from India.
(Photo courtesy of Lord Shore of Stepney)

36. Two Glenn Martin Baltimores flying in loose formation over the Western Desert. Photo taken by Colin Turner.
(Photo courtesy of Sir Colin Turner)

37. Colin Turner in London, January 1944.
(Photo courtesy of Sir Colin Turner)

38. A raid on a railway marshalling yard at Catanzaro, Italy, on 7 September 1943, of which Colin Turner says: "We were supposed to bomb some 6000 feet above the target, but owing to the weather, as you can see we dropped the bombs from about 1200 feet. We had to miss the hospital at the bottom left. As a result of the low-level attack, our aircraft was badly hit and the plastic nose in which I was sitting was almost completely blown away and I was wounded with dozens of pieces of plastic. We returned safely to our base in Gerbine, Sicily, on one engine and the undercarriage down."
(Photo courtesy of Sir Colin Turner)

39. Hector Monro, who retained an association with the RAF for 60 years, and was Air Commodore and Hon. Inspector General of the Royal Auxilary Air Force, up until his retirement in 2000.
(Photo courtesy of Lord Monro of Langholm)

Part Four

THE ROYAL ENGINEERS
AND OTHER SERVICE ARMS

As well as those serving in a fighting arm, there were of course many people serving in areas in which different regiments and units provided a 'service' which helped the efficient running of the Army. These 'service arms' were extremely varied and those employed within them were often given challenging and unconventional duties to perform. The Royal Engineers is probably the most important service provider during any major conflict, but this section also includes the accounts of soldiers who served with the Royal Electrical and Mechanical Engineers, the Royal Corps of Signals, the Royal Army Ordnance Corps and the Royal Army Service Corps.

DENIS HEALEY

Ex Defence Secretary and Chancellor of the Exchequer Denis Healey served during the war from September 1940 to December 1945, mainly in combined operations in the Mediterranean, for which he was mentioned in dispatches and awarded an MBE.

Denis Healey was born in 1917 and grew up in Yorkshire. He entered Balliol College, Oxford, in 1936 and in the summer of 1939 was given a travelling scholarship to visit Greece. During his trip across Europe he saw much evidence that the continent was preparing for war. In Eleusis he was arrested for being a Nazi spy because he was taking photographs near the Greek naval base at Salamis. The fact that he was wearing shorts contributed to their suspicion: he was promptly released.

On his return to England Denis Healey volunteered for the Army and was accepted by the Royal Artillery, but had to wait for his call up. Bored with waiting, he joined the Home Guard in Keighley but was eventually instructed to attend the Royal Artillery field training unit in Uniacke Barracks, near Harrogate. While there it was discovered during a medical inspection that he had a rupture, so he had to report to hospital for an immediate operation. After a period of sick leave he was sent to the Artillery depot at Woolwich to await a posting. His first posting, however, wasn't quite what he had expected. In the early months of 1941 he served at the Railway Traffic Office on Swindon station. His job was to count every service man, or woman, who got on, or off, the trains.

After the scar from his operation had healed he was sent to an officers' selection centre in Scarborough. Commissioned in to the Royal Engineers, he went to Derby to do a course in movement control, where he found himself concerned with planning and organizing the movement of armed forces by land, sea or air. After the course was over he spent several months as Rail Traffic Officer in Hull, Halifax, York, Leeds and Sheffield.

In the summer of 1942 he volunteered for training in combined operations to become an assistant military landing officer in a Beach Group. This training took place in Scotland. During this period he got his first bit of practical experience, when he accompanied an American cargo boat for the landing at Arzeu in Algeria, part of the operation to capture Oran from the Vichy French. During the trip he developed bronchitis and, on returning to England, went to hospital before finishing his training in Scotland.

On 13 April 1943 his fully trained Beach Group finally set sail from Glasgow to take part in major operations in the Mediterranean. Ten days later they disembarked at Algiers and moved up the coast to the Gulf of Tunis, where they became part of 78 Division, who were preparing for the invasion of Sicily. He eventually landed in Sicily at Avola three days after the main force, so he did not take part in the action there.

He was later posted to 231 Independent Brigade as Military Landing Officer –or beachmaster –for an assault on the Italian mainland north of Reggio. The idea was to cut off the Germans who were retreating from Sicily before they had a chance to reinforce those drawn up against the Allied landing at Salerno. 231 Brigade was composed of three regular battalions under the command of General Urquhart. However, due to a sudden storm, the operation didn't go entirely to plan and the flotilla of landing craft had to spend the night at Messina, where Denis Healey was responsible for unloading the entire brigade in darkness. This delay meant that the assault would have to change location in order to keep up with the retreating Germans. They would have to land much further north at a place called Porto di Santa Venere. On the evening of 7 September they set sail again, but all these unavoidable circumstances meant that timing and planning had 'gone to hell,' as Denis Healey recalls in his autobiography, *The Time of My Life*.

> The darkness was complete when I came on deck at half past two. Our landing craft was frozen in its relation to the dim shapes of other craft, so that it seemed we were stationary and the sea was flowing

past us. Flashes of green phosphorescence winked out of the receding foam. With difficulty I could construct a black range of mountains ahead. The Commandos should that moment be landing to test the German defences and to secure the beaches for our assault battalion, due to follow an hour later.

Half past four –still no sign of fighting. The darkness was almost imperceptibly reduced, the mountains larger, with a faint white glow at their foot. On the bridge the Brigadier was trying to contact his leading battalions.

'Hello Drake, hello Drake –are you dry yet, are you dry yet? Over to you, over.'

'The Devons are ashore, sir.'

The quiet repetitions continued. Then, like the cast of a fishing line, a soundless red arc of tracer, and another. Everyone watched intently, trying to interpret. Slowly it became clear that nothing was going according to plan. None of the units ashore had yet found a recognizable objective. But opposition seemed slight.

I went down into the operations room and put on my equipment. I felt sober, suppressing my excitement. With my dispatch cases, mapboards, haversack swinging around me I felt absurdly overdressed.

When I came on deck again it was half light. A grey coast of steep high hills on my left, and a long low jetty running out ahead to meet us on our right. We all crowded up against the ramps. There was a small town ahead of us, the beach enclosed between the hills and the jetty, a few craft already discharging and troops running into the streets behind.

BANG! A loud explosion somewhere. I saw spray settling back into the sea astern. BANG! Another explosion this time sent spray like drizzle over us. We crouched down and adjusted our helmets. It was mortar fire from some concealed position in the hills.

At last the craft swished into the shingle, down rattled the ramps, and we ran ashore.

It was still about half an hour before dawn. I could see a number of landing craft beached down by the water's edge, their ramps lowering, waiting for track to pour their vehicles over. Something was seriously wrong. Two craft should have beached half an hour before, carrying howitzers and bulldozers, towing sledges loaded with hundreds of yards of wire track.

All the timing had gone to hell. The Commandos had landed nearly two hours late three miles from the correct place, and no one had yet seen or heard them. The assaulting battalion with the Assistant Military Landing Officers and the naval beachmaster, who should have made a reconnaissance for beach exits, had landed on the wrong beach, an hour and a half late.

In fact everyone, assault battalion, AMLOs, beachmaster, reserve battalions, vehicles, and brigade headquarters reached the main beach at the same time. And the Germans had simultaneously occupied the hills above us, where they had perfect positions for their mortars.

As a result we had an extremely unpleasant time on the beach, with many casualties. The naval commander, Admiral McGrigor, had his launch sunk under him, General Urquhart collected shell splinters in his backside, and I myself had my first experience of being dive-bombed.

The enemy mortars were still lobbing bombs at us when everyone dropped flat. Dive bombers were falling on us out of the sun. I heard two, three descending drones and the grass suddenly blew in my face, the bushes swayed towards me.

I felt myself lifted off the ground, there was a tinkling followed by thuds as debris hit the earth again. I had not heard the explosion.

Then WHOOM, WHOOM, WHOOM, WHOOM, WHOOM. I counted the bursts, my muscles taut.

Stones and earth showered around and I felt a heavy blow on my right ankle. Then the drone faded. I got up and brushed off the dirt. My ankle was numb and not very painful.

The mortar bombing continued all day and night. We were sitting targets for the enemy on the hills above, who could see our every move, while we could never see them.

Then the Germans moved on. We shipped our two hundred casualties back to base in Sicily. The brigade was snatched away immediately for the landing in Normandy, while I returned to my normal work.

Following these dramatic events, Denis Healey was given a job on the staff in Bari. He was then posted to Naples. In January 1944 he was appointed Military Landing Officer to the British assault brigade for Anzio. The planning for this was carried out in the great baroque palace at Caserta.

Shortly before the operation he was involved in an accident when travelling in a lorry towards Castellamare, on the way to load up. The lorry ran into a concrete post at sixty miles an hour and he was thrown through the windscreen, cutting his throat and breaking one of his front teeth. The dentist was unable to use an anaesthetic on him and broke a drill while giving treatment. He recalls this as 'the worst pain I suffered in the war'.

All this aside, the landing at Anzio went exactly to plan and the Germans were taken completely by surprise. Of course, as history is proof, although the landing went well, subsequent operations from the beach-head were less than satisfactory.

After Anzio and a spell back at Naples, Denis Healey was sent to the east coast of Italy, where he served with the Polish Corps for the capture of Ancona.

After the capture of Ancona he rejoined the Eighth Army at Siena. In November he was sent to Pesaro, south of Rimini, to plan a major landing in northern Yugoslavia, which was intended to prevent Tito's Partisans from capturing Fiume. However, the Partisans arrived before the Allied forces were due to start landing and the operation was cancelled.

He spent the last months of the war in Florence, with headquarters of 15 Army Group. After the German surrender he made a trip into Austria before returning to Britain, where he immediately began thinking about a future career in politics. In fact, his ambitions were aroused a year before, when he received a letter from Ivor Thomas, the Labour MP for Keighley. Mr Thomas, having spoken with his parents, was aware of his political views and invited him to be put on the list of potential Labour candidates. He agreed and after being offered a choice of two safe Conservative seats, opted for Pudsey and Otley. So once the war in Europe was over, he was given three months' leave for the election, and was able to attend the Labour Party Conference on 21 May 1945. The speech which Denis Healey made during the conference so impressed the party that he was invited to apply for the job of International Secretary of the Labour Party, after his – predicted –defeat at the general election. In fact his defeat was not as great as expected, cutting a huge Conservative majority to 1,651.

In the week before Christmas 1945 he finally left the Army, married Edna Edmunds and began work as International Secretary to the Labour Party at Transport House.

In 1952 Denis Healey became the Labour MP for South-East Leeds. He was appointed Defence Secretary under Harold Wilson in 1964 and Chancellor of the Exchequer in 1974. In recognition of his services to the nation he was later elevated to the peerage as Lord Healey of Riddlesden.

IVAN NEILL

During the war years Ivan Neill worked as a more conventional Sapper than Denis Healey. He was the MP for the Ballynafeigh Division of Belfast between 1949–1973, the same year he was made a Knight. He was also Speaker of the House of Commons from 1969–1973.

During the early part of the war Ivan Neill was employed by RE Services in a civilian capacity. The main programme of work with which he was involved was the provision of ground defences against enemy air raids. He was responsible for constructing gun emplacements for Bofors anti-aircraft guns, and accommodation for the gun crews, in the area surrounding Belfast. This was all completed before the first heavy raids came in April 1942, and by the summer of the same year he had been commissioned into the Royal Engineers.

> Another urgent job was the provision of accommodation for the incoming USA Army air-forces. I saw the beginning of this work, but in mid-June my commission into the Corps of the Royal Engineers came through and I was appointed Garrison Engineer (Defences) for the Belfast area. I had hardly time to settle into the job when I was posted to the School of Military Engineering, Ripon, Yorkshire. This was a very profitable time for me and when I returned to my unit in the autumn I was promoted to A/CRE. This proved to be a very challenging job for me as with the growth of the troops arriving from the States we were faced with a heavy demand for accommodation. In a frantic effort Nissen huts and requisitioned accommodation were used to meet the demand. When the pressure eased off somewhat I

129

was appointed D/CRE in North Belfast, and my responsibilities were growing.

Very soon after I found myself in Elgin, Morayshire, having been posted to a training battalion where I first tasted the rigours of military life. We were being trained for the coming offensive in North Africa with bomb disposal as a major part of our training.

When the posting came the main group went to North Africa and a few of us were returned to our NI units. My stay was short, I was posted to Halifax for transport overseas to a unit in the build up for the war against the Japs. After a few weeks we found ourselves aboard a troopship in Liverpool destined for Bombay. The long journey out was very pleasant, with only one occasion when we had to don life belts. The journey took a full month, and we were glad to arrive at Bombay, collect the mail from home that was waiting for us, as well as a few other odds and ends, and continue the final lap of our transfer to a transit camp at Kalayan, north of Bombay. It was the tail end of the Monsoon and the camp was still under water. We had to climb out of our bunks and put our feet into gumboots in the first week.

Eventually the colonel came from Agra command headquarters to interview us for posting. When my turn came I was surprised with his first question: 'Where would you like to go?' My answer was simple: 'The driest spot possible'. 'Easy.' he said. 'Come with me up to Agra and when you see a spot of rain you will get down on your knees and thank God.' So with two junior officers we set off to Agra.

We waited for about a week and were then posted to Lahore. We went straight to the office and there was quite a fuss when we arrived: the chief engineer was expected any minute. The ACRE instructed us to go and take a look at Lahore and come back in two hours' time. When we reported back I was sent back to the USA Army base in Agra.

I took over the post of Garrison Engineer to serve the ground installations of the base. I made contact with my US opposite number and then met my own staff who were already in position: seven junior officers and four staff sergeants. The urgent job awaiting us was the completion of an aircraft hangar. We just got this off the ground –so to speak –when my CRE arrived to see me settled in. He stayed three days and then announced, 'If you need me, just give me a phone call and I will come up'. One very important instruction he gave me before leaving was to make sure the runway was kept clear of water during the Monsoon rains. I took a day to see the outfall from the airfield. It meant clearing a dried-up waterway which gave a four-mile runway to the Jumna River and this was cleared in good time before the Monsoon. At 1am on a mid-June morning I was awakened in my tent: 'Two feet of rain on the runway,' came the voice of my sergeant. We went to the likely spot where we thought to find the obstruction – a stone bridge on the outfall from the runway. There we found a large drum blocking the water outfall. We got a rope round it, tied it to my jeep and got it away with little trouble. We had the runways clear of water by 3am.

The saboteurs had been busy. This was something I had to deal with constantly. The next thing, the power cables to the control tower were cut asunder. Fortunately we had reserve – a mobile generator provided the power until we got the cables repaired.

During a duty trip to Rawalpindi a colleague and I travelled by RAF air taxi. After we had finished our business, we were informed that our plane would not be ready for two or three days. The local RAF men told us that if we were lucky we could catch a truck leaving Peshawar. We managed to get an early train and joined the truck leaving for the Khyber Pass. This was a rough ride, especially the last ten miles. There was nothing very exciting about the pass itself, but it was a very good defensive position.

Our return journey was a hurried retreat, as some of our RAF friends had given offence to the frontiersmen. Therefore, my colleague and I could not stay at Peshawar and went through to Rawalpindi. The plane was still not ready so we spent a weekend at Murree in Kashmir and travelled back to Agra on Monday.

Gradually I was learning some of the local routine and culture. We had civilian Indian staff who dealt with the contractors and routine daily work. I spent one day with the civilian staff. I chose a pay day and discovered there were eight fictitious unclaimed pay packets. I found out that this was the usual method the workers used to augment their income! Without realizing the risk I took, I said, 'This must stop,' but I think they found other ways.

On another duty visit to Calcutta my colleague and I took a plane, which left us in Dum Dum airport. After we got our business attended to, we had a day to look around Calcutta. I had a sudden attack of prickly heat, resulting from our quick move from the dry heat of Agra to the humidity of Calcutta. It remained unpleasant for the rest of our

131

stay but we continued on and took a good look around the city, including Chowringi bazaar. We saw the Black Hole of Calcutta and visited a memorial church to British missionary William Carey, who did wonderful work in the area in earlier days. There was no plane available so we had to return by train. Calcutta has a large railway terminus with heaving throngs of homeless lying everywhere. As we moved to board the train we literally had to step over small families living on the platform –the sight has never left my eyes.

With the build-up of the forces for the war against Japan now in place quite a number of planes were flying through on their way to Nagpur. The work at the air base was very busy with supplies building up in Burma.

Suddenly, August 1945, with the nuclear bomb dropped on Japan, the war was brought to an end. Things changed quickly, the base was now running down and demobilization was now going forward. Unfortunately for me it was halted at my group 23. I had to be patient until it got going again a few months later, when my demob came through. So it was pack-up time and on my way to Deolali to wait for a homeward bound troopship. (We were 3 weeks in transit camp before a ship was available).

It was a comfortable homeward journey with pleasant thoughts of seeing our loved ones again, but because there was a case of polio on board we were further delayed in a quarantine camp at West Kirby, and I finally got home on St Patrick's Day 1946.

RONALD KING MURRAY

Ronald King Murray, later Lord Murray, who was Labour MP for Leith Edinburgh from 1970–1979, served with the Royal Electrical and Mechanical Engineers (REME). He was Lord Advocate from 1974–1979.

War left the impression on me of a drab wilderness of muddle, drudgery, courage and self-sacrifice illuminated by flashes of heroism, inventiveness and tactical flair. The part I played was mundane throughout. As a university student I sought to join the Navy but was told that I was too young at the time for naval recruitment. As I had qualifications in maths and physics it was suggested that I attend a services' university summer school in England in electronics to improve my naval recruitment prospects. However, those who completed the course were earmarked for Army or RAF service. After some months I was admitted to an RAOC course in what was then called radio-location, later radar. After training I attended an officers' training course and eventually was commissioned in the newly-formed REME and posted to a technical college to teach basic electronics to REME recruits. Becoming restive after a year or so I applied for overseas service and was drafted to India where I joined a division camped in the jungle preparing for combat against the Japanese. After a few months it was converted into a permanent jungle training division for troops en route to Burma (radar not being a priority). Service in another training division in the jungle of central India followed.

In the autumn of 1944 I was successful in obtaining a posting to an active service unit, the 1st Battalion Hong Kong & Singapore Heavy

Anti-Aircraft Artillery, consisting of Indian troops recruited between the wars for service in Hong Kong and Singapore, part of South-East Asia Command. For the first time I was with a field unit equipped with radar. In the summer of 1945 we were part of an amphibious force with landing-craft preparing to invade Japanese-occupied Malaya when the atomic bombs were dropped on Hiroshima and Nagasaki, ending our venture.

Apart from sporadic blitz-type bombing I had only two direct experiences of hostilities. The first was in October 1939 when with a fellow student I went to the top of Calton Hill, Edinburgh, on noticing unusual daylight air activity. There we witnessed the later stages of the first Luftwaffe raid on mainland Britain which attempted to destroy the Royal Navy ships at Rosyth near the Forth Bridge. As we watched, a Ju 88 bomber flew less than a mile in front of us low over the houses, escaping eastwards. We could clearly see the white swastika against the plane's black fuselage.

My second experience was more disturbing. I was in a troopship in a convoy going through the Mediterranean to India via the Suez Canal in 1943. It was said to be the second so routed since the North African campaign. There was still active warfare in Italy and Greece. Having evaded a German U-boat wolfpack in the Atlantic the convoy left Gibraltar in broad daylight. Due south of Sardinia, which was still German-held, we were attacked by a squadron of German planes. The troops were below decks as –inexplicably –bombing was anticipated. Naval torpedo-carrying planes attacked us. Packed into H-deck near the bow and well below the waterline we could clearly hear first one torpedo, then another, coming straight for us, getting louder and louder. One passed within feet, just missing our bow, but hitting the next ship, which fortunately managed to beach on the North African coast with minimal casualties. The convoy's gunners succeeded in shooting down three or four of the attacking planes.

On being demobilized in 1946 I embraced the comparative rationality of peace with gratitude.

JOHN OSBORN

John Osborn, who was Conservative MP for the Hallam Division of Sheffield from 1959–1987, served during the war with the Royal Corps of Signals: he was knighted in 1983. His story not only shows us another side of soldiering, as a signaller, but takes us to yet another corner of the world, which was in some way affected by the global upheavals of the Second World War.

Within the last six months I have attended two interesting reunion dinners. I was the Course Officer of 170 Course at the 150 Royal Signals OCTU at Catterick, of which one of the cadets was Geoffrey Howe, now Lord Howe of Aberavon. Last November (2000) was the 55th anniversary of the course pass out parade. This spring (2001) I attended one of the regular reunion dinners of the Sheffield Artillery Volunteers. A characteristic of the Labour City Council, and some of the Labour MPs, was its support of CND, and opposition to the services using public spaces. The TA in Sheffield during the 1960s and 1970s valued an association with a former TA Officer, as the only Conservative MP in the area.

I was in the Rugby School OTC at the outbreak of the Second World War, and the boys helped fell trees for aerodrome construction, as well as assist farmers sow and harvest a variety of crops. Unfortunately my housemaster was killed on ARP duty during the blackout at a roadblock. The services of the school OTC were required when the Local Defence Volunteers were formed soon after Dunkirk; it was soon known as the Home Guard. After all, the school OTC was a disciplined force, we had uniforms and rifles, and we were used to forming fours and appropriate parade ground drill. Had there been an invasion, at about the time of the Battle of Britain it would have been a useful force, but at dawn we patrolled strategic points such as bridges and power stations. Our task was to look out for German parachutists whose role would have been that of a sabotage force. I was on ARP incendiary bomb duty and saw Coventry being bombed. I visited it a few days later on a bicycle and was shocked and distressed with what I saw. This prepared me for the shock of returning to my home in Sheffield by train from Rugby, and as the most senior boy conduct a party of five on bicycles to our homes in the West End from the railway station in the centre. The bomb damage of two nights prior to our return had been devastating. It was about this time, whilst leading a patrol from the school OTC, that there was a Heinkel bomber with its engine on fire and obviously in difficulties. We opened fire with scarce rifle ammunition and, although it duly came down a few miles away, I received a strong reprimand, as we had authority to open fire on enemy parachutists only and not German bombers.

When I went to Cambridge University in October 1941, although I was reading Natural Sciences, I joined the Armoured Corps, as I had been recruited by a cousin of my father for the 12th Lancers. At the time he was commanding officer, subsequently to become General Lumsden and killed in an air accident in North Africa. Any commission would have been subject to passing through the RAC OCTU.

By the summer of 1943 I had gained Certificate B at the Cambridge University OTC and a Part II Tripos in Metallurgy with a number of reserved occupations available to me. There were many air bases near Cambridge and I had met many serving in the RAF as well as the US Air Force. I volunteered to join the services, but because I had a natural sciences degree the War Office selection board would not allow me to join the RAC, but directed me to a technical service, and it turned out to be the Royal Signals.

In the autumn I did my initial training under the Rifle Brigade at Fulford Barracks, York, before doing pre-OCTU training at Wrotham in Kent in very wintry conditions. I passed out of the 150 Royal Signals OCTU in Catterick in October 1944, several months after the D-day landings in Normandy. For the next two months I was stationed at various transit units in Kent expecting to be posted to the battles in western Europe. I witnessed the impact of the V1 and then V2 rockets in the south-west London area.

Just before Christmas 1944 I set sail in a troopship from Liverpool for India or the Far East. On occasions I undertook watches on the bridge and was made aware of the presence of enemy submarines close to our course in the Atlantic Ocean. On arrival at Freetown in Sierra Leone I was transferred to the Royal Signals unit in Accra, Gold Coast, for acclimatization before going to Nigeria. It appeared that, having read natural sciences, I had been first in electronics and wireless in my OCTU course. I was therefore required to take over the long-distance and heavy wireless transmitter section of Nigeria Area Signals attached to the Royal West African Frontier Force. After some six weeks I went by road through Togo and Dahomey to Lagos and it was an experience to meet a French garrison in a French colony in a most difficult part of the world at that time. The colony had, by then, been cut off from France for nearly four years.

I had never seen a heavy wireless unit in my life until I took over this section, but the existing services were maintained for the next twelve months whilst I was officer in charge. I had to provide additional services including two-way radio telephonic communication so that GOCs in Nigeria, Gold Coast and Sierra Leone could speak to each other. These conversations went out in clear and there were then no scrambling facilities. It was a great strain for me as a mere subaltern to stop conversations between generals, but I had their support when it was realized that the *West African Pilot*, hostile to British rule, was listening to and reporting these conversations when they were indiscreet. The editor, whom I knew, many years later became president of Nigeria.

At that time West Africa was still the white man's grave. Antibiotics such as penicillin were not available, air conditioning did not exist and many officers and other ranks had to be repatriated for health reasons and quite a few died. I learned about the challenges facing the colonial power at that time.

Soon after VJ Day, and the return of West African troops from India and Burma, there was an uprising of the public services against the colonial power. I had to provide radio communication to over forty areas with major white populations using 19 sets and 22 sets which were not designed to cover distances of over 1000 miles, but with the help of skilled wireless operators from the campaign in Europe this was achieved.

There were occasions when military discipline was undermined by witch doctor and Ju Ju. One of my senior African NCOs died up country on leave, and a District Officer diagnosed 'death due to supernatural causes'. The rivalries between Ebo, Hausa and Yoruba in my unit were but a foretaste of a civil war some thirty years later.

The whole experience was a salutory one and served me in good stead when in the 1960s I was PPS to the Secretary of State for Commonwealth Affairs, Duncan Sandys.

In the spring of 1946 I returned to England mainly for health reasons due to my congenital mastoid in my right ear which within ten years had to be operated on. I became an instructor with the rank of captain on wireless theory and practice at the 150 Royal Signals OCTU in Catterick. I was in charge of major exercises of which the best known were Exercises *Three Day* and *Cromwell*. The heavy snow in February 1947 made it necessary to send cadets on foot with wireless sets on their backs through impossible snow drifts, as no Army vehicle could go out on the road. I had my first lesson, of many in later years, of the impact of the media especially under a Labour government. Instructors soon learned to drop the disciplines of the wartime years.

82 West African Division, were expecting to embark for –presumably –service in Malaya, or elsewhere in the Far East, when the atom bomb was dropped. John Osborn was sent to a jungle battle camp near Ibadan, but, after outwitting the senior staff on a jungle infantry exercise and being the only jungle warfare trainee to have done so in three years, he was put on light duties at the local club.

After his demobilization in the autumn of 1947 John Osborn started on a management training course in his home city of Sheffield. He had no particular intention to join the TA, but after learning that a new gunner regiment, 323 LAA Regiment RA (TA), was having difficulties handling and operating wireless sets of which he had had considerable experience in West Africa and at the Signals OCTU he attended evening drills and some exercises in uniform, but only as a volunteer instructor. At summer camp he learned that his attendances had been recorded and was told that if he joined the TA he would receive a sum of money considerably in excess of what he had earned as a management trainee over a similar period of time. He joined the TA a year after 'demob' and subsequently became a battery commander with the rank of acting major, but says that in military circles in Sheffield 'I am still known as Major Osborn'. In 1951 he accepted a directorship in the family business following the death of his father that year. Finding himself taking on more civic responsibilities, and then in early 1952 getting married, he decided to resign his commission. However, his CO advised him that this would not be possible because of the war in Korea. He learned that if he did resign his commission he would be conscripted into the Z Reserve. There was a vacancy for a battery commander in a new battery, R Battery, so he took up this new challenge. He finally resigned from the TA in 1955, but has maintained a strong association with his former service, and indeed there were both a Royal Signals group and a Royal Artillery group in the House of Commons. He explained that his military background also gave him advantages on political visits. For instance, in Mauritius in the late 1960s he took part in a survey in an Army Air Corps helicopter, and saw illegal drugs being grown in the centre of sugar plantations, to which there was 'appropriate follow up.' Then, on a visit to East Pakistan in 1970, at the time of the Pakistan civil war, he was the guest of an Artillery regiment, whose guns were trained on the Eastern border of India.

WILLIAM WILSON

William Wilson, who was Labour MP for Coventry, and then Coventry South-East, from 1964–1983, joined the Royal Army Ordnance Corps (RAOC) in March 1941, but found, not for the last time during his Army service, that he had actually been sent to the wrong place.

My calling up notice told me to report to Leicester Race Course on 13 March 1941 to join a training unit of the Royal Army Ordnance Corps.

I duly reported and, after giving my name, I was told 'You are not stopping here.' These very first words arose because I had been sent to the wrong unit. I should have been sent to Hinckley, a few miles from Leicester and nearer to Coventry. I was immediately moved to Hinckley.

At Hinckley there was delay in accumulating enough recruits to start a training company. As a result I spent three weeks in the cook-house washing up and doing other domestic duties. However, I experienced a happening never to be forgotten. One day in the cook-house a sergeant came in saying he wanted four big fellows. I met this requirement and the sergeant told me, 'You'll do Wilson, as last night there was a big raid on Coventry and an airman has been captured.'

The four big fellows were paraded. For the first time in my life I had a rifle in my hand. The sergeant said, 'Put a good show on. The colonel is watching.' I understood 'attention' and 'stand at ease' but when the sergeant cried out 'for inspection port arms' he might as well have spoken in Chinese for all I understood. I had to look at the fellow next to me to see what he was doing.

The parade ended and we were marched in single file to Hinckley Hospital. There, with a loaded rifle, I was taken into a small room in which the captive German airman lay in bed. Thus, a recruit with two weeks' cookhouse experience, I was in face of the enemy! The captive was in so much plaster that if all the doors and windows had been opened and he had been told to get back to the Fatherland, he could not have alighted from the bed.

I wondered what I should do if he did try to escape. I thought 'do I shoot at him?' I thought I am bound to miss and the bullet might finish up hitting me.

I cannot say I felt any enmity for the airman, although he might have played a part in destroying my home and family.

My training was completed in June 1941 and I was sent to the huge ordnance depot at Chilwell in Nottinghamshire. There for the only time in my life I had the Monday morning feeling. I was in the statistics department of the depot. After almost 12 months a major said to me, 'You don't think much of your job do you Wilson?' I said, 'No, a schoolboy could do it.'

I was soon on my way. I had played for the Midland Army Rugger team against the combined counties of Nottinghamshire, Lincolnshire and Derby in mid-week and two days later I was on my way to Scotland to join the HQ of the First Army. This was May 1942.

The First Army was part of 'Torch' in Algeria and Tunisia. We landed in Algiers on November 12th and thereafter I was near enough to the war to know I was in it. However, although I was in the first air raid on Algiers, I always felt I had been in more danger in Coventry, where on the night of the November Blitz I was one of the first casualties when I was extinguishing an incendiary bomb which exploded.

I had qualified as a solicitor in June 1939, but the war came and I had not really practiced as a solicitor by the time I joined the Army.

However, my legal knowledge came to my aid in Algeria. For a period we were billeted in French Army barracks in Laverdure. These rat-ridden barracks were in the hills miles from anywhere. One night each of us were given a tin of bully beef for our main meal. I said to my mate, 'These are too big for one meal. Let's save my tin till tomorrow. We do not know what tomorrow will bring.' I put my tin in an open cupboard by the ironing table I used as a bed. I did not give the bully beef a second thought until I was charged with being in the unlawful possession of a tin of bully beef. Army regulations state any spare food shall be taken back to the cookhouse. Military law is clear. The onus of proof is on the prosecution. I was marched before the camp commandant. Evidence was given about the tin of bully beef being found next to my ironing table bed. I told the camp commandant 'if the tin of bully beef had been found in my kit bag I would have to explain it. Anyone could have put the tin in the cupboard. There is no evidence that I put it there.' I was acquitted without a stain on my character. I was the first person I had ever defended. The result was a forerunner of my defending when I returned to civvy street.

I stayed in the First Army until it was disbanded at the end of 'Torch'. I served in Sicily and then Italy in the autumn of 1943. Although I was in the first air raid on Naples (I lay under a truck thinking 'see Naples and die') and in subsequent air raids, I still felt that the citizens of Coventry were in greater danger.

I was in the HQ of the Allied Forces in Italy.

We moved northwards to Caserta, Rome and then Siena. At Siena at the end of 1944 I was posted to the HQ of the Fifth United States Army in Florence. Why I was posted I never knew.

I was in Verona when the war in Europe ended. The HQ moved to Lake Garda.

At Lake Garda the immediate thought was 'where now?' Austria seemed a probability. I was asked, strangely enough, 'Where do you want to go?' I said, 'Yugoslavia or Greece.' In due course I was given a foolscap sheet of paper authorizing 'Corporal William Wilson 10538120' to travel to HQ Land Forces Greece.

I duly arrived in Athens where I was told, 'We do not know why you have come and we do not know what we are going to do with you.' Leicester Race Course was repeating itself! I returned the next day and was told, 'We are going to put you in the Greek Army.'

I was transported to an historic Greek village about 15 miles from Athens. I lived in a Greek house with civilians. Although I messed with British soldiers I was the only British soldier in a Greek Army unit. We talked a polyglot language of Greek, German, English and Italian. I served in this unit from July 1945 to May 1946.

When Greece was admitted to the European Union, I said in the House, 'I served for nine months in the days of destruction in the Greek Army and my affection for Greece, and the Greek people has increased with time. I am glad in the days of construction to welcome Greece into the Union.'

While I was in the First Army the senior RAOC officer was Brigadier Terry Clarke. At the time of the general election in 1945 it was reported in the British Army newspaper that Brigadier Clarke was a Conservative candidate. I wrote to him and told him that I hoped the best party won. When I went into the House in October 1964, the Brigadier was a member of the opposite side. On the troop-ship in October 1942 the prospect of us meeting in the House of Commons was hardly in our thoughts.

My Army number 10538120 played a part in the Divorce Reform Act 1969. In the autumn of 1968 I went to enter my name in the Private Members Ballot. I had already agreed that I would promote the Divorce Reform Bill if I won a place. When I was asked if I had any particular number for my place in the ballot I rang all the changes in my Army number. All had gone. I said, 'Put me down for the first vacant number.' That number drew place '4' in the ballot. The Divorce Reform Bill was on its way. We did not get the Bill through in that session, but all the hard work was done and in the next session the Bill went through.

William Wilson, 10538120, ended his Army service with the rank of sergeant.

ROBERT REDMOND

Robert Redmond was the Conservative MP for Bolton West from 1970–1974, and, although he was serving with the Royal Army Service Corps (RASC), he spent much of the war working with Special Operations Executive (SOE).

On 14 September 1936 –four days after my 17th birthday –I enrolled into the 10th Battalion (Liverpool Scottish) The King's Regiment Liverpool, Territorial Army. I could not do so before that day as I was too young. About a year later the battalion became The Liverpool Scottish, The Queen's Own Cameron Highlanders, and in January 1938 I received a commission. To have been admitted into such a highly respected unit and then to be commissioned was, without doubt, a matter for pride. It still is.

In July 1939 I attended a TA officers' course at the Royal Military College, Sandhurst. This course lasted a fortnight. I can remember little about the officers of the directing staff, but I shall never forget Company Sergeant Major Dowling, Grenadier Guards and Sergeant Egan, Coldstream Guards. Those two chaps and what they did to us on the drill square have left an indelible impression and I believe they served me well, not only in my service career, but in life as a whole.

On 25 August 1939 I was embodied as part of the advance party of the TA and I served from then until May 1946. In 1941 it became apparent that a physical problem was going to prevent my serving efficiently in the infantry and I sought a transfer into the Royal Army Service Corps. With the RASC I went out to the Middle East and to the Eighth Army in the Western Desert. After two years of advance, retreat and advance again, it seemed to me that if a war was necessary, a desert was a good place to have it. With the enemy now driven out of North Africa, the idea of moving into Europe and European terrain had little appeal. To my surprise, however, I was admitted to a course at the Middle East Junior Staff School. From there, I was among twelve other chaps who were appointed to MO4 GHQ MEF. This was the name, at the time, of the Special Operations Executive in the Middle East.

SOE is usually presented as glamorous and dangerous as if all those engaged in it were outstandingly courageous. In certain theatres –not only in France –this reputation is well deserved, but for most of us working from Cairo and later from bases in Italy, it was routine and far from the kind of thing one might expect. Nevertheless, work with the Partisans in Yugoslavia and Albania was important. The activity of No 1 Special Force in Northern Italy, in particular, was probably the most successful and effective of all the SOE operations worldwide. My job was –in modern jargon –in the logistics of supply and support to the resistance groups in these countries.

Before the war I had been active in the Junior Imperial League who were the forerunners of the Young Conservatives. I honestly and sincerely believed in the importance of politics and of our democracy. The political aspects of what one saw, particularly in the Communist parties of Europe, strengthened this political awareness. It was, therefore, natural that I should seek a postwar career in politics. I became a Conservative constituency agent. After training, my first job was at Wigan where I met my wife, whom I married when I moved to Knutsford. After seven years there, I went into industry, but still maintained my political interest, becoming Chairman of the Knutsford Constituency Conservative Association.

By 1968 it seemed that it might make sense to seek a seat in Parliament and I was adopted for the marginal seat of Bolton West. My four and a half years in the House of Commons were rewarding and I became very cross when those ignorant of what the life of an MP is make stupid remarks about it.

In addition to political work, I have given long service to the Royal British Legion. I was for some years President of the Alderley Edge Branch and, later, was for eight years Chairman at Knutsford. I am now President there.

Part Five

THE INFANTRY

Here we look at the stories of parliamentarians who served as infanteers, largely in a rifle company of an infantry battalion. Having said that, because of the nature of the Second World War, their experiences were, once again, often less than traditional and extremely varied.

PAUL BRYAN

Paul Bryan, who was awarded both the DSO and the MC during the war, became the MP for Howden in Yorkshire in 1955. After studying at Cambridge University before the war, he worked for a firm in the East End of London. He enlisted in the territorial battalion of the Queen's Own Royal West Kent Regiment (RWK) in July 1939, as a private soldier, and was commissioned into the same battalion –the 6th – in November 1939. This was unusual, as normally when someone was commissioned from the ranks they were sent to another battalion. In March 1940 he became the battalion intelligence officer, just in time for their departure for France with the BEF.

At the beginning of May 1940 he was summoned to an intelligence officers' course, and while he was there the Germans launched the Blitzkrieg. His semi-trained and semi-armed battalion was sent to defend an impossibly wide front. Consequently, the colonel and most of the battalion spent the rest of the war as PoWs. Paul Bryan joined the retreat and eventually found his way to Nantes on the Atlantic coast, where he discovered several more survivors of the battalion.

Once back in England, the remnants of the battalion –three officers and twenty-four men – were sent to the moors near the village of Wark, about eight miles from Hexham. They were later joined by the battalion transport officer and fifty drivers, and 200 reinforcements accompanied by a new lieutenant colonel, 'Swifty' Howlett. Paul Bryan was promoted to company commander of D Company.

Two years later, on 8 November 1942, Paul Bryan and the 6th Battalion RWKs, took part in 'Operation Torch', the invasion of Algeria. The invasion force landed at several locations and, although the Vichy French troops put up some initial resistance, they soon capitulated. Paul Bryan's own part in the invasion was somewhat unfortunate, in as much as, in the darkness, the Navy managed to land his company on the wrong beach, from where they could plainly hear the sound of battle some way in the distance. The following day the battalion sailed for Bougie, where they were the first to assault the beach: luckily, they were unopposed.

During the next stage of operations they sailed further up the coast to the port of Bône, where they were attacked by a German Ju 88, while disembarking from destroyers.

Paul Bryan's company marched 25 kilometres to Lake Fetzara, where they took up defensive positions and waited for the rest of the battalion. In time, French lorries and buses took them up the coast another eighty miles to Tabarka.

Although the Allied landings in Algeria had taken the enemy by surprise, fresh German and Italian troops were soon landing in Tunisia. As the Allies moved east and the Axis forces moved west, eventually they clashed at a village called Djebel Abiod. Here there was a fierce battle and the RWKs repulsed several attacks by enemy tanks.

The exposed defensive position at Djebel Abiod was held by the battalion for nine days, between 17 November and the night of the 26th–27th. They were then relieved by 8 Argyll and Sutherland Highlanders.

As the brigade continued towards Mateur on 28 November, with the Argylls leading, the route took them through a narrow defile, between two imposing hills known as Green Hill and Bald Hill. The Germans had set an ambush and within minutes the Argylls had lost around 150 men and all of their Bren gun carriers.

Consequently, 6 RWKs were given the task of capturing Bald Hill, and 6 Commando, Green Hill, with the Buffs in reserve. The Germans were in too strong a position and the battalion lost eleven officers and 150 other ranks killed, wounded or missing. Shortly after this, 'Swifty' Howlett was promoted to command the brigade and Paul Bryan became second in command of 6 RWK.

The second attack on Green Hill, this time by the Buffs, was supported by a complete regiment of twenty-four 25-pounders, two huge American 155 mm 'Long Toms,' a battery of four 5.5" medium guns, a battery of mountain artillery and a company of 4.2" mortars. This was the heaviest volume of artillery support yet used in the campaign.

The second attack also failed and, after heavy loss of life, the brigade was ordered south to an area near Beja, because fresh German troops supported by Mark VI Tiger tanks were approaching from Tunis.

As second in command Paul Bryan was in charge of the administration of the battalion, and his chief concern was in getting supplies distributed over several miles of wild hilly country.

After a successful encounter with an Italian force, the Germans arrived ten days later with their tanks and quickly overran the French on the right. Paul Bryan's D Company, with the aid of three Churchill tanks, counter-attacked and drove the enemy back, capturing many prisoners.

In the spring of 1943 General Montgomery began his final advance towards Tunis, with the Eighth Army chasing Rommel across the desert from the east, and the First Army, continuing from the west. Bryan's brigade accompanied the First Army and the Germans were determined to make a stand. In fact they even tried a counter-attack, which cost them heavily. Once again 6 RWK were heavily involved and took many prisoners.

Next, the brigade had to capture a craggy hill called Djebel bou Diss which the enemy held in strength. Fighting took place at short range and even hand-to-hand, and although the Germans tried to counter-attack, after three days bou Diss had been captured.

A week later their target was the famous Longstop Hill. By now Paul Bryan's battalion was so decimated that even cooks and storemen were armed for the attack.

Following an intense bombardment by 400 guns, the RWKs and the Buffs carried out a night attack. Later the Argylls, supported by the Churchill tanks of the North Irish Horse, took over the attack and reached the crest of Longstop, only to discover there was a second, even more heavily defended, crest further on. The second crest was later captured by the Buffs. By the end of this battle, 6 RWK was so decimated that they could no longer operate functionally in the North African campaign. Paul Bryan was awarded the MC.

After the campaign in North Africa Paul Bryan was promoted to lieutenant colonel, and would command the battalion during the advance through Sicily and Italy. He had thus achieved the remarkable feat (perhaps unique) in the British Army of rising from private soldier to lieutenant colonel in the same battalion, without ever having left it.

Paul Bryan led the battalion into Sicily, where they fought at Centuripe and Monte Rivoglia, after which he was awarded the DSO. Later, in Italy, they took part in the operations around Cassino, a period which he recalls in his autobiography *Wool, War and Westminster*.

On the morning of March 19 my battalion moved to the village of San Michele while I and the company commanders went forward to the mountainside overlooking Castle Hill. We were to take over this feature from a battalion of the Essex Regiment in the 4th Indian Division. As we neared the battalion headquarters I left my company commanders behind in the shelter of a hollow and climbed up the craggy slope to find the Essex CO, who had established himself under the cover of an overhanging rock. After brief greetings he got down to the business of describing the situation and we stepped out onto a ledge to survey the scene. As we stood there together looking at his map I heard a sharp crack, he fell at my side –yet another victim for yet another German sniper. Fortunately he was only hit in the arm but that was certainly the end of this battle for him.

I scrambled down the scree and rejoined my company commanders, but during the long rough walk back to the battalion we were under constant shellfire. Captain Weatherley was killed and Captain Birch was wounded and was to die later. Despite these disasters, as dusk fell, the men of the battalion made their way up the mountain track and during the night got into their new positions.

Our layout could not have been more bizarre. By far our most important duty was to occupy and hold the ruined Cassino castle. This consisted merely of a strong ruined tower and a courtyard which was surrounded by a thick wall, part of it ruined, some 10 feet high. Perched on its rocky crag behind and 300 feet above the German held parts of Cassino town, some of the enemy positions to the west and south were within 100 yards of the wall. Moreover, the Germans looked down straight into the courtyard from Cassino monastery, so movement was virtually impossible in daylight. The castle commanded a valley which led from Cassino town up towards the monastery, the most natural line of progress for any attack on Monastery Hill.

The plan was to devote one company to the defence of Castle Hill and the rest of the battalion would be round about a certain point

165 which was on the hillside immediately opposite, where I established my battalion headquarters. In view of the importance of Castle Hill I put my second in command, Denis Forman, in charge there.

While the battalion was getting into position, Brigadier Bateman, to whom I was reporting, arrived to introduce himself –a charming man for whom during the next week I acquired a great respect. He told me that the Divisional General wished one of my companies to do an attack that very night on a certain position known as Yellow House. It did not take me very long to persuade him that this was not a possibility. The troops had not even yet come into place. They had never seen their surroundings by day, let alone the objective they were meant to capture. The terrain they were asked to cross, a steep hill with a savage surface of rough boulders, rocky outcrops and stony escarpments, would be hard enough to tackle after proper reconnoitering and in daylight.

The general himself arrived in due course and Donald Bateman passed on to him my reasons why the attack was out of the question. He was less easily convinced and after a frosty exchange with Bateman the conversation ended with his words: 'I would not like to be in your position if Yellow House has not been captured by tomorrow morning'. To his eternal credit Bateman did not turn a hair.

Next night D Company had to carry out the fearsome attack. Owing to minefields and other hazards, the only way to deploy a company on to the side of the hill preparatory to an attack was for the men to emerge in single file through the castle gate. Needless to say the enemy had a fixed-line machine gun on the gate and no doubt an artillery registration too. If they had any idea we were coming they would stop us before we started.

Our men finally got assembled on the hillside but they had not been climbing long when there was a most enormous explosion –mines. There were many casualties. Alerted, the enemy brought down heavy artillery fire. In the end the attack had to be abandoned.

On the next day things went better for us. It was clear to me that, as the capture of the castle was one of the few Allied successes, there was bound to be a counter-attack. I therefore had the two most obvious approaches carefully registered by the guns of the Corps.

On the code word 'Ginger Rogers' 600 guns would shower their shells in one area. On the code word 'Fred Astaire' on another.

Sergeant Major Dixon from our side of the valley had his machine-gun platoon with their guns on fixed lines ready to back up the artillery.

It all worked like a charm. At dawn the signal came that an attack was imminent. I gave the code word –I can't remember which. All hell broke loose. It was too much even for the famous parachutists and forty of them came up to the castle with their hands above their heads. We were in need of that sort of tonic.

After we had been in the Castle Hill area for a week the planned attack was abandoned. The monastery held out until 18 May, after yet another bloody attack –this time by the Poles. Our casualties in this grim week were eleven officers and 120 men.

After Cassino Paul Bryan was posted back to England. The battalion continued through Italy and finally Austria, under the command of Gordon Defrates. Bryan ended the war in command of 164 Officer Cadet Training Unit (Eaton Hall), Barmouth, in Wales. He was the first non-regular soldier ever to command an OCTU.

He was the Conservative MP for Howden in Yorkshire between 1955–1983, and Boothferry between 1983–1987; was a Minister of State for the Department of Employment during the 1970 Edward Heath government and was knighted in 1972.

CLIVE BOSSOM

From the adventures of the Royal West Kent Regiment, we now turn our attentions to the Royal East Kent Regiment, known as The Buffs, in which Clive Bossom served between 1939 and 1948, attaining the rank of major.

Clive Bossom, later Sir Clive, was the Conservative MP for Leominster from 1959–1974. In 1937 his father Alfred Bossom, who was the MP for Maidstone between 1932–1959, wrote a book in which he predicted the war. So, to be prepared, his son joined his county regiment, The Buffs, as a supplementary reserve officer. He attended two short summer camps, passed the written Sandhurst exam and was fortunate, therefore, to receive a regular commission on 1 September 1939. Two weeks later, on 16 September, the battalion set out for France and he was sent to the depot at Canterbury to receive a crash course in the 'art of war'.

Clive Bossom now recalls his service with the regiment in France, both with the BEF in 1940 and during the invasion of 1944, and thereafter in the Far East.

A few months later I was posted to our base camp at Le Mans, France. I was slightly disillusioned with my first command – one elderly corporal who obviously had discovered the delights of French wine, a handful (in every sense of the word) of unwanted scallywags and one mad, temperamental cook. Even with my newly experienced crash course on military knowledge, I was hard-pressed to keep my fifteen men fully occupied with training and trying to turn them out to look anything like guardsmen.

After a few weeks of this I thought I deserved forty-eight hours' compassionate leave. I wrote myself a pass allowing me to visit my recently acquired American step-grandmother, Madeleine Dittenhofer, who was living gracefully at the Hotel Crillon in Paris. Unfortunately once there I ran into a senior staff officer in the hotel lobby who enquired whether I was on his staff. When he was informed I was on 'compassionate leave' he immediately despatched me back to the depot in Canterbury. As a result I missed Dunkirk by several weeks!

Back in the UK I was posted to a company of the 11th Battalion The Buffs stationed near Mereworth Castle in Kent. Lorna and Esme Harmsworth, great friends of mine, lived in the castle. They invited me over for tennis and a swim and insisted I stay for an early supper. At supper all the young sat at one end of the long dining room table, at the other end sat Esmond Rothermere, deep in conversation with two of his editorial staff from the *Daily Mail*. Being extremely inquisitive I edged up as near as possible to try and eavesdrop on their very serious conversation. Only partly could I hear but the gist seemed to be that Churchill had informed all Editors that they should break the story of Dunkirk as slowly and gently as possible. On no account make any dramatic announcement which could cause an immediate panic.

I returned to my Mess and announced to those still present that the French and Belgian Army had surrendered, the BEF was in full retreat and that the German Army was almost at our gates. Having made this dramatic announcement I retired to bed, only to be awoken brusquely at 3 am by two very grim intelligence officers from Army HQ who demanded to know how and where I had got this information. I was in a real dilemma. I did not want to implicate Viscount Rothermere, who certainly had not breathed a word to me about Dunkirk, so I simply told the truth, explaining how foolish I had been to eavesdrop and even more foolish to pass on this garbled version of what I had overheard.

Soon after that my battalion was converted into a gunner regiment and I spent the next few months on numerous courses learning about artillery. Come the invasion, we returned to France with the 49th Division, slowly proceeding to Le Havre. Here we were stuck outside the city due to minefields, mud and very strong resistance.

Once again I had the urge to visit my step-grandmother (she had failed to leave France). I gave my brigadier a heart-rending story. He was not at all moved, explaining there was no such thing as leave during a siege, but he was willing to turn a blind eye if I 'got lost' for a few days. Somehow I reached Paris which was *en fete* as the Free French and the Americans had just arrived. Although Madeleine had been interned for a while she had been so difficult that she had been released and allowed to live at the Hotel Bristol, also occupied by a number of diplomats. To my amazement I found she was not suffering from malnutrition as Arturo Lopez had befriended and helped her with Black Market food. This second 'compassionate leave' mission was certainly not justified!

She told me that, shortly before I arrived, to 'rescue her from starvation', she had met in the hotel lift a handsome young Englishman who told her he had been at Harrow with my elder brother Bruce. He said he had tried in vain to persuade him to join him in the Spanish Civil War. This naïve lady did not even ask herself what was an Englishman doing in Paris during the German occupation. John Amery was executed as a traitor on 19 December 1945.

It so happened that I was an exact contemporary, both at Eton and in the House of Commons, with his younger brother, Julian Amery. We became lifelong friends and I always admired his bravery, despite all the terrible publicity about his brother; he contested Preston in the 1945 general election. Julian had an outstanding war record, particularly in the Balkans.

On rejoining the Division, my General, 'Bubbles' Barker, gave me a new and challenging assignment. He was very worried by the nightly pounding the front line was receiving from German heavy mortars. Moreover they were very mobile and hard to locate. So Barker invented the 'Anti-Mortar Unit'. I was given *carte blanche* to pick forty-five men, and we succeeded in getting a workable if somewhat Heath Robinson unit together in a very short time. It consisted of signallers armed with 22 wireless sets, stationed with the most forward infantry troops. Each time a mortar fired they took a simple compass bearing which they radioed back to my mobile HQ truck where we plotted the source from the intersecting bearings. I also had the use of a small Canadian unit who were experimenting with a kind of radar, and on call there were two light aircraft flown by delightful daredevil Polish pilots. I never got a great thrill going on these reconnoitre flights as the pilots loved flying right over the German lines. On landing our plane usually looked like a pepper pot from the enemy small arms fire. With all this input of information we were able to pinpoint an area where the mortars might be, proceed to bring down all the Corps' artillery firepower, thereby leaving a very large hole with the hope that we had despatched the German mortars. Anyhow my unit most certainly came into its own before and during the Battle of Arnhem.

I ended the War in Dortmund where I was suddenly posted as second in command of 2nd Battalion the Buffs, then in Burma. On embarkation leave my posting was cancelled. The War Office informed me I was being sent on 'a special mission'. I got very over-excited as I had visions of some cloak and dagger operation. Imagine my amazement and amusement when I found I had to escort two small Persian kittens to Mountbatten's HQ at Kandy, Ceylon, for her ladyship. I flew out with the troops' mail in great comfort in a Sunderland flying boat, landing on the Nile near Cairo, Bombay and Colombo. After the cold winter of 1945 the warmth and beauty of Kandy was unbelievable.

After two months I joined my regiment at Singapore which had recently arrived from Burma. For a time we looked after part of Changi Jail which was crowded with Japanese prisoners of war. One thing that shocked me was the really brutal discipline administered by the Japanese officers and NCOs, but at least it meant we never had any trouble from the Japanese prisoners.

The battalion was then dispersed over southern Malaya. At that time the local communists had not yet begun fighting. My main problem was to keep some of the men, who had fought a hard war in Burma, fully occupied. The last thing they wanted to do was to start so-called training. They only wanted to go home and get demobbed. I found that sport of all sorts saved the day for them. The situation was greatly improved when the battalion was sent to Indonesia to do a 'mopping up' operation. Although the war had finished there were a number of Japanese soldiers who had disappeared into the hills and had not heard the war was over!

I personally had an interesting time liaising with two Dutch units. The men in one unit had been well trained in England, but Queen Victoria must have bequeathed them their equipment. It was one war out of date! The other Dutch unit had been trained by America and had unbelievably ultra-modern equipment, but they lacked discipline and training. These young Dutchmen were very disillusioned as they thought they would be warmly welcomed back to their 'old' colony. This, though, was far from the case. The Indonesians were all but hostile to their former masters.

Lastly I had eighteen months in Hong Kong, an experience I shall never forget. I have returned on many occasions wearing 'different hats', right up to the week of the handover in 1998. Again I was fortunate I was given the job of looking after 259 young Danish volunteers who came out to my battalion. King Frederick of Denmark was Colonel in Chief of The Buffs, so he sent out these highly motivated and intelligent young men who soon spoke good English, many even learning Cantonese.

Clive Bossom retired from the Army in 1948 and was keen to get into politics. He fought the general election of 1951 for Faversham and again in 1955, failing to win by 59 votes. He was eventually successful in 1959 at Leominster in Herefordshire, and remained an MP until 1974.

ERIC COCKERAM

Eric Cockeram served with the Gloucesterhire Regiment during the war, attaining the rank of captain. Having been in the OTC at school, he enthusiastically joined up 6 months ahead of when his call-up papers would otherwise have arrived. At first he joined the King's Regiment, then stationed at Freshfield near Formby in Lancashire. This was a week before Christmas 1942. His military contribution to the war effort came to an abrupt end on 30 July 1944, while serving with the Glosters, when he was very badly wounded by a hand-grenade in Normandy and spent the next 6 months in hospital and convalescence. He has been disabled ever since. His story begins on D-Day, as the Glosters unload from their landing craft. However, as he goes on to explain, a new secret weapon that had been issued to each man before the assault, would cause them a certain amount of discomfort.

> On 6 June 1944 I was a 19-year-old lieutenant commanding a platoon. The day started with me feeling desperately sick as we got tossed about in a flat-bottomed landing craft in the English Channel, but worse was to come when we landed. Since we were not in the initial wave, but part of the follow-up later in the day, the 2nd Battalion of the Gloucester Regiment had been equipped with folding bicycles which were strapped on top of our knapsacks which had to carry everything else such as a waterproof ground sheet, a blanket and a minimum of personal requirements such as dry socks. Last of all, a spade was strapped on top of this pile so by the time we jumped off the landing craft into the water to land on the beach, it was a miracle that we didn't sink in the sand before reaching the shoreline.

The idea of the folding bicycles (at least in the minds of someone in the War Office) was that we should land, unload our folding bicycles which had a central hinge which enabled the two wheels to pack next to each other, and then we were supposed to swing the rear wheel through 180 degrees, tighten the thumb screws and peddle away as fast as we could to take over and relieve some troops in the front line. Since before we had travelled 100 yards or so we came under shell fire and the worst place to be when being shelled is above ground we quickly ditched our bicycles and used the spade to get below ground in slit trenches. We quickly learnt that it was better to march at a brisk pace being ready to run into a ditch in the event of shell fire rather than cycle along a road which was in any event crammed with tanks, flails and troop carriers.

We were supposed to capture Bayeux on the evening of D-Day but in fact it was dawn the following morning, 7 June, before we entered the town which surprisingly had suffered remarkably little damage except for the railway station and marshalling yard which had been heavily bombed prior to June. This was part of the Allied plan to cripple the French railways and so the German means of bringing up reinforcements to this part of France, so most of the railway system in Brittany had been crippled well in advance of the landings.

After capturing Bayeux and pressing onwards a few miles, we came across some resistance and so dug in to allow us to consolidate before advancing further. Here we ran into an unanticipated problem, namely cows. They roamed the fields freely and when we were being shelled by the Germans, the cows ran around frightened and making a great deal of noise and it didn't take long for quite a proportion of them to be wounded or killed and a dead or dying cow emptying its bowels is not the best thing to have next to a slit trench in which you might have to live for the next 24 hours. So at night we had to resort to burying these cows or at least putting sufficient earth over them and the mess they made to smother the foul smell, which, since it was mid-summer, attracted the attention of flies which circled around us and the cows. It was not a pleasant experience nor one which we had anticipated.

I considered myself fortunate that I was not involved in the British Expeditionary Force in 1939/40 (still being at school at this time). It must have been a pretty testing experience to be constantly under pressure from an enemy that was vastly superior both in numbers and equipment. By contrast in Normandy in 1944 the roles were reversed and we were vastly superior. Not only did we have command of the sea for a year or two prior to June 1944, we also had command of the air and we saw very little German air activity. As a 19-year-old young lieutenant at one point facing Villiers Bocage I actually had both aircraft and artillery coming overhead to bomb and shell the German positions in front of us, and with radio was required to act as forward observation officer for the shelling. In those days this was quite an experience for a 19-year-old and demonstrated the superior fire power available to the Allies compared with the Germans who were unprepared and slowly retreating.

One hears the phrase from time to time that someone had 'a good war'. This obviously means that, not only did they not get killed but they also did not become a prisoner of war. A 'good war' usually consists of joining up near the beginning, seeing the whole job through, being the right age for promotion so that after six years, one comes out as a colonel or above (or equivalent rank in another service). All credit to anyone in this category but those of us who were still at school at the beginning of the war were teenagers for most of the while, and who only saw two to three years' service, clearly only made a limited contribution.

Eric Cockeram was the Conservative MP for Bebington from 1970–1974 and Ludlow from 1979–1987. His political appointments included being PPS to the Minister for Industry, the Minister for Posts and Telecommunications and the Chancellor of the Exchequer.

MARCUS WORSLEY

Marcus Worsley was the Conservative MP for Keighley in Yorkshire from 1959–1964 and Chelsea from 1966–1974. During the war he served with the Green Howards, a regiment largely recruited from the men of Yorkshire. Arriving into the regiment late in the war, he didn't get to see active service, and has very mixed emotions about the value of the whole experience. Born in 1925, Marcus Worsley was not called up until 1943. By then the tide of war in the west had turned and it was no longer a question of whether, but of when, the final victory would come. 'Military experience in the Second World War,' he notes, 'was inevitably a matter of one's age. Had I been even a couple of years older I would probably have seen many a shot fired in anger.' On reflection, and no doubt given time to think, he admits he may have been better suited for service with the Royal Navy: so why did he choose to volunteer for the infantry in the first place?

Out of a perhaps quixotic sense of local loyalty I joined up in my father's (Yorkshire) regiment, the Green Howards. At that moment there was a shortage of men in the Navy and conscripts were then going to sea. To avoid that and join the Green Howards I had to volunteer for I think five years and three in the reserve. I have often wondered if I did the right thing. The Green Howards of course was, and is, a magnificent regiment, but as it turned out I never served with an active service Green Howards battalion; I missed serving with school friends and I admire the Navy; but who knows?

Anyway the Army endeavoured to turn me into an officer (which put an end to my volunteer status). In the end they succeeded, but by the time a pip appeared on my shoulder the Allies were on the Rhine.

Towards the end of my officer training we were at a battle camp for a week with no papers. During that week Belgium was freed.

At the end of the war the government was anxious to avoid flooding the labour market and devised a system whereby everyone was given an 'Age and Service Group' number which dictated the time of release. Mine was 55; had it been 54 I should have been released much earlier.

So I spent a further two years in the Army after the end of the War, a total of four years in all, more or less filling in time. From the point of view of defending King and Country, it wasn't up to much, but I suppose no experience is wholly without value. Soon after VJ Day I was posted out to India and to the Royal West African Frontier Force. Two divisions of West African soldiers had been recruited to fight in Burma and places East. With VJ Day they were no longer needed, but ships were short to get them home. The A & S Group system did not seem to apply to Africans, but it did to their officers and NCOs, so off they went and with them their experience; many had been district officers and so on. They were replaced by a mixed bag, a few weary regulars, some wonderful Poles who could not go home and a preponderance of white-kneed youths, of whom I was the senior at 21.

The result was I suppose predictable. The Division's men came from all four former (then) colonies. Our only remedy when, say, the Nigerians mutinied was to call on the Gold Coast men, give them truncheons of some kind and tell them, 'Those bad Nigeria boys go mutiny. You good Gold Coast boys go bash 'em,' and/or vice versa.

It taught me that civil society is a lot more fragile than it is sometimes thought to be. We have seen too many examples since!

So my military service was wholly without glory and I am bound to say without much satisfaction either.

As well as being an MP, Sir Marcus Worsley has been High Sheriff, and Lord Lieutenant of North Yorkshire.

WILLIAM DEEDES

From the ranks of these famous county regiments we now turn our attention to those who served in the Rifle Brigade (RB), or the King's Royal Rifle Corps (KRRC): not to be confused, as great rivaly has always existed between the two. One of the most famous of these is William Deedes, who is equally well-known as a journalist and author. After leaving Harrow in 1929, William (Bill) Deedes became a correspondent for the *Morning Post*, and in 1935 he went to Africa to cover the war in Ethiopia. In 1936 he was appointed political correspondent, but six months later the paper was bought by Lord Camrose of the *Daily Telegraph*, which already had a political correspondent. William Deedes therefore became a general reporter with particular responsibility for civil defence and air-raid precautions.

As the war approached William Deedes volunteered for the Territorial Army and joined the Queen's Westminsters, which formed part of the KRRC. His battalion, which was largely made up of journalists and actors, had its headquarters at Buckingham Gate. After being called up in August 1939, he was offered a commission and assumed the duties of a second lieutenant and platoon commander. His platoon was given the job of guarding vulnerable points, such as Staines Railway Bridge.

In the summer of 1941 the battalion moved to North Yorkshire to train as part of an armoured division. They eventually became a motor battalion in the 8th Armoured Brigade, which included three tank regiments, the 4th/7th Dragoon Guards, 13th/18th Hussars and the Notts (Sherwood Rangers) Yeomanry.

Although the three tank regiments in the brigade went over on

D-Day, the motor battalions followed later. However, they were soon taking part in battles from the Falaise Gap to Arnhem.

On the road to Geldern on 3 March 1945, while leading XXX Corps, the company which William Deedes now commanded made the front page of *The News of The World* after meeting up with a force of Sherman tanks from the American Ninth Army manned by black American troops.

On 2 April the company was given the job of securing a crossing over the Twenthe Canal near Hengelo. All the bridges except one had been blown and when the riflemen of the company assaulted the last bridge they were caught in the middle of fierce German crossfire. The two platoons on the bridge were decimated, while the third platoon, which was still forming up to join the assault, was pounded by mortar fire. The casualties in the company were so severe that, only a month before the end of the war in Europe, they ceased to be an effective force. For his part in the action William Deedes was awarded the MC.

After the war he returned to the *Daily Telegraph*, but his growing interest in politics, and a vacancy at Ashford in Kent, in 1946, eventually led to his election as a Member of Parliament in 1950. He remained in the House until 1974, and his appointments during that time included being Parliamentary Secretary to the Ministry of Housing and Local Government; and Parliamentary Under-Secretary for the Home Department. He was also a Minister without Portfolio from 1962–1964. He was made a life peer in 1986, as Lord Deedes of Aldington in the county of Kent.

QUINTIN HOGG

Born in 1907, Quintin Hogg, better known to the world as Lord Hailsham, went from Eton to Christ Church, then to All Souls College, Oxford, before embarking on a career as a barrister. He was first elected as the Conservative MP for Oxford in 1938.

When the war began he was already in his early thirties but wanted to join the Army before his call up. He was commissioned into the Tower Hamlets Rifles, and as a platoon commander his first military task was to guard vulnerable points in the East End of London. In time they were moved to Hainton, near Market Rasen in Lincolnshire, where they were assigned the tactical role of a motor battalion, even though they had no military transport. His own platoon was designated to be the carrier platoon, without any Bren gun carriers. In the meantime he was given the task of organizing a motorcycling course, to train dispatch riders for the battalion. First, he had to teach himself, so he purchased a secondhand BSA in London, but on the way back to Hainton slipped on some black ice and arrived in the back of a lorry with a broken rib. Nevertheless, after a short spell in hospital he went on to complete the task in hand.

During the period known as the phoney war, as an MP, he was occasionally absent from his battalion, in order to participate in important debates, especially those that concerned the war effort, in particular the famous Norway Debate which was instrumental in the resignation of Neville Chamberlain and the establishment of a coalition headed by Winston Churchill on 11 May 1940. Similar to other MPs who served in the forces he was highly critical of the government's conduct of the war: in the nine months he had been with his unit they had received neither field training, equipment or

167

transport. There had been no weapon training other than with .22 ammunition on a miniature rifle range, and they hadn't been issued with small arms ammunition anyway. He had himself been issued with a .45 Colt and three dum-dum bullets, which, according to the laws of war, he was forbidden to use. Apart from attending a young officers' course at Hendon Police College, which ended with a bayonet assault-course against some stuffed figures, he still had no more real military experience or training than achieved in his 1925 infantry Certificate A at Eton.

Things gradually improved after the Bren guns, their carriers and the ammunition arrived. Then, after the fall of France, the battalion was sent to defend a stretch of the Lincolnshire coast against a possible invasion. But, shortly after this he was ordered to report to the War Office in the Intelligence Division.

His recruitment to the War Office as a GSO III (General Staff Officer Class III) was to a branch of the Intelligence Directorate called MI(R), the 'R' standing for Research. At its disposal were scientific and technical experts, whose function was to devise new weapons – the 'sticky bomb' being one. He didn't stay with the unit long because he wanted to get back to the infantry, but gained considerably from the experience, learning about various existing anti-personnel and anti-vehicle devices, including land mines.

During his time based in London, he was able to attend the House of Commons on a regular basis and, on instructions, prepared a paper on the long-term strategy of defence after the fall of France. The paper so impressed Dalton, the Minister of Economic Warfare, that he offered him a job in his ministry, which he turned down in eagerness to return to his battalion.

In January 1941 he sailed from Merseyside with a draft of officers and arrived off Port Suez in the middle of March. He then went by train to a transit-camp at Gineiga, from where he hoped to rejoin the Tower Hamlets Rifles, who by this time had been incorporated into the RB as its ninth battalion. Instead, he was posted to S Company of the Second Battalion of the RB, stationed at Port Said. The battalion shortly moved to Mena, a tented camp near the pyramids and the Sphinx.

Soon, however, Rommel had swept past Tobruk, passing the Egyptian frontier at Halfaya Pass and Sollum with a mixed force of Italians and Germans. Many of Hogg's comrades in the THR were killed or captured.

Now acting as a platoon commander, Hogg moved forward to a position south of Buq Buq, where he took over from a young ensign of the Scots Guards. He had instructions to hold the position, so he ordered his men to dig slit trenches. Almost as soon as the platoon had started to brew up a new order arrived, instructing them to proceed another fifteen miles further west. They were to pass through the forward picket line in order to act as an infantry screen while the Sappers blew up a dump of some 500 tons of RAF bombs which had been left behind during the retreat. The subsequent explosions went on through the night and troops situated up to 25 miles away had thought a battle was in progress.

They soon got into the routine of night patrolling at platoon strength. The normal procedure was to travel in vehicles towards Sollum, which they would then conceal behind suitable cover. They would then proceed on foot right up to the outskirts of Sollum or even beyond. But it seemed that the Italians evacuated their day positions during the night and retired to some safer spot, which meant that, in spite of a number of false alarms, they never encountered the enemy during these patrols.

Then, as a prelude to an advance on Sollum, Hogg was ordered to clear a minefield, which had been left behind by the Scots Guards. By painstakingly locating each mine with a bayonet, they lifted 150 of these objects and sent them to safety, with no one getting injured in the process.

They advanced in column strength: 'S' Company, plus signallers, a few 25 pounders, and some Australian anti-tank gunners. A parallel column composed of the Coldstream Guards supported by Matilda tanks moved along the escarpment on their left flank in a sort of pincer movement at the top of Halfaya pass.

The Italian defenders had soon surrendered and Hogg was tasked with taking these prisoners to the rear. It so happened that while his platoon was still shepherding the Italians to the rear, Rommel made a counter-attack against the troops which were now holding Sollum and the Halfaya Pass. Soon the British were in full retreat again, but he was left holding the Italians. Not wanting to be captured, he flagged down every passing vehicle, and boarded the Italians in twos or threes on each of them. Amazingly, when the headcount was made after stopping at their platoon position, all prisoners were still present: 117 other ranks and six officers. However, after their advance, the Germans had reoccupied Sollum and Hogg's platoon were back in the same slit trenches they had dug when they first took over from the Scots Guards.

A few days later, his platoon position was attacked by Messerschmitt II0s. Unfortunately, two of his Bren guns were dismantled at the time, being cleaned after a sandstorm. The third, unlikely to work anyway because of the sand, was placed on an anti-aircraft mounting. He yelled a warning, sent his platoon under cover and manned the last Bren himself. Three times the enemy planes attacked, and only once did the Bren gun respond positively. During the encounter he received an injury to his knee.

In the first instance he went to the regimental aid post, miles away at battalion headquarters, to get his wound dressed and bandaged. He fully expected to go back to his platoon, but he was sent to the advanced dressing station, about 140 miles away. There he was given a clean bandage, a cup of tea and sent to the casualty clearing station at Mersa Matruh, about 250 miles from where he was hit. On his return to the battalion about two months later, he told of the disgusting conditions at the CCS, which was run completely by male staff. The colonel was not amused and ordered him to write down what he had seen. His letter was passed to HQ in Cairo, who responded by a complete remedy of the situation, which included the fact that in future the CCS would be run by women staff only. He considered this to have been the most useful thing he ever did in his life, especially as it came at a time when casualties were increasing.

Shortly after this he was sent to hospital again, this time with sandfly fever. By the time he got back to his unit they were on their way to the high desert, somewhere near the frontier wire and not far from Sheferzen. By now he was second in command of the Company.

In August 1941 he was posted to HQ MEF in Cairo, where ranked captain and with the rating of General Staff Officer Class III, his work was concerned with communications: supervising the timetable of troop-trains. After this he went as a liaison officer to the Ninth Army, with their headquarters at Brumana, just above Beirut. By the summer of 1942 he had been promoted major.

In September he contracted jaundice and was sent to the New Zealand military hospital. He lost over two and half stone in about a fortnight. Even after his recovery, his medical grading was permanently altered to A2, which meant he would no longer be able to serve in an active theatre of war. He therefore applied to return home and resume his duties as an MP.

In 1950 he succeeded his father as Viscount Hailsham and sat in the House of Lords, but in 1963 renounced the title for his lifetime and returned to the House of Commons, where he served until 1970 as the member for St Marylebone. He was First Lord of The Admiralty from 1956–1957, deputy party leader and then leader in the House of Lords 1957–1960 and 1960–1963, and Minister for Science and Technology 1959–1964. In 1963 he contested the party leadership, but lost to Sir Alec Douglas-Home. He remained an MP but also went back to his law career. He accepted a life peerage in 1970, as Lord Hailsham of St Marylebone, and served two terms as Lord Chancellor.

JAMES RAMSDEN

James Ramsden, who was Conservative MP for Harrogate, in the West Riding of Yorkshire, between 1954–1974, served with the 60th KRRC. He joined the Army in April 1942, although he had previously been a member of the Eton school OTC, and was sent to Peninsular Barracks in Winchester. After commissioning he joined the 60th at Strensall in early 1943. At the age of twenty, he spent the year before D-Day training to take part in the invasion, as a scout platoon commander in the 9th Armoured Division. In the end, however, the Division never went to war itself: it was broken up and sent piecemeal to Normandy. James Ramsden's Company from 8 KRRC went out in early August to reinforce 8 RB, the motor battalion of the 11th Armoured Division. This Division had already experienced a month's hard fighting all over the front – Hill 112, 'Goodwood' and most recently 'Bluecoat' – the Presles ridge. They were now on the right of the Second Army next to the Americans. The Division's sign, a black bull on a yellow ground, had been so ubiquitous that a captured German general had thought it was the symbol of the entire British Army. 'Twenty years later,' says James Ramsden, 'I was an Army minister and went back to Normandy to hear the Staff College DS analysing these battles and describing their experiences; my own look meagre by comparison.'

G Company 8 RB, to which he was sent, had by now lost about a third of their people, including four or five officers. All but one of the platoons were being commanded by sergeants, and the arrival of Ramsden's company brought them back up to strength. Sergeant Kisby, a battle-hardened veteran of the desert, had been in charge of the platoon to which James Ramsden was dispatched. The previous platoon commander had been killed a week before. James Ramsden now goes on to describe the Division's advance through Europe.

The Division's last effort on the British right had all but achieved the break-out from the beach-head, and the Americans on their right had done it. So the Normandy battle was loosening up, and resolving itself into a series of skirmishes with retreating German rearguards, some of which could still be sharp. To cope with them we were organized into mixed groups of all arms: a troop of tanks, three or four Bren gun carriers, a gunner FOO in a tank, and a platoon of infantry riding in half-tracks, say fifteen or sixteen vehicles and about sixty men. Three of these groups took turns to go in front as we advanced. They were christened 'Vanguards'.

The first day was typical. We were in close country, all little fields with high banks and thick hedges, no chance for the tanks to deploy and spread themselves out. So we had to advance up the road, a section of carriers in front, the tanks close up with them and the rest of the column strung out behind. The pace was suitably cautious and for the first few miles all went well. Then there was a dull clunk and a tearing noise and a tank went up in flames. So the village in front was held and G Company would have to clear it. While the infantry were getting ready I went with some carriers to look for a way round the flank. We found a farm road, but it soon got too narrow and my carrier shed one of its tracks, a not infrequent occurrence. I had a look over the bank. There were some slit trenches and a German soldier. Had we got a hand grenade? We had. Rifleman Howard, my wireless operator and Bren gunner, who will feature in this narrative, had another look and said it had worked. But we had to leave the carrier and most of our kit. I got in with Sergeant Kisby who was in the village street with the attack, alongside the foot soldiers. They cleared the village, not without cost to themselves, but most of the enemy had already made off to lay another ambush.

Such was more or less the pattern for the next ten days, during which we advanced about eighty miles and had some encounters. Kisby and I were sent out on foot and were chased back by a Tiger tank. The company history says one round took the skin off my nose. It might have, it was a nice clean nick, but I may have done it getting through the hedge. The tank's tracer looked just like when a child lights a sparkler firework. Sergeant Kisby was wounded soon after by a shell, Phil Board my driver was sniped and I had six shots at a running German with a pistol, which all missed, like the Tiger's did. All this got us as far as L'Aigle where we were the first in, double-banking some Americans.

There we had a few days rest. Amiens apart, the next stop would be Antwerp, only another ten days on but this time over three hundred miles ahead, such was now the pace of the advance. Once across the Seine there was better tank country and the Vanguard tactic was shelved. 3 RTR were in front all the way and cracked on, bypassing road-blocks and strong-points. G Company mopped up for them, and if the country got closer the carriers closed up to give the leading tanks some reassurance against panzerfausts.

We were doing this in a built-up suburb just outside Antwerp when Rifleman Howard took the opportunity to absent himself and disappeared into a house. He came back later looking cleaner and more relaxed, saying he had had a bath, which may have been a euphemism. Meanwhile I was being ordered to resume the march and was under serious admonishment for not proceeding. But I could sympathize with him when we reached the city itself, all crowds and kisses and civilians climbing on to vehicles, quite a bore really after a long drive with not much sleep.

Amiens, vital because of the Somme bridges, had involved a twenty-mile night march, a novelty for an armoured division. It was late evening and we were hoping to bed down when orders came in the words 'Its moonlight tonight'. In fact it was pitch dark and pouring with rain. There was one village in the way and I went on with the tanks' signal officer to make enquiries in French. No Germans, and we reached the city in the half light of dawn. How do tanks attack a city? 'Knock on the door and see if they will let you in.' Rifleman Howard was present and correct. When I looked back he was tearing things up and throwing them over the side. 'What on earth is that'? It was his Communist Party membership card and his copy of the *Soviet War News*.

After a day or two in or near Antwerp waiting for petrol, we had orders to drive straight on up through Holland and across the Rhine to Apeldoorn, but this did not work. The intelligence was faulty and the whole scheme had to be re-cast as the Arnhem operation, which the Guards Armoured did instead of us. We did boring infantry soldiering between them and the rivers. I got my carrier blown up on a mine which laid me up for a day or two and burst my eardrum. The Army treated this by putting drops in my eyes, a fact which I recorded in one of my letters home, and which got me a pension when later on I went deaf.

All in all, after the exhilaration of 'the Great Swan', that wonderful dash from Normandy, what had followed was anti-climax, even the progress from the Rhine to the Elbe, which was Normandy all over again, all rearguards and roadblocks. 'Moonlight tonight' was tried again, but didn't work this time. There was an unusual episode when we had to leave our carriers in the car park and go across the Weser in boats to help the rest of the company man a bridgehead, while the Sappers built a bridge. This was the only time we ever saw the Luftwaffe. They destroyed the bridge, killed most of the Sappers and made things uncomfortable for us. It was the only time G Company experienced an organized German counter-attack while I was with them, and that was soon broken up by the gunners. I had to say goodbye to Rifleman Howard, who had stayed back in the car park with the wireless and was rather badly wounded by a shell.

Christmas 1944 had been disrupted by Von Rundstedt's brilliant counter-attack through the Ardennes. We had been meant to spend it back in Poperinghe while the tanks exchanged their Shermans for the new Comets. Instead there were two hasty marches back round Brussels to the Meuse crossing at Dinant, where my company commander found himself responsible for the bridge, much encumbered by rear units of the Americans and by a growing exodus of refugees. We patrolled forward and found no enemy, but four of them in a captured jeep jumped the carriers' roadblock and were blown up on a string of mines. Thick weather had been favouring the German advance; but on Christmas day the skies cleared and looking out across the snow from a hill just outside Dinant we watched as they were bombed by Lightnings and finally repulsed by the assault of an American Armoured Division.

By the spring we were quartered in Schleswig and back to peacetime soldiering. A general election was in progress at home. My platoon formed up and asked me how I thought they ought to vote, not that Rifleman Howard would have been in any doubt. It was the first political question I had ever been asked to address. I shall not recount what I said, nor how most of them voted, though I did get to know. After all the ballot is supposed to be secret. I then rejoined the

175

60th, expecting to go to the Far East, but the bomb was dropped and I was able to go to Oxford instead.

During his time as an MP, James Ramsden was, among other things, PPS to the Home Secretary, Under Secretary and Financial Secretary at the War Office, Secretary of State for War and Minister of Defence for the Army.

PHILIP GOODHART

Philip Goodhart was Conservative MP for Beckenham from 1957–1992. He served with both the KRRC and the Parachute Regiment from 1943–1947. Arriving in the Army at such a late stage of the war, he would become involved with one of the main operations that continued after the end of hostilities, and in many ways was a consequence of it. Palestine had been garrisoned by a strong British force, but it was now time to hand it over to a new Jewish government and, at the same time, leave some sort of stability in the area. Philip Goodhart now describes some of his experiences in the Army, which, as you will soon discover, had a somewhat shaky beginning.

I made my mark within days of joining the Army at Christmas 1943. At that time all recruits had to undergo a mechanical aptitude test which consisted of assembling twelve bits of equipment laid out on a lengthy table. By the time I took the test about a million recruits had been assessed; about 100,000 like me had got nothing right, but I discovered later that I was the first recruit out of a million who had the entire testing kit thrown away as they had been unable to disassemble the equipment I had forced together.

I was, however, far from being the worst recruit at No 15 Primary Training Centre at Fulford Barracks in York. It coincided with the abandonment of all education standards for recruits and half of my fifty colleagues in the platoon were totally unable to read or write, a somewhat shaking experience for someone who had spent the first three and a half years of the war comfortably at school in America.

I then moved to a platoon of a battalion of the KRRC –a regiment which had once been the Royal American Regiment. After my mechanical aptitude debacle my prestige was somewhat restored as I became the sparring partner of the Army featherweight champion. In America the world featherweight champion, Willie Pep, had recently developed a new style of defensive boxing and in round after round Sergeant Blatchford, the Army champion, was unable to land a solid punch. The closest I came to enemy action was on leave in London; after an inebriated evening I went to bed in the Dorchester Hotel. When I woke up I was on the floor, the window had disappeared and so had the building next door, thanks to a flying bomb.

When the War in Europe ended I was second lieutenant at the Rifle depot in Winchester. When the result of the election, with its massive swing to Labour, was announced, the whole depot echoed to the chant 'Move to the left in threes, left turn'. I was very non-political and in the Mess remarked to the Colonel, 'I suppose that means that we will have brighter programmes on the BBC'. He looked at me coldly and said, 'Without doubt that it the stupidest remark I have heard all day'. I expect he was right.

Soon afterwards I joined the 1st Battalion of the Parachute Regiment which was supposed to become a Green Jacket battalion. We were going to Palestine where the 6th Airborne Division was leading the anti-terrorist campaign. After the losses at Arnhem the battalion had to be rebuilt with young recruits who were anxious to prove that they were as tough as the Arnhem veterans. On the Sunday morning before we were due to sail no less than sixty stolen vehicles were lined up outside the barracks at Bulford ranging from a farm tractor to a double decker bus. In 1945 it took real ingenuity to be able to steal sixty vehicles in a single night.

When our departure was postponed for a week the citizens of Andover demanded that they should be protected against us. We sent a picket to patrol the streets. As my relations with the battalion adjutant were far from satisfactory I was chosen to command the picket. This interfered with my plans to say farewell to my Wren girlfriend and my supervision of the picket was deemed to be inadequate.

The adjutant thought he would find a suitable punishment for my inadequacy and therefore I was appointed messing officer for the troopship that carried us to Palestine. It was a dry ship and I was the only officer who had regular official contact with the ship's officers who had unlimited supplies of drink. All the cooking and serving of the meals was done by the ship's staff so for a fortnight my duties consisted of deciding which of my fellow officers should get a drink in the evening. My military career prospered and soon after we landed in Palestine I moved to an interesting job at brigade head-quarters.

There were plenty of bombs and plenty of bullets. There was also a great deal of friendly fire. One evening outside the camp at Sarafand I spent half an hour huddled in a ditch where tracer bullets criss-crossed a few inches above my head. It turned out that two sentry posts had spent the evening firing at each other. In Jerusalem a rock dislodged by a guard had started a fire fight in which 32,000 rounds of ammunition were expended. Not a single person was hurt.

We suspected that some of these friendly fire exchanges had been put on so that quantities of ammunition could be sold to the Arabs or the Jews, but some of the exchanges were real. Fights between 6th Airborne Division soldiers and soldiers in the 1st Infantry Division were frequent and ferocious with the death toll rising towards double figures. At one stage I accompanied the general commanding 6th Airborne Division on a peace mission to see General Gale who was commanding 1st Infantry Division to see if we could reduce the number of casualties we were inflicting on each other.

I thoroughly enjoyed myself in the Army.

While in Parliament Philip Goodhart's appointments included being Parliamentary Under-Secretary of State for the Northern Ireland Office and Parliamentary Under-Secretary of State at the MOD: he was knighted in 1981.

JAMES SPICER

James Spicer, who was knighted in 1988, was Conservative MP for Dorset West from 1974–1997. Although he was commissioned in to the Royal Fusiliers, he eventually saw active service during the campaign in North-West Europe, while seconded to the Ox & Bucks Light Infantry. Even before this, his experiences during and before the outbreak of war had been extremely varied. He had risen from being an Air Raid Messenger in London to a platoon commander in the Army at the time of the Battle of the Bulge.

I was born in October 1925 which made me 19 when the war ended in August 1945. So, by any normal standards, my memories of the war should be those of a schoolboy growing into adolescence, and then possibly just completing my basic service training when the war ended. Fortunately for me, I managed to step on the 'accelerator pedal' and so 'enjoyed' a war full of excitement, but dominated as far as I was concerned by two aims. The first was to make quite certain that I got into the Army before the war ended, and the second to do everything possible to fit myself for an Army career. Covering a period from 1938 through until VJ Day is not easy 'straight to camera', so in order to assist me, and hopefully anyone who might read this little epistle, I have added in diary dates which serve as markers.

<u>September 1938, The Czechoslovakian Crisis</u> At the age of 12 I was pressed into service by my father (who was the honorary treasurer of our local hospital) to help filling sandbags and placing them around the hospital. I felt very grown up and, over a period of about ten days, became professional at filling and tying, though not at lifting!

<u>3 September 1939, War Declared</u> I have memories of air raid warnings on that day and I envisaged thousands of bombers flattening London. Nothing happened and we entered into the period of the phoney war. However, one momentous event for me. I gained my first stripe in the OTC at school at the end of my third year as a member of the Corps'!

<u>May/June 1940</u> The Battle for the Low Countries and France, culminating as far as the British were concerned in the evacuation from Dunkirk. I longed to be part of that heroic venture, but no one offered me the chance! However, on 13 May came the announcement of the formation of the LDV (Home Guard). My only ambition from that moment on was to join this volunteer force. I knew the CO of the local battalion quite well and badgered him on a daily basis. Sadly, he knew that I was only 14 and he constantly told me to come back in a year's time!

<u>June 1940</u> I finally realized that there was no hope of my getting into the Home Guard and so I enrolled as an Air Raid Messenger. This gave me a steel helmet, a blue overall uniform and a great sense of pride. From June until September we had very little bombing on the west side of London, but we did have constant air raid warnings.

<u>September to November 1940</u> A dramatic change and suddenly there *were* bombs, there *were* casualties and there *was* a job for Air Raid Messengers to do. We had only isolated 'sticks' of bombs, but some casualties and enough work to make me feel that I had a worthwhile job.

<u>1941</u> By March of this year the air raids had dropped right away as the Germans turned their attention to the Balkans and thereafter to Russia. It was time for me to move on and I went to the Home Guard once again. By then they were a far cry from the original LDV and at the age of 15 I was allowed to join a commando section which had a mobile role and was reasonably well equipped. I stayed with the Home Guard until just after my 16th birthday in November 1941 when I was commissioned into the Cadet Corps. This was a great step forward and after a couple of months I even persuaded my parents that, in addition to my battle dress, I should have a service dress with

a Sam Browne belt. This new appointment worked in well with my daytime activities. I had failed Latin at School Certificate level and my parents thought it was important for me to pass the exam before I was called up in 1943, so I went to a Latin crammer in Chancery Lane. Mr Marcy was a great character, but possibly past his prime. I (and most of the others) did very little work, a fact that was brought home to me in June 1942 when I sat gazing blankly at the examination paper. I walked out, thought about how best to break the news to my parents and then telephoned an RSM I knew in the East Surrey Regiment to ask if he could help me to enlist. Off to Kingston Barracks where a colour sergeant (pre-warned by the RSM) didn't query my age and date of birth. So my Army date of birth became 4 July 1925 and I held on to that birthday desperately throughout my Army service.

September 1942 to March 1943 My call-date was finally confirmed for 3 March 1943 and that left me with the question of what to do with myself for that six-month period. I still had my Cadet commission, but I felt I needed to toughen myself up in preparation for my recruit training. Without too much difficulty, I managed to get a job working in a scrap metal yard and that certainly did the trick!

March 1943 My 'friendly' RSM insisted on accompanying me down to Canterbury where I was to do my recruit training with the East Surreys. He handed me over to my training sergeant and I began six weeks basic training. This passed quickly and I then moved on to ten weeks infantry course, still at Canterbury. During this time I went before a War Office Selection Board and thereafter moved straight from my infantry training to Pre-OCC at Wrotham in Kent. There we learnt (if necessary) to ride bicycles, motor cycles and some driving and maintenance. My main aim was to get away as quickly as possible to OCTU which I managed to do early in September.

September to December 1943 The Isle of Man was a perfect place in 1943. There was conscription for men but not for women and in addition to that, there were very strong contingents of ATS, WAAF and quite a good selection of WRNS as well! We worked hard and played hard and I think I grew up! I passed out in December 1943 and was commissioned into the regiment of my choice –the Royal Fusiliers.

<u>January to October 1944, UK</u> I was posted to Colchester and bidden to do recruit training. This was a frustrating time for me because by then we all knew that an invasion of Europe could not be delayed much longer. We were based at Colchester, but early in April were evacuated to Blackpool so that our barracks could be used for the invasion forces. I spent D-Day in Blackpool, frustrated and miserable that I was not able to take part in this great enterprise.

<u>October 1944</u> Just before my 19th birthday, I finally received my embarkation orders and took off for Belgium as a reinforcement officer. I was posted not to the Royal Fusiliers, but to the Ox & Bucks Light Infantry in the 53rd Welsh Division. They were a first class battalion and had seen some bitter and costly fighting in Normandy.

The period up to Christmas 1944 was fairly uneventful and I and the men in my platoon were looking forward to a comfortable Christmas in a little town in Belgium called Lierre. Then came the Ardennes Offensive and within days (missing our Christmas!) we were helter skelter down to the Ardennes to meet the German attack. In the dense woods above the town of Marche we had some fierce fire fights in quite horrendously cold and snowbound conditions. Although our casualties were not high in number, we sadly lost our splendid company commander, Richard Vicker, who was killed. Then our 2 I/C, David Taylor, took command, but was evacuated, wounded, the following day. His replacement was Captain Dick Sears, who after two or three days with us was also killed. All in all, a sad business.

Then, early in the New Year, it was back up to the north to prepare for the final offensive in the Reichswald Forest and down to the Rhine. The Germans fought hard in the Reichswald and deployed the best of their remaining forces, including battle-hardened parachute battalions. Again we suffered casualties, but my particular platoon was really quite lucky. From then on we advanced quite rapidly towards Hamburg with the occasional fire fight and tragically, even at this late stage, some casualties.

<u>VE Day, 8 May 1945 and beyond</u> The full horror of war came home to me in Hamburg. I have never seen before or since such devastation and, in the face of so much human misery, former prisoners of war,

German civilians and our own forces seemed to draw closer together in a battle to survive and bring back some normality.

June 1945, Operation Pickford With many hundreds of younger officers, I was picked up and dumped back in London ready to go to the Far East. The Great Central Hotel at Marylebone became 'home' to some 600 of us. We all had our gratuities, we all thought we were off to fight the Japanese, and we were all determined to make the best of a short time in London. Then came a dock strike (unbelievable to us in a time of war!) and then finally the dropping of the atomic bomb on Hiroshima.

That, in shorthand, was my war. I achieved my main aim of playing some small part in it. I also managed to jump a generation in terms of my Army service. Looking back, I can honestly say that I wouldn't have changed one single part of my experiences during the war. I wanted to grow up fast and, with some luck, plus a devious approach to my real age, was able to do so.

Part Six

THE GUARDS

In this section we study postwar MPs who served during the Second World War in one of the Guards regiments. The Foot Guards are among the oldest regiments in the British Army, and consequently have a long and proud history and tradition. It's therefore not surprising that many of the young men, emerging from university, or public school, who would later grace the political arena, should wish to enlist in their ranks.

WILLIAM WHITELAW

Perhaps the most famous politician to serve in the Scots Guards was Willie Whitelaw, who stood against Mrs Thatcher for the position of Tory leader in 1975, but in defeat became Deputy Leader, and then Deputy Prime Minister, until a mild stroke forced him to retire six months after the 1987 general election.

William Whitelaw was brought up in Nairn in Scotland by his mother, after his father had died as a result of wounds he sustained in the First World War just after the birth of his son. At the age of eight he was sent to preparatory school in Berkshire, and from there progressed to Winchester College, and finally Trinity College, Cambridge, in 1936. The threat of war persuaded him to join the university Officers' Training Corps and pass the necessary certificates. After taking his degree in 1939, he went on a summer attachment with the Scots Guards battalion at Windsor. As a result of this, soon after the war started he was granted a commission in the Scots Guards without having to undergo any further officer training: he was now 21 years old.

He spent the early part of the war with the Guards Training Battalion at Pirbright in Surrey, after which he was sent to the old Croydon Airport as one of the officers on guard. The Guard there consisted of two subalterns and a retired captain who had served in the First World War and who had a splendid moustache. The younger officers christened him 'Blomberg' after the German Field Marshal. He was forever accusing the young lieutenants of idleness, and seemed to think the way to cure it was a walk around the sentry posts. It took roughly one and a half hours to walk around the perimeter of the airfield and sometimes they were ordered to do this up to four times a night. On one occasion, deciding he could no longer tolerate the young Whitelaw's idleness, he ordered him to go around the guard continuously all through the night. It so happened that the Captain wasn't due to return until 4 am, so encouraged by the Sergeant on Guard, William Whitelaw made the decision to take his Morris 8 instead of walking. All went well until, in the early hours of the morning, it began to rain. The car got bogged down in the mud and it took the efforts of all the available sentries to rescue it and get it back to base just before the arrival of the Captain, who remained totally unaware of Mr Whitelaw's deceit. The next day much amusement was caused by 'Blomerg' praising his subaltern for 'A good night's work.' In his autobiography Willie Whitelaw stated that throughout his life, whenever he drove past the place where the airfield had been situated, he had 'a nostalgic laugh'.

In time Whitelaw was made a transport officer and was sent to the newly formed 3rd Battalion Scots Guards stationed near Loughton in Essex, which was eventually turned into an armoured battalion as part of the Guards Armoured Division. Whitelaw was appointed Technical Adjutant and their early training took place at Codford Camp on Salisbury Plain. On 6 February 1943 he was married at St Giles's Cathedral, Edinburgh.

Prior to the build up for D-Day the battalion, equipped with Churchill tanks, was sent to Ashford in Kent. Due to reorganization, the battalion –indeed the entire brigade –was split from the Guards Armoured Division and became the 6th Guards Tank Brigade.

In July 1944, six weeks after D-Day, the brigade had orders to cross the Channel to Normandy. By now Whitelaw commanded a squadron. His own crossing was hindered by a severe storm which caused many of the tanks in the ship's hold to break loose from their chains. They were forced to return to England to secure the tanks again, and made a later crossing in fine weather. He rejoined his battalion at Bayeux.

The brigade's 'baptism of fire' came very quickly, on 30 July 1944, at the Battle of Caumont, a day that would effect Whitelaw profoundly. He was commanding his squadron of fifteen tanks with five people in each crew. The battle would take them from the Caumont ridge and down into the *bocage* country, where tanks found it difficult to operate. Their infantry support was provided by a battalion of the Argyll and Sutherland Highlanders of the 15th

(Scottish) Division. The Germans were dug-in behind every hedge. It was therefore a question of spraying each hedgerow with machine-gun fire before moving across the intervening fields. This procedure made it a slow but steady advance.

Unluckily, Whitelaw's own tank went over a mine and the track was broken by the blast. He summoned one of his sergeants and, after running between the two tanks under enemy fire, resumed his command of the squadron from the sergeant's tank. Soon after this the Commanding Officer, Colonel Dunbar, ordered Whitelaw and his other leading squadron commander to advance to their first objective, Les Loges, ahead of the infantry. They advanced to their objective swiftly and were ordered to consolidate and maintain their position, but they were now isolated from their infantry and in a very precarious position. Whitelaw was summoned to an order group at battalion headquarters just before 6 pm. He instructed his troop commanders to guard their left flank, unappreciative of the risk that could come from the rear. Unfortunately, two Panthers, mounted with 88mm guns, were able to exploit the situation.

While at battalion headquarters Whitelaw became aware that his squadron was under attack. He immediately returned in a scout car, while Sydney Cuthbert, the second in command, went off to investigate in his tank. Suddenly Cuthbert's tank received a direct hit. It burst into flames and the turret lifted into the air landing on the ground beside it. On reaching the squadron, Whitelaw found two more of the tanks in flames. In five short minutes he had lost three tanks and several members of the squadron, all trusted friends who had trained together for years.

The Scots Guards received much praise and many congratulatory messages following their opening action of the war. They had penetrated deep behind enemy lines and virtually destroyed an entire enemy division. However, for Whitelaw the success was always tainted by the tragedy, and he always felt a sense of guilt that he had not guarded the rear more effectively. Those five minutes triggered a deep change in his attitude towards life and towards his fellow human beings.

After Caumont he was promoted to second in command of the battalion and some months later awarded the Military Cross. The battalion moved through Belgium, Holland, and finally into Germany itself, where among other things he was ordered to take the surrender of Lütjenburg, on the Baltic coast.

As many fellow officers departed after being demobilized, William Whitelaw became a regular soldier and was appointed a staff officer to the 1st Guards Brigade, which was preparing for an attack on the Japanese mainland. After the Atom Bomb was dropped the brigade was relocated to Palestine, where British forces were under constant threat from Jewish terrorist attacks.

However, in 1946, after the death of his grandfather, and his inheritance of family properties near Glasgow, he resigned his commission in order to be with his wife and two young daughters. Ranked major, his final appointment was in command of the Scots Guards Company at the Guards Training Battalion at Pirbright.

Willie Whitelaw entered Parliament in 1955 as the MP for Penrith and the Borders. Before working with Mrs Thatcher, he had already served in both Harold Macmillan's and Edward Heath's governments. Mr Heath appointed him the first Secretary of State for Northern Ireland when direct rule was imposed in 1972. He was made a viscount in 1983 (Lord Whitelaw of Penrith), after which he served for 5 years as Leader of the House of Lords.

STEPHEN HASTINGS

Another Scots Guard was Stephen Hastings, Conservative MP for Mid-Bedfordshire 1960–1983. In 1939 Hastings went straight from Eton to Sandhurst to train for a regular commission. He was later sent to the Training Battalion at Pirbright, and eventually the Guards depot at Chelsea Barracks.

In March 1941 he was posted to the 2nd Battalion in Egypt, which became part of 22nd Guards Brigade. The 2nd Battalion took part in numerous operations against the forces of Rommel in 1941, such as 'Brevity' in May, 'Battleaxe' in June and 'Crusader' in November. From this period he notes:

> During the long lull between 'Battleaxe' and 'Crusader' the Battalion held the narrow stretch of desert between the escarpment and the sea below Halfaya Pass. Right Flank Company, in which I commanded the forward platoon, repulsed a strong probing attack by infantry and armoured cars. It was a time of active night patrolling in which I was frequently engaged and for which I was subsequently mentioned in despatches. 2nd Scots Guards was then turned into a motor battalion, supporting armoured formations.
>
> The object of 'Crusader' was to relieve Tobruk and drive the Afrika Korps out of North Africa. However, the subsequent tank battles in the desert began to illustrate the vast difference between British and German tanks.
>
> At one point in the battle 2nd Battalion protected the supply columns of 4th Armoured Brigade, part of the 7th Armoured Division, which was equipped with light American Stuart tanks. These were thrown against the 5th Tank Regiment of 21st Panzer

Division, which was supported by field artillery and a complete infantry regiment. The brigade sustained terrible losses, but somehow managed to destroy some twenty Panzers into the bargain.

As a result of 'Crusader' the Axis forces were driven beyond Benghazi and north of Agheila, where the battalion sustained losses in a misconceived night attack which nevertheless nearly turned the enemy's seaward flank.

In March the Afrika Korps counter-attacked in a wide sweep by 15th and 21st Panzer Division. After a running battle during which the British armour was heavily mauled the front was finally stabilized at Gazala where 2nd Scots Guards formed part of a heavily defended box known as Knightsbridge.

Stephen Hastings then learned that David Stirling, also a Scots Guards officer, was recruiting for his SAS Regiment, then known as L Detachment. He volunteered and was accepted. Stirling's attacks on airfields behind enemy lines were already becoming legendary.

Based in a tented camp at Kabrit on the Bitter Lakes, L Detachment also included his future parliamentary colleagues Fitzroy Maclean and Carol Mather. Maclean, who was already a Member of Parliament, would later become Head of Churchill's mission to Tito, and a respected author. Carol Mather, who was commissioned into the Welsh Guards, had already worked with Stirling in the Middle East with the Commando Brigade until its disbandment.

In July 1942 Hastings accompanied the SAS into an area of desert 60 miles south of the coast and 150 miles behind enemy lines. For the next two months they operated from a series of ridges in the desert, 30 or 40 feet high, which could conceal their vehicles and equipment. From here, their target was the main coast road, Rommel's main line of communication. In small groups travelling in jeeps mounted with Browning, or twin Vickers K machine guns, they carried out raids against the German supply columns moving towards El Alamein.

His first expedition met with disaster when the three jeeps in his patrol were strafed by Italian fighter aircraft, leaving two of them burning in the desert, long before reaching their objective. The patrol included George Jellicoe, Carol Mather, and six gunners, two in each jeep. Jellicoe was a seasoned commando who had previously carried out a raid on a Cretan air base, which had accounted for twenty-one German aircraft. By driving into a crevice, Jellicoe managed to save his own jeep and the nine men of the patrol were able to return to their rendezvous point, safely avoiding enemy patrols.

During this period L Detachment carried out a bold raid on the large airfield at Fuka near Marten Baghush, known as LG 12. The airfield was a staging area for all planes approaching or leaving the front and intelligence had reported it constantly full of aircraft. It was guarded by two battalions of Italian infantry.

The attack took place at night in the form of a 'jeep charge', as twelve vehicles, led by Stirling himself, sped towards the outer defences of the airfield. The vehicles advanced ten abreast with one flanker behind each side of the line. Carol Mather drove the jeep on the left flank and Stephen Hastings the one on the right. Once through the defences and on the signal of a Very light, the jeeps changed formation, closing into pairs. As the flankers, Hastings and Mather became the final pair. This was in order to bring all their fire to bear. The manoeuvre had been well rehearsed before the operation, as it was vital that none of the jeeps broke formation, or it would be in danger of crossing its neighbour's line of fire.

In this formation they drove through the middle of the airfield and through the dispersal area, blasting away at the aircraft on either side of them with their Vickers machine guns. Aircraft exploded into flames: Stukas, Junkers 52, Dorniers. Occasionally the vehicles would stop, a figure would dismount, plant a Lewis bomb on an aircraft, snap the fuse and return to the formation. As the attack progressed, a few of the jeeps were knocked out by enemy fire and the formation began to break. Returning across the airfield Stirling's jeep was knocked out, but after being picked up he ordered those remaining to turn around and have a second run, to try and destroy a few more aircraft: the official count was forty destroyed.

After their success at Fuka, disaster followed for the SAS on 13 September 1942. A major operation had been planned in which they were to take an important part. A force of 200 men were ordered to capture Benghazi and destroy its port, 600 miles behind enemy lines. Simultaneously, a force of commandos would assault Tobruk and the Long Range Desert Group (LRDG) would attack the airfield and barracks at Barce. Until now the SAS had worked in small groups and David Stirling was heavily opposed to the plan, but he had to submit to the dictates of GHQ.

Stephen Hastings was told that during the operation he would have to capture a mole in the harbour on which there were several heavy anti-aircraft machine guns. Having disposed of these he was to blow up an oil depot near the base of the mole, all with just fourteen men.

As the SAS formation drew near to Benghazi, Fitzroy Maclean, now acting as intelligence officer, discovered that the Germans had been pre-warned of the attack and were heavily reinforcing the area. Worried by Maclean's report and the appearance of German reconnaissance aircraft, David Stirling radioed Cairo for a change of timing: he was refused and the operation went ahead as planned. Consequently, most of the SAS troops didn't get anywhere near Benghazi; instead, they fell into a well-prepared ambush.

Having escaped from the ambush, more trouble followed the next evening. After camouflaging their vehicles in a wadi, they laid up during the day, while German and Italian aircraft searched overhead. One of the soldiers in the Free French Squadron became impatient and fired a shot at a persistent Italian bomber. The bomber called up reinforcements and the position was bombed and strafed until dark. Most of the soldiers managed to scramble safely into the scrub, but many of their remaining jeeps and trucks were destroyed.

After more than a year with his battalion and nine months with the SAS, and due to chronic bronchitis, Stephen Hastings was sent to Cairo, deemed unfit and appointed ADC to Richard Casey, Minister of State in the Middle East and a member of the War Cabinet. Six months later, after being passed fit again, he joined the Algiers station of Special Operations Executive (SOE), just in time for Operation 'Anvil' the invasion of the Cote d'Azur on 15 August 1944. Accompanied by two other agents, his job was to contact the Maquis somewhere in the Basses Alpes and report on their needs. On discovering that the Maquis in the area already had everything they needed, they abandoned their assignment and drove north through the liberated towns and villages, a drive which eventually took them into Paris itself.

From France Stephen Hastings, now a captain, was sent to Bari in Italy to join No 1 Special Force SOE, as a British Liaison Officer (BLO) working with the Partisans. On 2 February 1945 he parachuted into the Ligurian Apennines of north-west Italy, south of the River Po. From there he moved north, into the 13th Partisan Zone, a large area of mountains near the town of Piacenza. He was accompanied by Lieutenant Giorgio Insom, who was half Italian and half

Russian, and Sergeant 'Chalky' White, their radio operator. Insom had previously been an officer in the Italian Army, but had joined the British after the armistice. Once in Italy they joined Colonel Peter McMullen and Major Basil Davidson, at a village called Alpepiana, where they recruited a small band of Partisans to act as bodyguards, porters and couriers.

From Alpepiana they made their way across the snow-covered mountains to the village of Groppallo, which was the headquarters of 13th Zone. Here they met Il Colonello Marziolo, commander of the Partisans in the area. He was in charge of three decimated divisions, of 100 or 200 men, divided into various brigades: the Division 'Justitia e Liberta,' who were left-wing anti-Monarchists, bitterly suspicious of the communists; the Division 'Prati', who were Christian Democrats; and the First Division 'Piacenza,' who were Communist Garibaldini.

Their main task was to try and weld these disparate groups into a coherent force, which could eventually be used to attack Piacenza, once the Allies had broken through the mountains into the valley of the River Po. As each of the Partisan divisions had different political views, this was not an easy task. However, by April 1945, 13 Zone had a satisfactory central command, agreeable to all parties concerned. Their secondary task was to provide intelligence about German and Fascist units in the area.

On 5 April the signal came to mount their all-out effort, as the Eighth and Fifth Armies were about to break through the Gothic Line. The Partisans first attacked a German and Italian force of company strength, near Castell Arquato. Here they captured the bridge, which was needed before they could advance on Piacenza. The Partisans next attacked the enemy garrisons at Groparallo and Monte Chino, where a castle on the hill was strongly defended. It was finally abandoned by the Germans on 19 April.

At the end of April the Partisans began their advance on Piacenza. The plan was to establish a bridgehead over the Po. The battle for the city lasted from the 25th to the 29th, when the remaining Fascist and SS troops fled. By this time the Americans had provided them with three Sherman tanks: but it was essentially a Partisan victory. For his own part, Hastings was awarded the MC.

On returning to England after the war, Stephen Hastings returned to the Scots Guards, and was put in command of a company in training at Hawick and then in North Wales. He then applied for a position with the Economic Division of the Control Commission for Austria, located in Hiezing, and was accepted. He was later sent as a staff officer –GSO 3 Transport –to 46th Division at Styria, and then as Chief Instructor to a mountain training school on the Schmeltz above Judenburg. In the spring of 1948 he was appointed GSO 2, Staff Duties, at headquarters, British Troops Austria, near Klagenfurt. But after ten years of professional soldiering, he resigned his commission in 1949.

He later joined the Foreign Service as an officer in the Secret Intelligence Service, which eventually prompted him to stand for Parliament. He was elected as the MP for Mid-Bedfordshire in 1960 and retired from the House of Commons in 1983, the same year in which he was knighted.

ANTHONY MEYER

Anthony Meyer joined the Scots Guards in April 1941, after which he spent three months at Sandhurst, followed by periods with the Training Battalion at Pirbright, and a brief stay in the Tower of London, taking turns to mount the guard at Buckingham Palace. Finally, he was posted to the 4th Battalion, which was under canvas near Frome in Somerset. He was subsequently posted to Brigade Headquarters, and then Divisional Headquarters of the Guards Armoured Division, as a Liaison Officer. In April 1943, while he was Assistant to the General Staff Officer in charge of Training, Divisional HQ was struck by a virulent strain of jaundice, from which he was the only officer to escape. As a result, he single-handedly ran this part of HQ for about six weeks and was given special praise by the King and Queen during a visit. After this the Guards Armoured Division moved restlessly around Britain preparing for their role in the invasion of Europe. Anthony Meyer recalls his own days in France in his autobiography, *Stand Up and Be Counted*, in which he says:

> We eventually set sail from London Docks, where the towers of Canary Wharf are now rising, on Derby Day, 1944. There was a carnival atmosphere among the officers on board as we sailed down the Thames with the wireless blaring out the Derby commentary from Newmarket (where it was run during the war years). We hugged the coast of Kent that night, and awoke the next morning to the amazing spectacle of the sea lane from the Isle of Wight to the French coast, half a mile wide and eighty miles long, crowded with shipping in both directions, with barrage balloons moored every few hundred yards to keep German fighters at a respectful distance. By teatime we dropped

anchor a mile off the French coast and prepared to disembark. A large raft was brought alongside, and our vehicles, with all our worldly possessions loaded into them, were swung over the ship's side onto the raft. At this moment the wind began to blow. Within minutes we were in a full storm, and the raft swung wildly. Before long the ropes started to fray; within an hour the raft had broken loose and we waved farewell as it and all our possessions were swept from our sight towards the surf beating on the shore. It was clear that we were going to have a very uncomfortable war. We had four days of that storm. We did, after a day or two, get over our seasickness despite the diet of plum pudding and spam, which we had for every meal, being the only rations on board.

Eventually the wind died down and we were able to land, in amphibious vehicles this time. It was an emotional moment for me to land on French soil; it was an even more joyful moment for all of us to find our lost vehicles safely parked in Canadian Corps car park, with their precious contents intact; and we toasted our incredible good fortune with a bottle of champagne which Aylmer Tryon, the General's ADC, had been sent by an aunt in Australia. Afterwards we felt able to forgive Aylmer even his endless reminders, as we had lain storm tossed, that 'Worse things happen at sea'.

I cannot claim any deeds of great glory in the conflict. On the night before we set sail from London I had mislaid my only weapon, a very cumbrous revolver, in the scramble to dodge the V1s (buzz bombs) which were exploding around us in the docks. Just as well, as I should have been unlikely to hit anything with it except my foot. I did, however, make one notable contribution to the winning of the war. I had been assigned to what was known as the command post: a small group of officers, drivers, tanks and armoured cars accompanying the Divisional Commander, the diminutive but heroic General Alan Adair, very close behind the front line of advancing troops as we attempted, in vain, to break through the German anti-tank screen near Caen on 18 July 1944 (Operation Goodwood). My place was in a fearsome-looking Sherman tank, whose gun had been replaced by a dummy, but which was equipped for communication with Corps headquarters. Suddenly my earphones crackled: 'This is the Corps Commander; I am coming to see you. Where are you?' I hastily consulted the map, worked out the exact location, encoded it, and sent it off. I reckoned that General O'Connor would be with us in ten minutes. Ten minutes later two things happened simultaneously. The Germans found our position and dropped an almighty barrage of high explosives on us. We cowered safely behind our armoured turrets, battened down. My radio crackled again: 'This is General O'Connor. I have been to the map reference you gave me and you're ****** not there. Where the ****** are you?' Ten minutes later still, the bombardment had died down and a very testy Corps Commander arrived in a totally unarmoured jeep. To his dying day he never knew that he owed his life to my poor map-reading.

Four days later my war ended abruptly. We had been halted by mud and by German anti-tank weapons which had survived the most ferocious RAF bombing. I was in a rather lightly armoured communications vehicle when there was a very loud bang, followed by a good deal of daylight pouring in through the roof, and an awful lot of blood on the table beside me, which turned out to be my own.

For some days I hovered between life and death in a field hospital in Normandy. Brother officers who called to see how I was had written me off and were at a loss what messages to send to my wife, expecting her second baby in a month and desperate for news at home. However, I got back in one piece, only to relapse badly just as our son was about to be born. All in all it was eight months before I could be let out of hospital on a short lead. I did a lot of reading, and even got a very rudimentary grasp of economics; but I cannot claim that my involvement in politics started from then.

In fact it would be another 20 years before Anthony Meyer (later Sir Anthony Meyer) entered the House of Commons. He was the Conservative MP for Eton and Slough from 1964–1966, West Flint from 1970–1983 and Clwyd North West from 1983–1992.

DAVID GIBSON-WATT

Of the Welsh Guards contingent in the House of Commons, one of the best known, and certainly most decorated, was David Gibson-Watt MC and 2 Bars, who was Conservative MP for Hereford between 1956–1974. He served in North Africa and Italy with the 3rd Battalion.

The 3rd Battalion Welsh Guards landed in Algiers on 16 February 1943, to replace 2 Hampshires in 1 Guards Brigade, just in time for the advance on Tunis, as part of the First Army. They joined 3rd Battalion Grenadier Guards and 2nd Battalion Coldstream Guards, as infantry support for the 6th Armoured Division. David Gibson-Watt recalls:

> After a sea voyage of five days, 3rd Battalion Welsh Guards marched 17 miles to a big vineyard complex. Here the guardsmen treated the wine as if it was beer and, not surprisingly, some were very sick.

The brigade's first battle was at Fondouk, where they were required to capture the left hand side of a pass which cut through some heavily defended hills. At the same time the Americans would capture the right-hand side, thus enabling the armour to roll through the pass into the Kairouan Plain. As company second in command, David Gibson-Watt was LOB (left out of battle).

It was for his actions at Hammam Lif that David Gibson-Watt would receive his first award. Here the armour found that the hills were impassable, as they were held in strength. The Welsh Guards were required to attack and capture a ridge before operations could proceed any further, as David Gibson-Watt recalls:

Later, in the advance on Tunis, we were ordered to attack Hammam Lif, a scrubby hill to the north of Tunis. I commanded No 4 Company, on the right flank. On reaching the top of the hill, I was hit in the left forearm by a machine gun bullet. Putting on a first aid dressing, I led a platoon down a steep slope with thick bushes on it. I turned left at the bottom of the hill with my 25 men. We reached a large gorge where we halted. It was now dark, so, leaving Sergeant Rees in charge in a position behind the enemy lines, I managed to make it back up the hill and rejoined the battalion. The CO refused to let me go back to the platoon and I soon found myself in a train on my way to hospital.

Two weeks later David Gibson-Watt rejoined the Battalion at Sousse where he was made Adjutant and was awarded the MC.

In February 1944 the battalion took over from the 2/4 Hampshires on a remote mountain in southern Italy called Monte Cerasola. They held the position for ten days under constant grenade or mortar attack and several heavy infantry assaults. The battalion suffered badly, not only from enemy activity, but through the snow and ice which accounted for many cases of frostbite.

Twice we were attacked and, though we suffered a lot of casualties, we took about eighty prisoners. I had led the Battalion into position, and I was last out. I was awarded a bar to my MC.

A month later, we were holding a position in Cassino. When we broke out up the Liri Valley we advanced on foot at night towards Arce. Here we suffered very heavy casualties. In the evening I led my company in the dark, through the 2nd Battalion of the Coldstream Guards, and successfully took the left hill, allowing the tanks to advance through Arce. After this battle I was put in charge of a rest camp near Lake Trasimeno.

Later, at the end of the campaign in Italy, the Welsh Guards crossed the River Po and advanced several miles unopposed to the Canal at Bianco, where the bridge was blown up in their faces. It was at this time that David Gibson-Watt was awarded the second bar to his MC.

The battalion ended the war in Austria and on returning home David Gibson-Watt was made a company commander instructor at Sandhurst before leaving the Army. During his time in Parliament his appointments included being Minister of State for the Welsh Office. He was created a life peer in 1979.

DOUGLAS DODDS-PARKER

Douglas Dodds-Parker, who was an MP from 1945–74, was educated at Winchester and Oxford. He entered the Sudan Political Service in 1930 and was eventually posted to Khartoum as Assistant Private Secretary to the Governor-General. In 1935 the Italians began their invasion of Ethiopia and, while refugees poured across the Sudanese border, Douglas Dodds-Parker was employed in keeping their hopes of liberation alive.

On the outbreak of war with the Germans he joined the Grenadier Guards. He was commissioned immediately and sent to the Training Battalion at Victoria Barracks, Windsor. He was already thirty years old.

Early in 1940 a holding battalion was formed at Kempton Park race-course, where their duties included guarding Windsor Castle and Staines Railway Bridge. From here Douglas Dodds-Parker was sent to Cambridge on a course, later known as 'The Gauleiters'. MIR (Military Intelligence Research), the original special operations unit, had organized the course to bring together and classify officers who had specialist knowledge of foreign countries, who might be available for action, rather than intelligence. After attending the course he was employed by the War Office and given the formal task of representing the Mission concerned with Poland.

In late May 1940 he was sent to Cairo, in anticipation of Italian entry into the war, to lay lines of communication to Poland and Czechoslovakia, in the event that those which existed through Italy were cut.

When Italy declared war on Britain in June 1940 General Wavell ordered him to Khartoum, to report on preparations for action in support of the return of Emperor Haile Selassie to Ethiopia.

The Italians invaded the Sudan as far as Kassala, but they were soon contained by the combined efforts of the Sudan Defence Force and the 4th and 5th Indian Divisions.

By September the Emperor was in Khartoum and Brigadier Sandford was sent into the Gojjam to mark the route chosen for his advance to Addis Ababa.

Douglas Dodds-Parker took up his duties at Headquarters British Troops in the Sudan, in the Gordon College building, and was sent along the entire length of the occupied frontier and down to the Boma plateau, to survey and report on the possibilities of using irregular troops in the theatre.

At this time the legendary Orde Wingate arrived in Khartoum, with the temporary rank of colonel in the Gideon Force, working closely with the Emperor himself. Douglas Dodds-Parker would enjoy a close working relationship with this brilliant, yet controversial, leader.

By January 1941 the Allied Armies were advancing on Addis on three fronts. During this advance among Douglas Dodds-Parker's concerns was helping Oliver Corvedale's propaganda unit to operate near Keren. Their task was to weaken Italian morale and seek recruits for the Emperor's Army. One way they did this was by borrowing broadcasting equipment from Richard Dimbleby's BBC unit, which they set up close to the front line. They used this to play recordings to the enemy troops, in particular appeals from the Emperor to the Ethiopian levies who were working for the Italians, to rally to him. Many did, bringing their arms with them. Corvedale also played music recordings and, although his commanding officer was a bit disgruntled by being woken up in the night by the overture from *Aida*, Italians captured at Keren later admitted that the music made them realize there were 'other things in life'.

The Allies were under pressure to bring the Ethiopian campaign to a prompt and successful conclusion in order to release regular forces which were desperately needed in the Mediterranean. The breath-taking victory at Keren, and a spectacular advance over hundreds of miles, brought the end within reach by early May 1941. By this time Gideon Force, with Wingate and the Emperor, were across the Blue Nile Gorge and approaching Addis. However, General Cunningham got there first and made arrangements for the Emperor's entry on

5 May, exactly six years after Marshal Badoglio had ridden into the capital on a white horse. Wingate decided that the Emperor should do the same, but Cunningham sent a car, which the Emperor accepted. Not to be thwarted, Wingate mounted the horse himself and led the victory march into Addis.

Dodds-Parker was sent up from Khartoum to arrange the details of the transfer of responsibility for the Emperor from General Platt's to General Cunningham's theatre of operations. He returned to England the day after the victory parade and bade farewell to Wingate after dinner on the previous evening: he would never see him again.

On his return to England, Dodds-Parker reported to Wellington Barracks and was put in command of a platoon guarding Churchill's shelter at Storey's Gate against possible parachute attack. However, his return to regimental duties didn't last long and, reporting to Colin Gubbins at Norgeby House in Baker Street, he soon discovered why he had been recalled from the Sudan. For the next 18 months he would work with SOE organizing air and sea transport for agents going in and out of enemy-occupied Western Europe. During this period, because of his knowledge of future plans, he was forbidden to go into the field and risk being captured.

The first operation of which he was fully in charge was 'Moonshine/Opinion', the first parachute drop into Belgium in May 1941. Dodds-Parker drove two agents to the airfield at Newmarket himself, where the pilot of the Whitley asked him if he would like to go along, as it was only a short flight. He accepted and, after handing over his wallet with security passes, he climbed aboard. The target area was in the Namur/Dinant part of Belgium. On arrival the first agent parachuted successfully, but the second agent got caught up on the tail wheel of the aircraft. Nothing could be done to retrieve the unfortunate man, who was spinning around a few feet behind the aircraft, which effectively reduced their speed during their return to base. On reaching Boulogne they were forced to fly south because of flak, and they were also fired on when crossing the British coast. The agent was already dead when they arrived back at Newmarket, but the first agent completed the mission and returned home a year later through Spain.

In the late summer of 1942 Dodds-Parker was appointed Operations Officer in the Mission being formed to organize the activity of agents being sent from North Africa into the south of occupied Europe. The Mission, code-named 'Massingham' was to establish a base for later operations into France, Corsica, Sardinia and Italy. He arrived shortly after 'Operation Torch', the invasion of North Africa in November 1942.

Promoted to lieutenant colonel, he was put in charge of this base, where training was given in survival techniques, signalling, coding, sabotage, and guerrilla methods. Parachute training was given nearby. It wasn't long before operatives were being sent into France and Corsica. They were also used on special missions in North Africa ahead of the Allied Armies as they continued their advance towards Tunis. After the fall of Tunis, some of the mission moved up to an abandoned enemy airfield south of the city, in preparation for the invasion of Italy. During the attack on Sicily in July 1943 'Massingham' put all its resources and experience at the disposal of the British 1st Airborne Division.

The part played by SOE in the Italian Armistice in July-September 1943 was codenamed 'Monkey'. Dodds-Parker was responsible for sending the historic file back to London of what had been achieved through a series of negotiations, secret communications and clandestine journeys by secret agents, until the King had finally arranged the Armistice, following the arrest of Mussolini.

It all began when Marshal Badoglio sent one of his generals to Spain to contact the British Embassy. Eventually two peace emissaries arrived via Lisbon and Dodds-Parker made his own villa available for negotiations, where he could be in sole charge of all coded messages in and out of Europe. In total secrecy he had to arrange messages to and from Eisenhower, London and Rome. The final stage was the most critical. The Italians had asked for six hours' notice, to allow for coordination of Badoglio's announcement of the Armistice from Rome at the same time, 6.30 pm, as Eisenhower's broadcast on Algiers radio. Dodds-Parker decided that the message should be sent off at 10.00 am on 8 September, the day before the landings at Salerno. This should allow enough time for decoding and passing it to Badoglio by midday.

Suddenly, there was a moment of extreme temporary concern, when at 9.00 am on 8 September he was handed an emergency message from Badoglio explaining his belief that the Germans had found out about the Armistice and suggesting that the whole project must be abandoned. Consequently, Eisenhower telephoned Dodds-

Parker from Carthage to ask if he was sure about the security of his codes. This was probably the most important decision he would ever have to make. Thousands of Allied troops were waiting to assault the beaches of Salerno –could they be heading for a trap? He replied to the effect that there was no reason to suspect the codes had been compromised. In the event, they had not been. Eisenhower dictated a message for him to send to Rome, and then, at 6.30 as planned, he made his announcement on Algiers Radio. Badoglio's announcement was made a little later and the invasion went ahead.

Eisenhower sent Dodds-Parker to Italy to meet the King and Badoglio, and discuss ways of helping to throw the Nazis out of Italy. His immediate aim was to disrupt enemy communications and thus slow down the build-up of German troops and armour in the area around Naples. There was a lack of trained agents in Italy, but there were plenty of Italians who hated the Fascists just as much as they did the Nazis, so many of these patriots with knowledge of the local countryside were recruited for irregular operations behind the enemy lines. Later Special Operations (Mediterranean) was set up at Bari and Monopoli to supply the growing irregular forces in the Balkans.

After 'Overlord' and 'Dragoon', the invasions of Normandy and the south of France, Dodds-Parker went to Paris, where Colin Gubbins was coordinating the part SOE would play in the link-up between the two Allied forces. There he operated with the Supreme Headquarters (SHAEF). He arrived shortly after the Battle of the Bulge had been won.

It seems that his political life began almost by accident. He was preparing to go to Palestine when, only a few weeks away from the 1945 general election, James Edmondson, the Member for North Oxfordshire, decided that he didn't want to stand again. He approached Douglas Dodds-Parker about the possibility of him taking his place and after some discussion he accepted. He was duly elected on 5 July and remained in the House of Commons until 1974. He served as Under-Secretary of State in the Foreign and Commonwealth Offices from 1953–1957 and was knighted in 1973.

ROBERT BOSCAWEN

Robert Boscawen was Conservative MP for Wells in Somerset from 1970–1983 and Somerton and Frome from 1983–1992. While in Parliament his appointments included being Vice-Chamberlain of Her Majesty's Household from 1983–1986, and Comptroller between 1986–1988. During the war, serving as a lieutenant with 1st Armoured Battalion Coldstream Guards, he was awarded the MC. Robert Boscawen commanded No 2 Troop, of No 2 Squadron, which set sail for France on Friday, 30 June 1944 and was destined to take part in the attempted break-out from the Normandy bridgehead on Tuesday, 18 July – 'Operation Goodwood.' He kept a vivid and detailed diary, describing events from the moment the battalion landed in Normandy until he was severely wounded, and the following story, which uses extracts linked together, is taken from this unique record.

On Saturday, 15 July all officers were summoned before the Commander. From that moment we knew our ordeal had started. After months of waiting before the invasion and training together for two years or more, this came as a great relief.

'Well,' he began, 'the great day has come at last. On Tuesday we go into our first battle. It is going to be a big show and ought to be a very good party.'

Lieut-Colonel Ririd Myddleton; under him the battalion had trained in armour. A shy man, he was well liked and trusted by all ranks. He then gave us the plan.

The position was that rather a deadlock had taken place all along the front. Caen had been taken, but the American advance in the west had made little progress. So in order to draw the German armour away from the Americans, to enlarge the bridgehead and to place us in a good position, the British were to put in an attack in the east.

XXX and XII Corps, both infantry, were to attack on Sunday and Monday respectively west of Caen, to draw the enemy away from the main attack. On Tuesday 18th, preceded by a terrific artillery barrage and the 'heaviest aerial bombardment of the war', VIII Corps, consisting of the Guards Armoured Division, 11th Armoured Division, 7th Armoured Division and 3rd Infantry Division, were to attack south from the new direction east of Caen. The Canadians were to occupy the suburbs of Caen east of the Orne and 51st Highland Division were to take Troarn on our eastern flank.

The plan was that after the barrage 11th Armoured Division would advance almost regardless of loss due south as far as the main Paris railway at Cagny, and then turn due west to take the high ground on the right flank near Bourgeubus. The GAD were to follow led by 2nd Grens, followed by 1st Coldstream and 2nd Irish Guards, to reach the railway at Cagny and then turn east to take high ground by Vimont, and so protect the east flank.

Monday was spent feverishly preparing for the battle. We listened to a continuous rumbling of artillery in the distance that showed us XXX and XII Corps were attacking. We spent the afternoon folding maps, studying aerial photographs, receiving and giving orders, and cleaning our guns. It was a day of anticipation, and I was glad when we set off for a night drive to north of Caen.

It was an awful approach march, cross-country on a very dark night with only tail lamps, and worst of all a thick cloud of dust everywhere. Eventually we arrived at about one in the morning drawn up in a long column in a field, west of the bridge over the Orne.

Tuesday, 18 July, Operation 'Goodwood.' It was a clear grey dawn with no mist. I woke up about six and lay waiting for the day to start. Suddenly the silence was broken by the crash of a nearby medium battery, followed by a rising crescendo of guns, soon breaking into a roar all along the line. A minute or two later the heavy drone of bombers could be heard. And there they came, hundreds of them, in an endless untidy stream, protected by a few Spitfires. Soon they were over their target, red sparks and white puffs of flak were going up all round them, and then one heard the muffled crumps of their bombs. On and on came the bombers, Lancasters and Halifaxes, one or other falling victim to the flak, with an orange flame and black smoke it fell like a stone to the ground.

After nearly an hour the heavy bombers stopped and Fortresses and 'mediums' took over, sprinkling fragmentary bombs on our centre line.

Breakfast of two sausages and tea, then we cleared up and got the tank ready. At a quarter to eight we broke wireless silence and 'netted' the sets. Then came the familiar whine of the starter-motor, as Jepson, my driver, warmed her up.

Around eight the 11th Armoured moved forward and the barrage slowed down. A couple of shells landed quite close, so we mounted our tanks ready to go. Soon after eight the battalion moved off in a long column line-ahead.

We crossed the Orne on a pontoon bridge and made across country for our start line. On the 'air' the Commander told us that already the first villages (Demouville and Cuverville), had been cleared by the 11th. No. 1 Squadron were leading, followed by Battalion HQ, ourselves (No. 2), and then No. 3.

Then the shelling started. It was there we had our first casualty. Our attached gunner Battery Commander (of the Leicester Yeomanry) was called up on the 'air', but there was no answer. Oliver Heywood, (who, as Signals Officer, travelled as the Operator inside the Commanding Officer's tank,) tried several times. Someone answered that he was knocked out followed by the call for '6', the doctor, which was countermanded with the word 'understood' from Oliver. So we knew he was killed. A few minutes later I passed him, caught by a shell while out of his tank. I was glad this did not upset me, and I very soon got used to unpleasant sights.

We eventually crossed the start line through our own minefield and, still line-ahead, moved south. To our left was a battalion of the 11th, (the Fife and Forfar Yeomanry in Shermans), firing at some houses. We passed over a lot of slit-trenches and pits full of dead and 'bomb-happy' Germans offering no resistance.

The country was a flat open plain of corn land, bordered on the right by shattered and burning buildings with Caen and the Mondeville steel works in the distance. We passed Cuverville and Demouville on our right and crossed a railway line running east to west. Then we stopped. The Grenadiers in front had been held up somewhere, no one knew quite what was happening. Later we discovered about eight of their tanks had fallen victim to 88 mm's and other anti-tank guns, and Sir Arthur Grant, their No. 2 Squadron Leader, had been killed.

Panthers had been reported to our left, and as my troop happened to be on the extreme left, I turned them in that direction and kept a good look out. Our tracks were nicely covered in the tall corn but we were a sitting target to any Panther in the woods. Vehicles of all kinds were crowding up behind, the 1st Motor Battalion Grenadiers, Harry Stanley's No. 4 Company in their halftracks, and some carriers of heavy machine gunners (the Northumberland Fusiliers). No. 4 Company were attached to us to provide close infantry support, the practice during training and until the end of this battle. Mixed up too were a few odd tanks of the 2nd. Recce. Welsh Guards. It was a lovely target and soon the shells and mortars started landing on us heavily, with their tearing crumps.

No. 1 Squadron came up with reports of three Panthers moving on the left. I scanned carefully with my binoculars but could see no movement in the trees about eight hundred yards away. Then Malcolm Lock reported a Panther opposite him and he got it with his Firefly, the 17 pounder Sherman. He did very well getting it. With one shot it 'brewed up' nicely.

By now the situation was far from clear. It was about 11 o'clock and it was obvious things were not going to plan in front. The Grenadiers appeared held up and all was confused, so in order to 'get on' the Commander ordered us, No. 2 Squadron, to move round the right flank and try to push on to our first objective, Cagny.

Nigel Pratt and Val Hermon's troops led off cautiously to the right, while I was left behind for a bit to protect the left flank from these Panthers. One of Val's tanks put a burst of m.g. into a ditch and out got thirty Huns with white flags. All the time tanks and guns were firing, but as one could never tell what at, this made everything very confusing.

About this time the Commander was told to get a move on as the farm to which we were advancing so cautiously was where Brigade HQ already were, such is the confusion of war. Dermot Musker, the Brigadier's protective Troop Leader, told me afterwards that all the big shots of 'brigade' had been walking about, talking and giving orders next to the farm, when he thought he saw something move in it. He put a shot or two into the buildings. A few minutes later over

211

a hundred Germans came out and surrendered. If they had chosen to fight, brigade would have looked very silly.

We pushed on south towards the railway. It was not known whether Cagny was in ours or enemy hands, but the squadron came round the corner of a small wood and there we saw a sight that rather shook us all.

Eight hundred yards to our front was the railway on a steep embankment, almost a tank obstacle. This side of it and to our left front was the remains of Cagny. Beyond the railway, the horizon was covered with burning Shermans. I could count nearly twenty (a whole squadron, burning in one field alone). Beyond was gently rising ground, evidently housing a barrier of 88 mm anti-tank guns. The railway was the end of the bomb line, so the 88s were unmolested.

The Commander decided then 'we must not add to this disaster' so must move under cover of the railway embankment round Cagny ready to push on to Vimont, our main objective. The Grens were engaged north of Cagny, it appeared with some Panthers, so we were to move south of it through a bottleneck between a wood and the railway. Nigel led through, followed by the remainder of the squadron, and me who remained in the bottleneck to cover them. It was a horrid place, a battered little railway station with a signal box and level crossing on my right and a wood surrounded by a stone wall on my left.

Further up the line where Nigel was, something was going on. A Panther had put its nose round the corner of a wood and shot at Nigel's and the Sergeant Major's tanks. I think it was firing down the railway, anyhow a few minutes later there was a bang on the top of my turret as something hit my tank. I quickly reversed away as I could see nothing and put down some smoke –typically it failed to go off –luckily the tank appeared undamaged and reversed back to the wall round the wood. I remember asking Jepson whether anything had come through, but he said it was all right in front. Good fortune had struck us as well as the others. The German tanks were evidently short of armour-piercing shot and their high-explosive shells made a bang and took the paint off.

We learned after that the Irish were having a stiff battle trying to advance round the north of Cagny, but the Germans were now dug in in strength, and without the infantry to deal with the anti-tank guns in the woods, progress bought serious trouble. So we had to sit and wait in this horrid place to hold Cagny until dark when the infantry would take over from us. Up till now I had not felt frightened, but sitting on that wall for four hours was a very disagreeable experience and I longed for darkness to come.

The whole squadron was spread out along the wall, my troop on the left (nearest the village), a shocking position but there was none better. Harry Stanley's infantry were mopping up the village. Sniped at continuously we replied with ineffective bursts of m.g., as we could not tell where the shots came from.

Soon the enemy got our range and we were mortared and shelled heavily and continuously. They landed all around us. No damage was done but they were very noisy and discouraging. Every now and then the horrible roar like a tube train of the nebelwerfer six barrel rockets came over and stonked us. Six hundred yards to our front was a thick hedge and beyond in the distance was the village of Frénouville with its church tower a target for our guns. (It could well have been the enemy OP.) It was noticed every time one of our spotting planes flew over, we were shelled. Later it was discovered that this was a captured British one used by the Hun OP. We heard that all our own were ordered to the ground, and sure enough over it came, only this time every gun let off and it was soon shot down.

Worse was to come. Two planes came low over us, and I realized they were Huns just as one was in front of me. I saw him release a bomb which came spinning down towards my tank. I took cover on the floor and hoped for the best. It landed at the back, but bounced away harmlessly and was crashing through the wood as I looked out of the top again, a U.x.B!

Then what we feared most of all occurred. We were being steadily mortared and bombed when I heard that sickening whizz and crack of an A.P. shot and saw a neat round hole appear in the wall behind. A beastly Panther or something was shooting at me but I could not see where from. Why none of us brewed up I don't know, but they missed and after a while the Panther went away.

I was relieved when about eleven o'clock the infantry appeared. Small lines of men crawled out and dug in to the front of us, and we started to pull out. It was the 5th Coldstream.

We were given a parting stonk of shells as we picked our way back between the craters. We formed into a long line and were led off back to laager for the night. On the way Sergeant White's tank from Nigel's troop stopped and would not restart. While we were shackling on our tow rope a Hun plane was machine-gunning something quite close with a spectacular display of tracer.

It was now pitch dark, we were left behind and we spent an anxious half hour looking for the rest, during it I cursed Sergeant White several times to myself. After considerable 'chos' we got into a laager position (drawn up in two lines), just east of La Prieure. I posted sentries and immediately lay down with the crew under my tank in the corn. It was nearly one a.m., and reveille was at four to break laager. After sixteen hours in a tank I was pleased to get out, and soon went to sleep. A long and unsatisfactory day, we had done all we had been asked to do, but of course were still a long way from our objective.

On Wednesday, 19 July we were reserve battalion during the day, so hoped for a reasonably quiet time, but after yesterday's disaster to 11th Armoured nobody was inclined to push on to our original objectives. We soon heard that yesterday our friends in 11th Armoured Division had lost over one hundred Sherman tanks, and ourselves, perhaps another thirty, while 7th Armoured were never able to pass through. Gone were any doubts –if they existed –about the stamp of foe we were against. The enemy in inferior numbers, and without air cover, regained their poise after the bombing and struck back. They had warning of the British attack and organized their defence in great depth.

Shelled intermittently, we lost a few men wounded in Battalion H.Q., including No. 3 Squadron's Sergeant-Major. We passed the morning in the same place until we had an order to move to a defensive position as enemy tanks were reported behind. We moved only to be told to come back again. Yet a second time we moved back to this position followed immediately by being sent to the north of Cagny behind the 2nd Irish Guards in case of a counter-attack.

A shocking position. We ended up on a forward slope in view of the enemy, as usual. Suddenly a tank in front of us was shot by a Panther, and it brewed up at once in a cloud of smoke. I saw some of its crew running away in the corn. It was disheartening to see these tanks burn up so quickly. The Germans called our Shermans 'Tommy Cookers', a fitting name. The generals and senior officers were angry if one called them this, and we were not meant to know what the Germans thought of Shermans. They were definitely no good for the job of attacking tanks; we needed a heavily armoured tank with a big gun like the German Tiger to do any good.

By Thursday, 20 July it was obvious that the much-vaunted breakthrough had completely fizzled out. But the attack had succeeded in bringing the enemy armour over the eastern flank and had contained the enemy's main forces, so, as it turned out, it wasn't wasted.

'Operation Goodwood' didn't achieve the breakout that the Allies had expected, because the Germans reinforced the area with their own armoured divisions. The startling reality is that during the operation VIII Corps only managed to advance six 'bloody' miles, for the loss of a large number of tanks. However, it did succeed in drawing the Germans away from the Americans, which enabled Lieutenant General Omar Bradley to attempt his own breakout on 25 July –codenamed 'Operation Cobra.'

After carpet-bombing the area with more than 4,200 tons of explosives, the Americans opened a gap in the German front line, wide enough for General Patton's Third Army to break through with whirlwind speed on 1 August. Although the Germans made a counter-attack at Avranches between 6–10 August, by the 20th they were in full retreat, leading to the liberation of Paris on the 25th.

However, not wishing to jump ahead of the story, the next extract from Robert Boscawen's diary takes us to 9 August, when he himself came face to face with a German Panther.

On 9 August Bill Gray (No. 2 Squadron CO) was summoned back to Battalion H.Q. for orders. [Bill Gray was later to become Sir William Anstruther-Gray MC. He was already MP for North Lanark since 1931 and became chairman of the 1922 committee.] The 11th Armoured Division were to be pulled out for a rest and we were to take their place. During the night 3rd Irish were to move up to the Sourdevalle ridge (in a salient beyond the Vire-Estry road), and take over from the Monmouths who were supported by a squadron of Hussars. Our Squadron was to be in support of the 3rd Irish while the rest of the battalion were to remain in reserve. The position we were told then was horrible. It was overlooked by a hill opposite, and by another hill on the left flank, being heavily shelled all the time. We were up against elements of 10th SS Panzer, 9th SS Panzer, and 3rd and 5th Para. Divisions: all good soldiers.

The night was sinisterly silent. I called the Tank Commanders together and told them to camouflage the tanks, then to dig a slit trench. To my front along the next hedge was the forward platoon of the Micks well dug in behind the bank. It was under Peter Doyle, a contemporary of mine at Eton. Further up the field were three knocked-out Shermans, hit from the hill to our left. Beyond them was a little sunken lane full of dead Germans.

It was now about six o'clock and I think our alertness had fatigued a lot. Our wireless was switched off, necessary for saving our batteries and for listening for enemy tanks. Mortar fire suddenly increased and the shelling became a barrage, to our front the chatter of machine guns suddenly broke out. An attack was coming in. I shouted to the Driver and Gunner to jump in, and switched on the wireless. I seized my headphones and binoculars, inevitably they got entangled.

The game was on. I'd spotted the whereabouts of the stag and we were now to fight it out. 'Seventy-five traverse left slightly, on, 200, fire at the dust'. It was only a reckless shot as I could not see the tank. However, I hoped it might frighten him a bit.

We were all in a huddle at the left-hand back corner of the field and Caulfield, 'Two Baker', was still stuck in the field behind. I came up on the air to Sergeant Emmerson: 'Hello Two Charlie, Panther moving across front from right to left. Move up into the field on your left and up to the next hedge, but do not go on to the forward slope.'

Emmerson moved through the hedge on my left and went forward to the next bank. I followed, but it needed a lot of backing and turning to get through the only gap in the bank, and wasted a valuable minute or two. I couldn't see where Emmerson had gone and had now lost trace of the enemy.

When I got through the hedge I saw that Emmerson had gone much too far, in fact off the ridge and was two fields ahead. Either he had not listened to what I said or I had not made myself clear, but he was always inclined to go bashing off like that. It was too late to stop him now, so I moved over to where he should have gone. I turned my tank to the right to face the enemy and took a look forward.

Just as I got there a cloud of smoke came out of the top of Emmerson's tank. Some men jumped out of it and lay rolling on the ground, one I saw had his clothes on fire, another ran for cover, two stretcher bearers from the Micks raced over to them. A cloud of white smoke now poured out of the turret.

There, not three hundred yards away, slightly to the right of the burning tank, I saw the turret of the Panther behind a hedge, his gun was pointing at me. I could just see the round hole of its muzzle. 'Traverse right,' my gunner saw it at the same time. They could not have seen more than my turret either.

It was a desperately exciting moment. The stalk was over, it was them or us. All I could say was, 'Fire'. The first shot went off, and at the same time I heard the roar of the A.P. as the Panther's shot whizzed past my head, while a sinister smoke ring appeared out of the black hole of its muzzle. My shot went low and kicked up a cloud of dust in the bank beyond. The next was also low, the third I saw hit fair and square on the front of the turret. But it appeared not to have the slightest effect, and was greeted by another 'whoozz' like the roar of an express train as it passes another. It could not have been far off its mark.

There seemed a long pause before the next shot and I looked down to see Guardsman Liddle having difficulty with a round. It had stuck on the way into the breach and he seemed to be taking an unearthly time to find the rammer. Both Guardsman Channon and I shouted at him to hurry up. I cursed the bloody little pop-gun for just bouncing off. Just then I heard an agonising yell from outside the tank and saw Bodsworth, the gunner of Two Charlie, standing covered in blood. He was in a terrible state. I could see he was horribly burnt and wounded. (I was in a dreadful dilemma, he desperately needed morphia, but the enemy was in our sights.) I knew I was too engaged to leave the tank. There was nothing I could do then except throw out the first-aid box and come to his aid later.

Meanwhile Channon had got off another three shots and the first had hit the Panther again. It did not fire now, and disappeared from view. Several days later when the area had been cleared of enemy, Bill found a Panther at the bottom of the hill below us. Two shots had hit it, one had hit the gun and had gone down into the driver's compartment and killed him. I don't make any real claim but it is possible that this was the one. I like to think so anyway, and no one else claimed it. If so, it was one of the few Panthers knocked out head-on in Normandy, certainly by a 75.

The next day's attack, Friday, 11 August 1944, I shall never forget. In the words of their CO, Colonel Joe Vandeleur, it was 'the most bloody of all those fought by the 3rd Battalion (Irish Guards).' That was certainly true for our own No. 2 Squadron. The two leading companies came under devastating fire and suffered seventy per cent casualties. The German guns and tanks on the far slope could not miss the Coldstream tanks and promptly destroyed them. In appearance it achieved nothing –except perhaps to keep the enemy off someone else –a crucial factor though in holding the SS Panzer Divisions to their ground.

Tuesday, 29 August. It was a great moment when we eventually crossed the Seine at Vernon, the beginning of the great advance to Holland. I had a feeling of pride and achievement as we rattled over that pontoon bridge into North Eastern France.

Thursday, 31 August. The day's objective was to cross the Somme south of Amiens, while the 11th were to take Amiens. I was lucky to be leading the Battalion and set a pretty good pace. In front the Grenadiers had practically no opposition until the Somme, except shooting up an occasional convoy. The Recce Welsh and 'Household Cavalry' were well out in front shooting up Germans struggling vainly to escape. What happened on the river was confusing but the Grenadiers and Irish had crossed with a little skirmishing and the Grenadiers lost two tanks. At first we raced up and down trying to find a bridge to take our weight and eventually crossed at the villages of Fouilloy and Corbie, and I was proud to be the first tank in the battalion to cross the Somme.

Sunday, 3 September, the Liberation of Brussels. When the leading troops arrived it was found that the Germans had left that afternoon, and the free Belges were in control, rounding up the remainder. The Germans had set fire to the Gestapo records at the Palais de Justice when they left and the glow lit up the sky. The Welsh Guards were first in. The Grenadiers were halted for a short time for permission to enter. A certain amount of light skirmishing took place and the Irish had a fight round the Palais de Justice, but there must have been many Germans still left hiding.

The lights went on in the city and all windows and doors were flung open. My tank halted, behind the one in front, in the centre of the town by the Bourse (their Stock Exchange), and immediately I was smothered with kisses, flowers and wine. We were dragged away from our tanks into houses, and given a royal feast. We drank glass after glass, and we had to be self-controlled not to be laid out.

For the next two days the spearhead of 21st Army Group, XXX Corps, halted in and around Brussels, Louvain and Antwerp. It needed a pause for supplies of petrol to catch up, to enable them to continue their advance towards Germany before the enemy had a chance to recover.

Having taken part in most of the great historic moments that had followed D-Day, Robert Boscawen was about to play his own part in what has perhaps become the most famous, and certainly most studied of them all Operation 'Market Garden.' The plan, very much devised by (now Field Marshal) Montgomery himself, the Commander in Chief of 21st Army Group, was simple enough. By dropping 3 airborne divisions behind enemy lines and capturing all the bridges from the Maas to the Rhine, the Allies would be able to sweep north and turn into the industrial heartland of Germany itself and bring the war to an early climax. The plan, although a bold one, could well have worked if the German resistance in the area consisted of the second-rate troops which intelligence reports had suggested. However, shortly before the operation got under way and unknown to the Allies, cadres of the 9th and 10th Panzer Divisions had moved into the area to refit.

The final target for Operation 'Market Garden' was the bridge over the River Rhine at Arnhem in Holland. The job of capturing the bridge and holding it until reinforcements arrived was given to the British 1st Airborne Division, commanded by Major General Roy Urquhart. The Division consisted of two parachute and one glider-borne infantry brigades, with a Polish parachute brigade to follow up. However, concealed in the woods to the north of Arnhem were the tanks of the 9th and 10th Panzer Divisions, and troops of II SS Panzer Corps.

With 1st Airborne established in Arnhem, the job of the Guards Armoured Division was to force their way through German territory to forge a supply route for reinforcements and equipment. Robert Boscawen accompanied the armoured column in its attempt to reach the troops in Arnhem –an attempt which of course 'famously' failed. In his diary, he describes the events that were taking place while the struggle at Arnhem itself intensified.

Orders for Operation 'Market Garden', the major ground and airborne advance into Holland, had been given to the battalion on

Saturday, 16 September. XXX Corps was to advance some sixty miles along a single axis linking up with the three major river crossings that formed the delta of the Rhine. The objective of the Guards Armoured Division was to establish itself around Nunspeet beside the Zuider Zee and so cut off from the land the remainder of the German Army in the west of Holland.

On Sunday, 17 September a moderately heavy barrage went down and then came the drone of aircraft, which lasted all afternoon. It was uncanny to think that during that short time a whole Army had been landed in Holland. At the same time the G.A.D., led by the Irish, advanced over the Escaut Canal to meet them. The airborne landings had taken place at Arnhem, Nijmegen and Grave, and up the centre line.

On the 20th, by a brilliant feat, the Grenadiers captured the Nijmegen bridge across the Rhine.

No. 2 Troop had been badly mauled on the previous Albert Canal line a few days before Market Garden, with Sergeant Brough killed. We were without tanks at the start, when on Sunday, 24th, the Germans cut the centre line and brewed up a hundred of our vehicles. In the morning the American (101 Airborne Division) put in an attack. The attack, however, failed and the road was still cut. They did not seem to know what was happening, but the enemy were reported to have a brigade across the road.

Meanwhile a few Sherman tanks of the Division's Forward Delivery Squadron had passed rapidly through us to put in a brave but disastrous attack with the Americans. The assorted enemy force from one of General Student's para divisions that had come across from the west was much stronger than expected and these tanks ran up immediately against some 88s.

In the evening the 7th Armoured Division put in an attack and by midday on the 26th the road was cleared and we moved on.

The news came in the evening of the 27th that Arnhem had been evacuated and of the 6,000 men landed only 1,200 had been brought back safe across the northern Rhine. It had been a very hard fight by the 1st Airborne Division against overwhelming odds, but they had held out for nearly nine days. They must have had a terrible time and it must go down as one of the hardest battles of the war. The bold plan had fallen at the last fence. Not in vain though, they had enabled 2nd Army to hold the Nijmegan bridge across the Waal or Lower

Rhine. (During the evening we listened to one of the most moving broadcasts I have ever heard by Stanley Maxted a Canadian War Correspondent who was among those few who came back over the Rhine. After nine days fighting with 1st Airborne in Arnhem his description of the withdrawal of these gallant men brought us near to tears. In single file, holding on to the man in front, boots wrapped in blankets, he told us they had walked silently through the enemy lines under steady machine-gun and artillery fire to the little assault boats which ferried them back across the swift current of the Rhine.)

So much has been written about Operation 'Market Garden' since, it is difficult to realize that at the time most of us had only the vaguest outline of the bigger picture. We certainly did not know that when 1st Airborne landed there were two Panzer divisions located in the woods north-east of Arnhem. These two, after the withdrawal of 1st Airborne, were able to turn full attention to eliminating XXX Corps' bridgehead over the River Waal, beyond Nijmegen. The battle was far from finished.

Monday, 2 October. At four o'clock we moved north through Nijmegen across the Waal and took over from the 2nd Irish, backing up (231st) Infantry Brigade of 50th Division who were holding the Nijmegen bridgehead on what we knew as the 'Island.'

The Germans had been counter-attacking heavily and the Micks had had a sticky time. (Freed from the threat to Arnhem the Germans were losing no time in seeking to lance this abscess over the Nijmegen bridge.)

Nijmegen is a nice clean-looking town and I should have liked to have spent a day there. However, we went straight through to the bridge. This was being shelled when I crossed. A truck was hit in front of my tank as I reached the entrance. The bridge, built in 1936, was vast and was remarkably little damaged. It was known as the 'Grenadier Bridge' after their brilliant exploit capturing it. When the four Gren tanks under Sergeant Robinson charged over in half evening light followed by Peter Carrington's tank, the Germans were hanging from the girders of the huge span firing down upon them. Demolition squads too were actually under the bridge with the charges but they were soon ousted by our Sappers.

On the other side of the bridge we stopped, filled up and cooked some supper. The battalion was to sit behind the Hampshires and Dorsets who were in 50th TT Division and were holding the line north of Bemmel: another name I shall never forget. Only a few miles of flat ground separated us here from the bridge at Arnhem, but it might have been a continent away.

We moved up with No. 2 Troop in the lead. The Squadron was put in the line with the 1st Hampshires in two orchards, two troops in each. We spent the night close together in the tanks with precious little sleep, each doing an hour's guard. All night we were shelled and mortared. At one moment a heavy concentration landed on top of us. The tank was hit once or twice, and I soon got a headache from the noise.

About five o'clock we stood-to and I walked up rather anxiously to the front of the orchard with the Tank Commanders to show them their positions. Then we moved the tanks up and sat there the whole day.

That night, about ten thirty, I was awakened by a terrific barrage. The Hun had started belting the orchard with everything he had. There were not only mortars and ordinary sized shells but heavy shells making a crater some five or six feet wide, 210mm, I should think. I saw the sparks of a mortar land about five feet from me. Just then a windy infantry sentry came running in shouting, 'There are enemy all round us'. I had everyone out in the tanks by now.

I moved cautiously up the orchard, my tank going in reverse I remember, turret traversed towards the enemy as I had not had time to turn round. There was a great deal of small arms firing going on and it was plain that the enemy had infiltrated into the orchard behind the barrage. We edged our way down towards the end and I expected to meet two or three Panthers. We were being fired at by Spandaus all round and the tracer came whistling past.

So we halted and let the orchard have everything we had. It was very reassuring to hear our own guns firing at last. We raked the orchard with Browning for nearly quarter of an hour, spraying in all directions, especially the flashes of the enemy m.g.s which appeared very close. Four or five Brownings lit up the orchard with their tracers, but we could see nothing clearly defined except the dark shadows of trees in the moonlight. It was only too apparent we were right amongst a heavy attack by German infantry. Our own had disappeared. The barrage had been too much for them. Apart from the high-speed crackle of the Spandaus I had been surprised to hear the slower beat of the Bren firing at us and so I was rather anxious about the two anti-tank guns that our own infantry had abandoned. The Boche could easily have turned them round on us. However, the Hun had had enough of our Browning and had withdrawn. I don't suppose he expected tanks. By the size of the barrage he probably had about a company attacking behind it, so our time hadn't been wasted. If they had cut the road behind us, it would have been a difficult situation to clear up next morning.

Wednesday, 4 October. At first light I went to find the infantry. They were in a barn; evidently they had had enough of the mortaring and pulled out. It was bad, but hard to blame them, for they had had an awful time, and few days rest since D-day.

Friday, 23 February 1945. We crossed the German frontier at Hassum and entered Goch, a badly battered small town. Desultory white flags were hanging out of a few of the windows. The Battalion harboured in a field around two battlestruck farms, a rather dismal place. The Canadian attack was going well and the 11th Armoured Division were attacking Udem and trying to go as far as the last Siegfried defences.

March 28. The news is terrific. I cannot believe it can last much longer. The whole front is crumbling and the armour is on the move. Orders came at three this afternoon 'Objective Hamburg via Bremen.' That which once seemed impossible has now arrived.

Friday, 30 March –Good Friday. We crossed the Rhine at Rees. A tremendous moment in one's life, as we moved slowly over the immensely long pontoon bridge the Sappers had built.

On Easter Day, Sunday, 1 April 1945, No 2 Squadron was put in the lead. Our objective was to seize the bridge across the Twente Canal between Hengelo and Enschede, two large Dutch towns on the German frontier. Both towns were reported to be strongly held. The Irish Guards Group would advance on the main road to Enschede to our right. Ian Jardine's troop was to lead, then mine, followed by Squadron H.Q.

At our 'O' Group, I could feel the excitement at this chance for the Squadron, and especially for Ian, to capture a bridge. Nothing would stop us. Sergeant Shipley, our troop sergeant now, pressed me for his tank to be allowed to lead the Troop for once instead of mine. Normally his, with the 17 pounder, would move last, but such was the morale and enthusiasm of the men to push on, I had to say yes. Sergeant Reading's tank was behind mine and Sergeant Bastone's with another 17 pounder in the rear. We started soon after seven and rushed along for about ten miles on minor roads in wooded country and through one or two straggling villages, so as to avoid the main opposition. The route twisted about and we made a number of sharp turns. At one point there was a long wood, set back a few hundred yards on the right of the road, from which it appeared we had come under slight enemy fire. My Troop was deployed to deal with this and I moved across a field so as to use my seventy-fives and Brownings on a few houses in the trees. We set them ablaze, and the 5th Battalion quickly moved up from behind to mop up and take a number of prisoners, while on we went. Ian dealt with similar opposition ahead when he entered a village, possibly Beckum, but he quickly brushed it aside with a few rounds of seventy-five H.E. into the suspect house that left it ablaze. A number of Germans appeared along the route showing no fight, while a few Dutch civilians waved and cheered. There were too the inevitable pathetic refugees, women and children, struggling along with bundles of belongings.

Unfortunately Sergeant Shipley missed a turning and fell behind us. He tried frantically to regain his place in the lead, and took a short cut across the corner of a field to our left. His driver failed to see the ditch half-way in time. I saw his tank bury its nose down in this and I knew we should not see him again that morning.

There were one or two armoured cars of the Household Cavalry close in front of us. We were in some confusion as to where the bridge was. Ian had tried without success to ask a civilian but the roads were most complicated with some detached houses and the map did not help, when we suddenly found the canal ahead. The road rose slightly and the canal appeared ahead of us at right angles with a high bank on the opposite side. There, too, was the bridge, half a mile or less to the left, and a road along the canal bank ran towards it. We had come upon the bridge from the wrong direction. A Dutchman ran out in front of my tank shouting at me the bridge was 'kaput' and some more I could not understand. It was too late to do anything but rush the bridge. We saw the bridge clearly, a steel bow span, about a quarter of a mile down with a crowd of Germans standing on it. We charged towards it. In front of me were Ian's three tanks and close behind me Sergeant Reading's and Sergeant Bastone's, then Jimmy and Dermot with the H.Q. tanks. We scattered the Germans with long bursts of M.G. fire from the Brownings on top of our tanks. I was aware of some trees on our left and a small black gasometer beside the bridge on the far bank, –I thought it might explode.

Ian rushed over the bridge with the armoured cars, his second tank close behind. I was just turning right onto the approach ramp to cross it when Sergeant Caulfield's tank in front of me stopped across the road. He was firing his 17-pounder to the left.

My driver halted and I found myself broadside on, looking down the barrels of four 88s beside the bridge, the place seething with Germans. The flak battery, each gun protected by earth mounds, lay just the other side of the road beyond the ramp up to the bridge.

A short fight followed. I hit one 88 with my seventy-five straight away, my Browning belt emptied so I let the rockets off. They flew towards the 88s. The bridge blew, I felt it go. Caulfield was the last across. I saw the 88 shots flying up at me, there was a whoof and the turret was engulfed from below in a whirlwind of flame.

I eventually broke free from the flames and threw myself into the ditch. It was dry, but something said to me, 'You're all right, get up and go on.' Guardsman Bland and I stumbled back for some two hundred yards to safety. The rest were trapped or shot down before reaching it. Another crew was running back near me and someone beat out the flames.

Like the fighter pilot Richard Hillary in his description of being shot down into the North Sea during the Battle of Britain, suffering shock and severe burning, in his book *The Last Enemy*, I remained conscious through it all, and like him unable to see. The quiet and efficiency of all, from our own kind M.O. in the front line, and along the distant chain, on top of a scout car at first, then through the Dressing Stations, and back at last to Base Hospital, then to England by Dakota aircraft. One of the senior nursing sisters of 21st Army Group Base Hospital in Brussels met me recently and told me she recalled they were somewhat worried about my condition. She singled me out at the fifty-year commemorations of the Normandy landings especially to tell me. However, they also told me at the time that my eyesight was going to be alright.

I was flown to Swindon Transit Hospital where my parents and brother first came to visit me briefly. Then taken by hospital train to Derby Hospital, an extremely uncomfortable journey I recall. Finally after a week or so there –President Roosevelt had just died but the war still went on –an ambulance took me south again by road, to the Canadian wing of the famous East Grinstead Victoria Hospital. There the legendary care and skills of one Archie McIndoe and the matron sister, Cherry Hall, with their wonderful team of dedicated girls and male doctors and nurses were quick to take me in hand. By then they had become immensely practised at restoring the remarkable pilots of the 'Few' and their successors, to a renewed existence – for some they even made the morale-boosting promise 'We'll get you back flying' –and did. So for myself, coming right at the end of nearly six years aerial combat in Europe, and an Army officer at that, I was just 'all in the day's work'. This hospital had been among the first to be allocated with the great new drug penicillin. It seemed as though the endless penicillin and saline baths kept me going.

Within a few days Hitler was dead, and for days afterwards all the patients in our ward, who could either walk or scramble about, pulled around trolley-loads of drinks, to be stocked up for the great day soon to arrive. Those who had done so much to achieve it were not going to be deprived of their share of savouring the victorious end.

For me it became a seemingly endless haul to be able to see anything again, and then to scramble around. But it came. We had to be slowly pieced together, shielded from unwanted infections, which for a time I fell foul of, and with operation after operation by teams of men and women, and volunteers who above all understood morale. Then short periods at home, and back again for more. We were indeed fortunate to be in such skilled hands, even if we didn't feel so at the time.

At the outset my mother visited me from London, standing her bicycle in the Guard's van of the Victoria train, almost every evening, when she was not having to travel abroad, despite her holding a senior post in the headquarters of the Red Cross at the time. She kept me aware of the world outside, and an occassional visit from a brother officer on leave were all a wonderful boost. It was of course immensely boring and depressing but it is not my intention to dwell on the mental torments that are bound to accompany every experience such as this. The kindest of volunteers who came and read books and articles to me I was deeply indebted to. A general election came and went, and many years later it gave me much cause for amusement to pull the leg of a fellow member of the House of Commons, Dr Evelyn King, whose election address was read out to me in Hospital and instantly caused me to say, 'Not him at any price.' His then constituency was not far from mine in the 1970s. In retrospect it is wonderful to recall that the then Queen, later the greatly loved Queen Mother, came to speak to me in the ward of East Grinstead and asked what I wanted to do when I could escape from their clutches.

It was more than a year before I could begin to struggle into normal life. The Army very fairly kept me on their payroll as long as one needed hospital treatment, but afterwards they were unable to use someone with such a low category. This country should be proud of the Private and Emergency hospital system that existed in wartime to mend the severely wounded, both military and no doubt civilian casualties too, long before a National Health Service had been brought into being.

At the end of the summer of 1946 I asked my mother to see if I could join one of the many Civilian Relief Teams that the joint war organizations of the Red Cross and St John had built up before the war ended to enter the occupied territories of Europe and beyond, which she was administering from London. She was delighted to arrange it and in September I set off to join this relief team in Hamburg in the British zone whose priority was to aid the tens of thousands of refugees, then called Displaced Persons, from all over Europe and Russia, who had ended up in Western Germany –mostly slave workers from the German war factories or inmates from the dreaded concentration camps. Hamburg itself had suffered probably amongst the worst devastation of any city in the world –Europe or the Far East –the terrible 'fire storm' created by the RAF in July 1943, several nights of massive incendiary bombing, starting a typhoon of wind, heat, and flame that has seldom been commented on or discussed since in Britain. Three-quarters of the city was destroyed and the casualties were in tens and tens of thousands. By 1946 there was a population living largely underground in miles and miles of rubble. There was no United Nations Relief then, that was for the future, and the other Allies were deeply involved in relief in their own zones. So there was an enormous amount for the British teams to do. It was also one of the coldest and longest winters of the century, and there were terrible shortages of food, both at home and abroad. The British Army, still very large indeed, gave up a days' rations a week for the German children in Hamburg which the relief teams had to handle.

The Displaced Persons had the priority. They had been largely moved into the massive 'Hitler' barracks outside the city for shelter and warmth, but they required frequent visits and medical supplies. There was little time to think about my own physical shortcomings. However, there was one notable event for me which provides a poignant and fitting moment to bring this tale of bitter destruction and tragedy to an end. Almost eighteen months to the day after I left them so abruptly, I was able to visit the Battalion I had served with for nearly three years of war. A visit to a large camp of Polish displaced persons near Lübeck brought it about. Not far beyond was Travemunde on the Baltic, where the 1st Coldstreams, now reverted to their true role of an infantry battalion, having said farewell to their armour, were guarding the frontier with the Russian zone opposite them. Although the personnel were enormously changed it was a great homecoming for me and I shall never forget the way I was received.

Part Seven

PLANNING AND INTELLIGENCE

As well as the soldiers who fought in the battles of the Second World War, or helped to provide the Army with the many services it required, there were also those who assisted in the planning of historic events, or helped by gaining or processing the information necessary to plan and carry out military operations. Earlier we have studied a number of individuals who were involved with planning or intelligence at different levels. However, in this section we look at the careers of former politicians whose primary funtions were in these areas.

JAMES ALLASON

James Allason was Conservative MP for Hemel Hempstead from 1959–1974 and was PPS to the Secretary of State for War from 1960–1964. He was a regular soldier, commissioned into the Royal Artillery in 1932, but transferred to the 3rd Dragoon Guards in 1937, and went on to reach the rank of lieutenant colonel. During the war he gained a lot of valuable experience while working in planning.

The outbreak of war found me as a subaltern in an armoured regiment in India. We trained for desert warfare and expected to be sent to Egypt, but the call never came, which was somewhat frustrating for professional soldiers.

After Pearl Harbor Americans flooded into India. One said to me 'You Brits here don't know there's a war on'. I replied, 'Have you had a German bomb blow a wall onto you?' He said, 'I'm sorry. I didn't know you'd been in the Blitz', so I did not explain that this had occurred in 1917.

In 1943 I went to the Staff College at Quetta, and was then posted to the Indian Joint Planning Staff in Delhi. One day a squat figure dressed as a lieutenant colonel in the Warwickshire Regiment came in and asked to see the plans for Burma. He had a yellow face, thin moustache and crew cut hair. So I played for time and found he knew no one in his regiment. Then my boss came in and immediately showed the plans. When the visitor left, I said that he was probably a Japanese spy, so we had the gates closed until we found that he was Enoch Powell, recovering from jaundice, our new Intelligence Liaison Officer on his meteoric rise from private to brigadier.

Another visitor was Major General Wingate, with his hair down to his collar and a mad look in his eye. Soon after he had to go to hospital, where Lord Louis Mountbatten visited him and enquired if he had everything he wanted. 'I want an Air Force,' was the snarled reply.

In January 1944 I arranged to accompany the Army Group Commander, General Sir George Giffard, on his tour of Fourteenth Army, to be followed by attachment to Fourteenth Army Headquarters. We flew to Ledo, in north-east Assam, to see off Brigadier Bernard Fergusson who was leading his Chindit Brigade on foot into Burma. Then we flew to the Arakan. We spent the first day there visiting 5th Indian Division facing the Japanese on the coast, then we crossed the steep Mayu range of hills by the only road, to reach 7th Indian Division in the valley beyond.

We stayed the night at the headquarters of Major General Frank Messervy, an old polo friend. He told how in the Western Desert when he was commanding 7th Armoured Division at the Battle of Alam Halfa his headquarters had been overrun by Rommel's tanks. He pretended to be a private soldier, explaining his DSO ribbon: 'Yes I was an officer once, but drink was my downfall.' So he was not closely guarded and escaped.

During the night there was gunfire to the rear; the Japanese had come right round behind us. I was told to take my General away fast. We were only delayed when dive-bombed by Zeros at the foot of the pass. I saw Giffard off by plane and spent the night at Corps headquarters. This time there was gunfire to the front of us, when the Japanese tried to cut the only road between us and 5 Div, but they were driven off by Corps troops. But 7 Div had been completely surrounded and the headquarters overrun, but this time Messervy had escaped uncaptured. The Battle of the Box had begun.

The only regiment of tanks was with 7 Div so the only tanks left were twelve reserve Grants with their crews. I knew Grants well, so suggested forming them into a squadron. I was given a company of Gharwalis for close protection and took my command to the top of the pass where we came under intermittent Japanese attack, but had a grandstand view of air supplies dropping on 7 Div.

After a few days a mortar bomb wounded me in the arm, cutting the artery. The main dressing station had been overrun by the Japanese, who murdered everyone, staff and patients alike. However, there was still a Field Surgical Unit in a tent nearby, and they sewed

232

up the artery, saving my arm. A frightened wounded Japanese prisoner followed me onto the operating table, who seemed to have a
guilty conscience. But he was of course treated with the utmost care.
I spent the next two months in hospital being patched up.

While I was in hospital Brigadier Mike Calvert's Chindit Brigade
flew into Burma in Dakotas and gliders. Lieutenant Colonel Peter
Fleming, our deception expert, took a lift in a glider, but it became
uncontrollable over the Chin Hills and had to be cast off, landing
some ten miles behind the Japanese lines. As an experienced explorer,
Fleming led them out successfully and wrote an amusing account of
it. Mountbatten remarked that he was glad to see his staff joining in,
until someone pointed out the awkward consequences if someone
with knowledge of future operations fell into Japanese hands, so the
practice was forbidden.

When I was released from hospital, I reported at Fourteenth Army
Headquarters. Wingate had been killed in an air crash a fortnight
before and the Chindits had then been ordered to move north to assist
the Chinese-American force moving south from Ledo. But they did
not seem to be complying, so I was sent to investigate. I knew that
Wingate had a private plan that he should capture some small town
and then proclaim that it was second only to Mandalay in importance. The Japanese would then lose face if they did not recapture it
and the British would lose face if they did, so would have to supply a
fresh division as garrison. Sure enough, I found Chindit Headquarters
still committed to this plan, so I suggested I see Bernard Fergusson to
discuss it. I flew in that afternoon. The brigade had been nearly three
months behind enemy lines and they were very tired, but Fergusson
was ready, as a last effort to capture Indaw, after which he would be
relieved. I told him that the last operational division had already been
committed, so if he captured Indaw he would have to hold it himself,
which we agreed was impracticable. I flew back that night and
persuaded Chindit Headquarters, so Fergusson's Brigade was flown
out and Calvert's Brigade moved north.

Mission accomplished, I returned to Fourteenth Army
Headquarters to be greeted with long faces. I had disobeyed an order
that I was unaware of. I was told to pack my bags and go. One night
after dining fifty miles behind Japanese lines, I was dining at the 500
Club in Calcutta.

I returned to South East Asia Command Headquarters, which had moved to Kandy. It was now integrated, so I had an American opposite number, a charming Rhodes Scholar, Lieutenant Colonel Dean Rusk, later Secretary of State to Kennedy. We worked hard on post-monsoon plans for Burma. Once I got so tired that I asked for weekend leave. Instead I was sent to attend conferences in Delhi and Calcutta, so got my rest reading Jane Austen on the long flights.

We started to look at the invasion of Malaya, and found we would need a refuelling airstrip to allow fighters to fly from Rangoon. I found an island called Phuket which turned out to be suitable, so I named it 'Operation Roger'. I understand that it is now pronounced differently.

In December 1944, after seven years overseas, I returned to England and called on my Whitehall opposite number to compare notes. He was just about to leave for the Yalta Conference, but his aircraft crashed into the Mediterranean and they needed another experienced planner in a hurry, so I was back in a job. Churchill used to bombard the Chiefs of Staff with queries and suggestions. They would pass these to the Directors of Plans, who would pass them, if appropriate, to my team. We met in the underground Cabinet War Rooms, but my office was in the War Office with the designation MO5. When a note landed on my desk starting 'Pray let me know . . .' and initialled WSC, I knew we had an urgent job.

The general election was looming and I wanted to stand, but I felt that the job I was doing was so important that I could not be spared. My naval opposite number, Commander Alan Noble, did not feel the same way when offered the Chelsea seat.

Our last job was to despatch an Airfield Construction Group to the Pacific to build airfields for Bomber Command so that they could share in the bombing of Japan, a project dear to Churchill. In the event they were diverted to Hong Kong, where they were no doubt useful.

On 15 August I went to my Army Director of Plans and said, 'Here is the completed plan for the formation of a Commonwealth Corps in Canada to train for the invasion of Japan in the spring of 1947. What shall I do with it?' He replied, 'You know exactly what to do with it'.

But the fighting did not end. It was British policy, but not American, that our allies should return to their Eastern possessions. Mountbatten had moved to Singapore, but his reports on Java were evasive, so eventually I was sent out with the priority 'Personal

Representative of the CIGS' to see what was going on. I arrived in Java in December 1945 to find that the British were being used to prevent the Dutch forces from trying to reoccupy their country. The Indonesians were in full revolt, so the Japanese Army had been rearmed and were fighting them to protect the British. An average of three Dutch women a night were being abducted and the Dutch forces were very restive.

On my way to the airfield my jeep driver was wounded by an Indonesian sniper, so I arrived in Singapore covered in blood. Mountbatten asked me to a cosy dinner and asked to see my report. He said, 'My dear boy, you have completely misunderstood the position but I will do you the honour of writing it for you.' I was so angry that I tore up his report on the way back to Raffles Hotel; I wish I had kept it. My report went to the Cabinet and all restrictions on the Dutch Forces were lifted, but by then it was too late.

Enoch Powell went to the Conservative Research Department. I said to a member there 'You should watch Enoch, one day he will be Prime Minister'. He replied, 'No, to become Prime Minister you must be popular with your colleagues'.

As for me, I later did another spell of two years in Cold War planning, then was sent to the Joint Services Staff College to learn about inter-Service planning.

OSCAR MURTON

Oscar Murton, who was Conservative MP for Poole between 1964–1979 and who was later elevated to the peerage as Lord Murton of Lindisfarne, also had a very different kind of war. Although commissioned as an infantry officer, he spent very little time carrying out regimental duties. Even before the outbreak of war his future as a senior staff officer was already under consideration.

While at school he was an under officer in the OTC, which was affiliated to the Leicestershire Regiment. He was commissioned into his county regiment, the Northumberland Fusiliers, as a territorial officer in June 1934. At that time he was working in London, so in order to continue his 'drills' he was attached to the 22nd Battalion the London Regiment (The Queens) based in Bermondsey. His company paraded at Hays Wharf, and was comprised mainly of London dockers. On drill nights the battalion paraded in civilian clothes, and all officers were required to wear bowler hats.

On returning to the north-east he rejoined the 4th Battalion of his regiment. Although employed as a very junior member of his family firm, he didn't have a great deal of responsibility: he therefore much preferred soldiering. In consequence, while still only a second lieutenant, he studied for the regular Army promotion examinations for the rank of captain. One thing led to another and in due time (still as a lieutenant) he became Staff Captain of 149 Infantry Brigade (TA).

In 1938, with the threat of hostilities and the consequent doubling of the Territorial Army, it was decided to train a number of nominated TA officers in staff duties, and the survivors of the course were summoned to the Army Staff College for a final 'polishing' in the summer of 1939. To his gratification he was offered an immediate appointment as a Brigade Major. Bearing in mind that he had only been promoted to captain three months before, it came as some surprise. However, after some hesitation he turned the offer down, as he was tied into his family business and had been recently married. Also, he could not be absolutely certain that war would come. Of course it did, and he was subsequently embodied with the battalion as a company commander in what had become a motor reconnaissance battalion. He didn't remain with the unit for long, as the commanding officer told him that he would soon be given a staff job and, rather than having to disrupt his team, he thought it best to post the young Murton with a draft to a motor training battalion forming in Tidworth under the aegis of the Rifle Brigade. There he was given a company comprising Northumberland Fusiliers, the Loyal North Lancashires, and the Tower Hamlets Rifles, as he now explains:

It was a strange mix of regimental cultures: Northumbrians and Lancastrians 'heavy' infantry with a coal-mining background, and 'Light' infantry mostly Cockneys from the East End. The general complaint of the Northerners was that the Cockneys were too 'smart' for them.

My regimental duty did not last long. By the beginning of December I had been posted to a general staff appointment at Headquarters Southern Command at Salisbury as a GSO3 (Captain) dealing with staff duties and training: the allocation of the equipment and training requirements of the formations of the Field Army located in the Command area of Southern and South-West England. At this stage I did perhaps regret my failure to take up that offer of a higher rank made a bare four months previously, but there was now no time for regrets.

Headquarters Southern Command expanded rapidly with its increased importance after Dunkirk and had moved out of Salisbury to Wilton House and its immediate neighbourhood. It had become a command of major operational importance.

After some months I was promoted GSO2 (Major) Staff Duties, with the duty of co-ordinating all requirements and the allocation of equipment to all formations in the Command, for the defence against possible invasion. I also became responsible for general staff policy, war establishments and war organization generally within the command.

I had now spent the best part of three years in Southern Command

Headquarters and I was fully expecting a change, either to another staff job and probably in a field formation, or to regimental duty.

In the summer of 1942 the posting arrived. I was to move some ten miles to Headquarters Salisbury Plain District! I was now a lieutenant colonel GSO1 and Chief of Staff to a major general. I had just turned 28 years of age, so it was quite a challenge. I became responsible for operations, intelligence, Staff Duties and training of all static units in the county of Wiltshire, e.g. the School of Artillery etc. and large contingents of the Home Guard. Two other tasks: co-operation and assistance to UK and US field formations located and training in the District; and also to participate in major exercises taking place throughout Southern Command both as an originator and as a senior umpire. This was for me very much a 'hands on' experience which I greatly enjoyed,

Early in 1944 my situation changed again. I was posted to the War Office in the department of the Director of Staff Duties as the GSO1 of SD1, one of the four branches. SD1 dealt with a formidable array of tasks and responsibilities, from formulation of the Army's General Staff Policy, to the war, and post-war organization of the Army, taking in on the way liaison with the two other Service Ministries and the Civil Departments of State. For good measure, this also involved the detailed organization of all troops in the UK Base both British and Allied: the latter more especially Polish.

It also became my task to organize the annual conference held at the Staff College, Camberley, chaired by the Chief of the Imperial General Staff and attended by all senior commanders from all theatres of operations, some thirty in all. I was responsible personally for the production of the minutes and their ultimate publication as a limited and numbered document. I dealt with two such conferences in my time in SD1.

Each morning, while at the War Office, the Director of Staff Duties (SDS) held a meeting of his brigadiers and lieutenant colonels, commonly referred to as 'Prayers'.

On one occasion he handed down the table to me a paper, saying, 'This is for you'. It was a minute from No 10 to the CIGS. Paraphrased it read:– 'For action this day. Pray inform me on not more than one sheet of paper, of the present organization, strength, military preparedness and possible future roles for the Polish Armed Forces at present in the United Kingdom. WSC.'

There were certain difficulties apparent to me. Not only was the subject complex and to some extent diffuse but I also knew that the CIGS required all papers and minutes to be provided in large type to ease the strain on his eyesight. My sheet of paper was shrinking fast and so was the time available to provide a coherent answer.

By lunchtime (but no lunch) I had marshalled the facts and produced a draft. Laid before my General, the comment made was, 'You will never get all that on one page. Condense it.'

By 3.00 pm I was back. 'That's better, but what about –?'

Off again and back once more. 'Right. Now take it along to the DCIGS.' Having changed the whole thing round for the second time it came as a great relief when DCIGS said, 'Fine. Have it typed and back to me, but hurry, you are up against the deadline'. Finally, into CIGS for signature.

Who dare say that we minions did not earn our staff pay?

My sister-in-law had become engaged to a Belgian in 1939, but plans for her marriage had been deferred because of the outbreak of war. However, in view of the fact that there had been no enemy movement for seven months against France and Belgium and Holland, she decided, much against my family's wishes, to proceed with the plans and travel to Brussels. Her wedding took place, but almost immediately afterwards the German invasion began. She found herself parted from her husband who had been called up for service and she herself became an evacuee entrained out of Belgium and ending up near Lourdes in the Hautes Pyrenees.

For two years her family heard nothing of her until a message came from a Belgian girl who had escaped to the United States saying merely that my sister-in-law was alive and well.

In early September 1944, a few days after the reoccupation of Brussels, I was ordered to fly out to Main Headquarters 21 Army Group to attend a conference in connection with the future employment of certain elements of the Polish Army. Main Headquarters had moved up to the outskirts of Brussels.

When I emerged from the meeting I found an officer of my own regiment waiting for me. He had identified the red puggaree band which the Northumberland Fusiliers (quite without authority) painted on their steel helmets and which I had left in a corridor, and he was curious as to the owner.

In the course of conversation I asked him what were my chances, in the limited time available to me, of attempting to trace my sister-in-law and her husband, should they be in Brussels. His reply was astonishing. He had not only met them, but had spent the previous evening with them. If I wished, he would take me to their apartment when my work ended that day. The city curfew applied only to the civilian population so there would be no problem. Nor was there any. After four years and four months of enforced silence it was a great reunion and I made my first acquaintance of two small nieces.

I had become deeply involved towards the end of the war in the preliminary planning of the shape and form of the post-war Army. I much enjoyed my work to the extent that voluntarily I deferred my release from service for a further year.

I was twice recalled for refresher courses subsequent to my release in connection with a future mobilization appointment. But that is another story.

AIREY NEAVE

Army intelligence officer Airey Neave had graduated in jurisprudence before going to France in 1940 as a lieutenant in the Royal Artillery, where he was taken prisoner at Calais. After escaping from a PoW camp in Poland, he was taken to the maximum security prison at Colditz Castle, from where he escaped and successfully returned to England. Using the intelligence he had gained through his experiences, he helped to establish an underground movement which trained aircrew in methods of escape and evasion in occupied territory, and, as an agent for MI9, helped to organize the rescue of some 4,000 servicemen from the continent.

In August 1940, after his capture at Calais, Airey Neave was taken to a PoW camp above the town of Spangenberg near Kassel in Germany, which was known as Oflag IXA/H. From here, in February 1941, he was moved to the vast encampment of Stalag XXa, near the town of Thorn in Poland, on the banks of the Vistula. At Thorn hundreds of British officers were kept in an old Polish fort surrounded by a moat, where they lived in damp, cold, vault-like rooms. NCOs and other ranks were imprisoned in another complex a short distance away. The Germans formed their prisoners into working parties, which were employed in the construction of roads and aerodromes, in the area around the camp.

It wasn't long before Airey Neave began to plan his first escape. In the main prison complex there was a hut where a captured British dentist worked. Officers from the fort who needed dental treatment were marched to the dentist every Thursday. No doubt due to a bad diet and his general weakness of health, Neave suffered from severely inflamed gums and so visited the dentist each week.

On the day of his escape, 16 April 1941, along with fellow prisoner Flying Officer Norman Forbes, he was marched under escort from the fort, as usual, to the main camp to keep his weekly appointment. The two men escaped through the toilets and made their way to the warrant officers' hut, where, with prior communication, bunks had been prepared for them. Their plan was to hide in the hut until the Germans, having supposed they had escaped into the surrounding pine forest, had eased off their search parties, at which time they would make their real bid for freedom.

The next morning, however, the whole camp was called on parade: perhaps the Germans suspected that they were still there. As the prison guards searched all the huts, Forbes and Neave lay under their bunks, tight against the wall and, even though the Germans searched nearby, they remained undiscovered.

Three days later, on 19 April, they joined a working party of a hundred and fifty men who were marched beyond the pine forest to a large farm, where they were split into smaller groups for different tasks. At midday the ration lorry drew up, in which two men from the camp had been concealed. Unobserved by the Germans, the two men got out of the lorry and mingled in to the crowd. Forbes and Neave hid in the roof of a barn while these two men took their places for the head count when it was time for the working party to return to the camp. Once the working party had gone, they changed from their British uniforms into workmen's clothes, complete with Polish ski-caps that had been made from Army blankets. Thus attired, they disappeared in to the Polish countryside.

After four days of evading detection, they were questioned by German guards near the frontier, who were suspicious of the fact that they didn't have any papers. They eventually admitted to being escaped British PoWs, but the Nazi official who questioned them preferred to believe that they were Polish spies and they were taken to Gestapo headquarters at the town of Plock, where they were inter-rogated and kept in the town prison. Their interrogation lasted for two days, during which time a notice was displayed on Neave's cell door which read 'Airey Neave, Spy'. They felt certain they would be shot at any moment, when suddenly they were taken back to the camp at Thorn and reinstated as PoWs.

Back at Thorn, a grim night lay before them. They were marched at gunpoint, with their hands above their heads, into the chill blackness of the moat, where they were made to sit in two semi-circular chambers in the outer wall, used as a store for rotting swedes and timber, and where the stench was almost unbearable. Eventually, half crazy from cold and hunger, the iron doors were opened and they were taken to a room in a kind of keep at the head of the drawbridge, where they slept quietly, physically and emotionally exhausted.

A few days later Airey Neave was woken by a guard in the middle of the night and, along with Forbes and a few other British prisoners prone to escaping, was taken off to the maximum security prison at Colditz Castle, from where it was believed that escape was impossible. The castle was used by the Germans to house Allied officers who had been particularly troublesome. Neave arrived at Colditz in May 1941.

All the prisoners at the camp, whatever their nationality, had one thing in common: they were determined escapers. It wasn't long, therefore, before Airey Neave became involved in tunnelling and helping with other escape attempts. Soon he was ready to make his own escape by simply walking out of the main gate dressed in a German uniform, which he made himself out of a Polish uniform bartered for chocolate. The insignia and finishing touches had been made by a skillful Polish tailor. The end result left a lot to be desired, but, after months of watching the movements of the guards, by August 1941 he was determined to go.

He went on parade in the courtyard at 9 pm as usual, with all the other prisoners. His makeshift German uniform was covered by a British Army overcoat. After the parade was dismissed, all the prisoners began to return to their quarters and the guards fell in to be marched away. He removed the overcoat, which was taken off him by another prisoner, put his German cap on his head, stuck out his chest and began to walk towards the gates.

At the gate in perfect German he informed the guard that he had a message for the Kommandant from Hauptmann Priem. The guard let him pass, but he hadn't gone far before the inadequacies of his uniform aroused suspicion and he was recaptured.

As he stood there at gunpoint, some thirty or so German officers and guards surrounded him and amused themselves with threats of shooting him for wearing a German uniform. However, once the Kommandant, Oberst Prawitz, arrived on the scene the threats died away and he was taken off to the solitary confinement cells, where he remained in utter darkness. He was later made to stand for many hours while the Germans joked about his comical uniform. A photographer was even summoned from the town to take pictures of the sorry spectacle, before he was eventually returned to the British quarters.

As autumn gave way to winter the prisoners broke the monotony by rehearsing for a variety show in the camp theatre. They also took advantage of the situation by preparing an escape route, which began beneath the stage. As the weeks passed, Airey Neave worked on a new and more authentic German uniform. This time he would take on the identity of an infantry officer named Schwartz.

On 5 January 1942, along with Toni Luteyn, a Dutch prisoner, Neave made his next escape. After 9 pm parade they made their way to the theatre, felt their way beneath the stage and carefully prised up the loose floorboards. This led to a hole in the ceiling of the passage below. They climbed through the hole and down a rope. The passage led to the door of the gate-bridge, through which was a narrow corridor that led them to the guard-house. Both dressed as German officers, they slipped outside into the snow and walked down to a path which led away from the castle, saluted several times by the guards. Once outside they headed east for the town of Leipzig.

Having got away from Colditz they ditched their German uniforms and took on the identities of Dutch electrical workers. They had false papers which permitted them to change their place of occupation from Leipzig to the town of Ulm in South-Western Germany. From Ulm they intended to make for the Swiss border. The ingenious Dutch officers at Colditz had acquired by bribery a timetable of the trains from Leisnig to Leipzig. They therefore knew that the first workman's train was due to arrive at 5 am, and by the time they had reached the station they had only half an hour to wait.

Just before 5 the station doors opened and the crowd of workers who had assembled outside surged forward to the ticket office. They followed in their wake and Luteyn, who spoke the best German of the two, stopped and bought two workmen's tickets to Leipzig. Shortly the train arrived and they climbed aboard with the others.

At 6 am the train drew in to the great station at Leipzig, from where they would need to catch another train to Ulm. However, the train for Ulm did not leave until 10.30 in the evening, so they had to pass the day in Leipzig. During these long hours Airey Neave almost gave the game away when in the waiting room he took a bar of Red

Cross chocolate out of his pocket and began to eat it. The workers around them stared and talked in threatening whispers. Chocolate had been unknown to the workers for many months. Even German officers of high rank had eaten little for some time. British PoWs, on the other hand, thanks to the Red Cross, were well supplied. To sit there eating this forbidden delicacy in the waiting-room of a great station not only made them an object of envy but of deep suspicion. They rose awkwardly and walked out of the waiting room into the town.

They returned to the station later that evening and Luteyn bought their tickets to Ulm, where they arrived at 9 am on the second day of their escape, having shared a compartment on the train with a burly man in an SS uniform, who occasionally chatted to them about Holland.

At Ulm they needed to catch another train to the town of Singen on the Swiss frontier. Luteyn made his way to the ticket office and calmly asked for two tickets. The girl in the office asked to see their papers. She then fetched the railway police who wanted to know why they wished to travel to the frontier zone. Luteyn explained that, although they were due to begin work in Ulm, they wanted to have a short vacation first. The railway police didn't suspect them of being escaped PoWs, but insisted that they should first report to the local State Labour Office, having only just arrived in the town. While the police escort waited for them at the front door of the Labour Office, they absconded through another door. However, they couldn't go back to the train station, so instead they bought a local map in the back streets of Ulm and headed across country to the town of Laupheim, from where they caught a train to Stockach, a village as near to the Swiss frontier as they dared to go.

In the early hours of 9 January they eventually walked through Singen in the blackout and headed south through a wood, marching on a compass bearing to the frontier. It was a fine, cold night and the moon was dull. They slowly advanced until they could see a gap in the trees and the lights of cars passing along a road. Not far to the east was what appeared to be a frontier post.

For an hour they crouched in a ditch beside the road and watched as a sentry paced up and down some forty yards away from them. On the other side of the road was a smooth plain of snow surrounded by distant trees. This was 'No Man's Land'; beyond it lay freedom. At half past four in the morning the sentry turned away and they agreed it was time to go. They crawled out of the ditch, across the road, and into the field. After what seemed an eternity they rose to their feet and ran forward into Switzerland. They first came to the village of Ramsen, where they handed themselves in to Swiss frontier guards.

Although they had made it safely to Switzerland, before they could return to Britain they would have to cross German-held territory again in order to reach Spain.

At the town of Schaffhausen Airey Neave bought a picture post-card, which he later famously sent to Oberst Prawitz, the Kommandant of Colditz, in which he wrote: 'I hope that you will not get sent to the Russian Front on my account.'

The two men were eventually taken to the town of Berne, where they were delivered to their respective Legations. Here, Airey Neave was met by Colonel Cartwright, the Military Attaché, who had been the hero of many First World War escapes himself.

In April 1942 Neave received an urgent summons to Geneva, where, along with Captain Hugh Woollatt MC of the Lancashire Fusiliers, it was arranged for them to escape over the Swiss frontier into France. Their subsequent journey took them to Marseilles and Toulouse, before crossing into Spain and making their way to Gibraltar, from where they took a troopship for their journey home.

Airey Neave landed on the quay at Gourock at noon on 13 May 1942. From Glasgow he caught the night train to London, which drew into Euston the following morning.

In June 1942 he began work with Colonel Jimmy Langley and for the next two years tried, despite tremendous obstacles, to help the men and women of the French Resistance in particular to establish escape routes by which Allied airmen shot down over the continent could return to England. In July 1944 he was back on French soil himself, his task to organize the rescue of servicemen who were hidden in the forests of central France and Belgium, which often involved going deep behind enemy lines. He was also involved with 'Operation Pegasus' in October and November 1944, when soldiers of the British First Airborne Division, who had survived Arnhem, we brought back across the Rhine.

At the end of August 1945 he was appointed to the British War Crimes Executive, an organization set up to collect evidence against the principal Nazi war criminals. In October, by now a lieutenant colonel, he became an official of the Nuremberg Tribunal, acting as a liaison officer between the Tribunal and the defendants. On the afternoon of 18 October 1945 he went with Mr Harold Willey, the General Secretary of the Tribunal, to serve copies of the indictments on many of the leading war criminals: these included Hermann Goering; Rudolf Hess; Colonel-General Jodl, Chief of Staff of the High Command of the German Armed Forces; and Grand-Admiral Doenitz, the Commander in Chief of Hitler's Fleet and the man Hitler had appointed as his successor. He visited these and others in their cells, advising them about their rights under the Charter of the Tribunal.

By the end of the war Airey Neave had been awarded the Military Cross; Distinguished Service Order; Croix de Guerre and the US Bronze Star. He entered Parliament in 1951 as the Conservative MP for Abingdon, but his career was cut tragically short on 30 March 1979 while he was serving as Shadow Northern Ireland Secretary. He was killed by a terrorist bomb as his car drove across the ramp to the House of Commons underground car park.

ESMOND WRIGHT

Professor Esmond Wright, who was the Conservative MP for the Pollok Division of Glasgow from 1967–1970, served in the Intelligence Corps and then the newly formed Bureau of Current Affairs, mainly in North Africa and the Middle East, arriving shortly before the Battle of Alamein. However, in common with many other contributors, his story is rather unusual, and its beginning already hints at the greater achievements that would grace his later life. It begins on the other side of the Atlantic, where on one occasion he was to be singled out by President Roosevelt.

I heard of the outbreak of war in September 1939 when I was awakened from my sleep in a cornfield west of Saskatoon in Canada. I, and my two colleagues who like me were graduate students in American Universities, had just visited an Indian reservation and had seen one of the most beautiful sights in the world, Lake Louise, near Banff, in the Canadian Rockies. On hearing of the outbreak of war, we made speed south and returned to the US at Opheim, Montana.

I was fortunate to win a Commonwealth Fund Fellowship to study in the US in 1938. The United States –and not least the Old South – was, and remains, at once a vast intellectual stimulus and a second home. Part of its appeal is the fact of space and size and the sense of man versus the continent, the land of the Big Sky and the Big Dream; there is nothing in those 3,000 miles from Manhattan to the Golden Gate but what white men have put there, built and preserved, within the last 350 years, much of it, in fact, within the last three generations. Part of its appeal lies in the sense of freedom, of free men and women and the free movement of goods and ideas in a vast and abun-

248

dant society. Part of its appeal lies in the mixture of the sophisticated and the pioneering, of idealism and open-mindedness that mark American life. Add the American University communities and their opportunities for research and scholarship. Part of it is the warmth and friendship of one's own friends in Virginia, living with a history of racial problems and of the still throbbing legacy of Civil War, that makes our own domestic history anaemic by comparison, but bringing to their problems a zest and a faith that problems can be solved, that are all but absent from Britain.

This was of course the America before the idea of Black Power was born, before the wild vendettas of Senator Joseph McCarthy, before the Vietnam War, before the 1954 Supreme Court decision that ended segregation. But about my own vision of America there is still the awareness of those 270 million Americans of all nations, creeds and colours, who have found it a land of opportunity and of liberty, the America of Jefferson and Emerson and Adlai Stevenson, the America not least of Robert E Lee. So I found, when I went to my own desert war, that I wanted in my kitbag, alongside Fisher's *History of Europe*, the *Oxford Book of English Verse*, and *Moby Dick*, a slim volume little known in Britain but which is one of the great pieces of American literature, Stephen Vincent Benet's *John Brown's Body*:

> . . . Bury the bygone South.
> Bury the minstrel with the honey-mouth,
> Bury the broadsword virtues of the clan,
> Bury the unmachined, the planters' pride,
> The courtesy and the bitter arrogance,
> The pistol-hearted horsemen who could ride
> Like jolly centaurs under the hot stars.
> Bury the whip, bury the branding-bars,
> Bury the unjust thing
> That some tamed into mercy, being wise,
> But could not starve the tiger from its eyes
> Or make it feed where beasts of mercy feed.

I had returned to the UK in 1940, after receiving my Master's degree from President Franklin Delano Roosevelt, who came to Charlottesville in June 1940 to honour his son, Franklin Junior, who was a student at the law school. When I stood up as my name and university were called, I got a special round of applause, since FDR had made a point about Churchill's and Britain's stand against Hitler in the early months of the war. I turned round to acknowledge the applause and a White House guard patrolling the aisle behind me came over and –to the delight and further applause of the crowd – shook my hand. Next day, at a party on the Lawn, Franklin Junior came over to me and said, 'I have a special message for you from my father. Tell that young Englishman that he got his degree from the President of the US and not from a White House policeman.'

FDR is, of course, now a figure of legend –and of controversy. The story is a familiar one, of the three men who, in Washington DC in 1932 saw FDR pass by. 'There he is, a second George Washington, going to build a new country.' 'No', said the second man. 'He's a second Abraham Lincoln, going to rebuild a battered state.' 'No,' said the third. 'That guy is like Christopher Columbus. When he set sail for America in 1492, he didn't know where he was going. When he got there, he didn't know where he was. And when he came back, he didn't know where he'd been. That's the President and the New Deal.'

I took a MA; a doctorate would have required at least one more year, and there was a war on. On return, Lord Eustace Percy, then the Warden of my college, asked me to stay a civilian but to lecture to troops. I declined, since I saw no reason for 'evading' the war, and instead volunteered for 'special duties'. I did my basic infantry training with the KOYLI at Strensall, near York, and was transferred to the Intelligence Corps, whose depot was then at Winchester. I sailed for the Middle East in April 1942. It was a long journey, since Rommel was driving across North Africa bound for the Nile, and there was a danger that we'd all end up PoW in the Sinai! So we called at Freetown, but unlike today, British troops did not go ashore. We had a wonderful month in Durban, South Africa, where no less than 4000 of us were taken in as guests by friendly people. The first wedding I attended was in Durban and I was treated more royally than the bridesmaid because I was 'going north'. Not all South Africans –the Boers' descendants –wanted to do so, and South Africa was – at least officially – neutral. But after opening a new camp at Pietermaritzburg, we sailed north and I reached the rear HQ at Alamein in August, just in time for the big show.

Thereafter, it was sand, sand and sand again –and still sand –in everything, in food and drink and clothing, endless sand, and sand again. The moment that I enjoyed most was about six months after

Alamein, when I was a sergeant major in Heliopolis and was told that, thanks to a reference I had made in a talk to running a friendly society –like the church funeral benefit club of which I had been treasurer (like my father before me) before the outbreak of war –I was to be transferred to the newly-created Bureau of Current Affairs. Someone was needed in the Eighth Army in the Middle East, it seemed, who could explain the Beveridge Report on Social Insurance and the Allied Services, which had just been published in London. As a result I was commissioned and I spent most of the war years in Cairo, Alexandria, the Lebanon and the desert, talking to troops on the political issues of the day. I spent a few months as a special observer with the Ninth Army at Antioch on the Turkish/Lebanon border, assessing the wisdom –and practicality! –of 'going through Turkey,' and another few months in 1945 in the Vardar valley north of Salonica in Greece, wondering how 'Communist' it would be when its royal family returned –they had spent the war years in Cairo. After the 'shooting' was over I lectured to troops in Trieste, when it was a 'Free City,' and visited Slovenia and Dalmatia. So in one way or another I left the Army with a reasonable knowledge of the geography and social features of the Middle East and of the Balkans.

Another vivid memory is of escorting Sir Ronald Storrs on a visit to his old friends of the First World War in Cairo and Alexandria; he had been the Oriental Secretary in the British Embassy in Cairo in 1914, and as such was the 'brains' behind the British alliance with the Sheriff Hussein of Mecca in 1916, which led to the campaigns of Lawrence of Arabia. In 1944 Storrs, by then an elderly statesman, was seen as a possible victim of assassination attempts either by pro-German Arabs or by the Zionist terrorists in the Irgun Zvei Leumi, which had just begun its campaigns that led four years later to the existence of Israel.

The major lesson of the war, however, was that the Army was a creature of myth and legend. I found few 'Blimps' in the War; most colonels and brigadiers of my acquanitance were bright and young and almost classless. The real leaders emerged regardless of class. But if there was one lesson above all –central to life, and especially so to politics –it was loyalty. It ceased to be a word, as it is to so many. On it, and on the expectation of it in others, your own survival liter-ally depended. And there were, at all points, some who would buck the machine, sometimes from the most sincere of motives, sometimes

251

from conscience, sometimes from sudden panic or cowardice, sometimes from vainglory, sometimes from selfishness, sometimes because they were cast by nature for the role of barrack-room lawyer. Politics is full of these too. The Army can deal more sharply with them –in all their variety of motive –than can civvy street. But in the Middle East in the 1940s, respect increased for the straight, normal, decent man who soldiered on through five long years in an alien world. There is a lot to be said for the Services, and for the idea of Service. This is the sharpest contrast of all between today's world and the world of the desert war. For me it was, in a measure, my real post-graduate school.

Esmond Wright was elected to Parliament in March 1967 as MP for the Pollok Division of Glasgow, but believes he won not because of any merits of his own but because George Leslie, a popular local vet, stood as a Scottish National Party candidate and got 10,000 votes – mainly from Labour supporters. Labour got 12,000 votes and Wright clocked up 14,000 votes. Unfortunately, Leslie did not do so well at the general election in June 1970, and Labour regained the seat, with a majority of 601. The Labour MP elected for Pollok in 1970 was James White, who had himself served with the Eighth Army during the war. He remained as the Glasgow Division's representative until 1987.

Part Eight

THE ROYAL AIR FORCE

Finally, in this section post-war Parliamentarians are studied who served in the ranks of the most junior of the three services, the Royal Air Force. Then, as today, there was more to RAF air crew duty than being a pilot, and once again the contributors to this section illustrate some of the many sides to this totally independent and self-contained branch of the wartime armed forces.

TONY BENN

Probably the best-known politician to have served in the RAF was Tony Benn, who was still studying at Westminster School when the war began. His father, William Wedgwood-Benn, had been both a Liberal and Labour MP, and a Government Minister, and in 1942 entered the House of Lords as the 1st Viscount Stansgate. While still at school the young Tony Benn had joined the ATC (Air Training Corps). Both his older brother Michael, and his father –at the age of 63 –had enlisted in the RAF. His brother would later win the DFC, and it was Tony's own ambition to follow his example by also becoming a pilot. His ambition was realized in 1943, when he eventually joined the RAF himself and was selected for pilot training. After short periods at RAF Elmdon, Birmingham, and RAF Heaton Park, Manchester, he was sent to a place called 'Hillside Camp,' near Bulawayo, in what was then Southern Rhodesia, to train on the PT-26A Cornell training aircraft.

During pilot training there eventually comes the moment when each student makes their first 'solo' flight. In Tony Benn's case this took place on Wednesday, 14 June 1944. He recorded the event in his diary and provided the following extract describing this crucial moment in his training.

> We taxied on to the tarmac and I got out and walked back with Crownshaw. He said we'd just have a cigarette and then go up again. I was very surprised, but put it down to a desire on his part to finish me off ready for another check tomorrow. However, we took off, did a circuit or maybe two, and then as we taxied up to the take-off point, he said to me, 'Well, how do you feel about your landings?' I replied,

'Well, that's really for you to say, sir.' He chuckled. 'I think you can manage one solo,' he said. 'I'm going to get out now and I'll wait here for you,' he went on.

So this was it, I thought. The moment I had been waiting for came all of a sudden just like that. 'OK, sir,' I replied. 'And don't forget that you've got a throttle,' he said. 'Don't be frightened to go round again –OK? And by the way,' he added –he finished locking the rear harness and closing the hood, then came up to me, leant over and shouted in my ear, 'you do know the new trimming for taking off?' 'Yes, sir,' I replied, and he jumped off the wing and walked over to the boundary with his 'chute.

I was not all that excited. I certainly wasn't frightened and I hope I wasn't over-confident but I just had to adjust my mirror so that I could really see that there was no one behind me. Sure enough it was empty and I was alone. I did my vital actions very deliberately and carefully, I looked round and paused, then opening the throttle slightly I swung into wind until my directional gyro read '0', for I had set it on the last circuit. Then I opened up to full throttle as smoothly and yet as quickly as I could. I pushed the stick forward and connecting the swing which developed with my rudder I loomed across the drome, swaying rather from side to side, but keeping her under control and well into wind.

The 'drome at Guinea Fowl is bad and we bounced about like a wheelbarrow but gradually I felt the pressure come off the stick and as the airspeed read 70 mph I applied a gentle pressure and we rose off the ground. I took my left hand off the throttle where I always keep it during the take-off and placed it on the trimming lever which I juggled with until I could climb 'hands off' at 75 mph. I tried to sing but I couldn't hear myself very well and I still couldn't believe that I was alone. I glanced behind me quickly to reassure myself and I felt as happy as a schoolboy.

Then I remembered my brother Mike's words: 'Whatever you do don't get over-confident; it is that that kills most people and I only survived the initial stages through being excessively cautious.' So I brought my mind back to the job, checked the instruments, looked all around and when we had reached 500 feet began a gentle climbing turn. It was very bumpy and the wind got under my starboard wing and tried to keel me over, but I checked it with my stick and straightened out when my gyro compass read 270 degrees. Then I climbed to

900, looked all round and turned again on to the down-wind leg. By the time I'd finished that turn we were at 1,000 feet, so I throttled back, re-trimmed, got dead on 180 and I felt pretty good about things.

There isn't much to do on the down-wind leg and I was tempted to put my elbow on the side of the cockpit and look professional, but once again Mike's words were in my ears and I thought that on a first solo a fellow has enough to do without wanting to look professional. I noticed that the circuit was almost empty of other kites –perhaps that one down there was going to take off, and there I could see one turning out of wind after landing. By this time I was –if anything –a little too far, so I silently cursed myself for letting my mind wander off the job on hand.

I opened up on the turn which I started very gently in good time to about 1,400 revs and we came in just opposite the path I had selected. I always thought that I would feel a sense of panic when I saw the ground coming up at me on my first solo, but strangely enough I didn't feel anything but exhilaration at the approach which had turned out so well. No need to use so much engine, I reflected, so I made the final adjustment to the trimmer and then rested my hand on the throttle for the first moment. I thought I was a little high as I crossed the boundary so I eased back to 800 rpm, and as I passed over, I distinctly saw Crownshaw standing watching where I had left him. Now we were coming in beautifully and I eased the stick and throttle back. A quick glance at the ground below showed me to be a little high, so I left the stick as it was, gave a tiny burst of engine and as we floated down I brought both back fully. We settled, juddered and settled again for a fair three-pointer.

I was as happy as could be. Remembering not to use the brakes too heavily, I applied them as we came towards the opposite boundary for I had touched down a little late if anything, but that's a small fault compared with under-shooting. I turned out of wind, hauled my flaps up and trimmed fully tail heavy; then I swung round on to the perimeter and, defeating the devil of over-confidence for the last time, I taxied slowly round to where Crownshaw stood. With him was another instructor from our Flight whose pupil, judging by the intense look on his face, was the one coming at that moment over the boundary. I saw him strain eagerly forward, his hands twisting the handkerchief he held this way and that. His pupil made a good three-pointer, but I shan't forget that man's taut expression and his shoulders thrown forward in an effort to see how it went. He relaxed as the fellow slowed down and smiled weakly to Crownshaw.

I taxied up, stopped and braked. Try as I did, I couldn't restrain the broad grin which gripped me from ear to ear and Crownshaw, seeing it, leant over before he got in and said ironically with a smile, 'Happy now?'

On 27 June 1944, only thirteen days after this event, Tony Benn received a telegram from his mother, informing him of the death of his brother Michael, who had been such an obvious inspiration to him.

In due course Tony Benn received his commission and was sent to Alexandria in Egypt, it was now April 1945 and the war in Europe was nearly over. He celebrated VE Day while on leave in Palestine.

He already had political ambitions, having joined the Labour Party in 1943, and when he was posted home in time for the 1945 general election he drove a loudspeaker van around his local Westminster constituency in support of the Labour candidate.

He subsequently transferred to the Fleet Air Arm, in the hope of being sent to the Far East, but the war was quickly over and he remained in England.

After the war he studied at New College, Oxford, and was elected as the MP for Bristol South-East in 1950. However, there was a problem concerning his future Parliamentary career. Now that his father had been made a Viscount and his older brother had been killed in the war, he would someday inherit his father's title: this would immediately disqualify him from serving in the House of Commons. He introduced a personal bill which would allow him to renounce the title. However, the bill was defeated and when his father died in 1960 he was required to leave the House. He continued the struggle and in 1963 re-entered Parliament, thanks to the 'Peerage Act' which enabled peers to renounce their titles for their lifetimes.

Tony Benn remained the MP for Bristol South-East until 1983, and was elected as the MP for Chesterfield in March 1984. As a government minister he has been Postmaster General; Minister of Technology; Minister of Power; and Secretary of State for Energy. He was Chairman of the Labour Party in 1971/72. He eventually stood down from Parliament at the 2001 general election.

JAMES MOLYNEAUX

Jim Molyneaux, who was the leader of the Ulster Unionist Party from 1974–1995, served in the RAF from 1941–1946. He was MP for Antrim from 1970–1983, and Langan Valley 1983–1997. During the war he found that coming from Northern Ireland caused him some dilemma when wanting to join the forces. He was made a Knight Commander of the Order of the British Empire in 1996 and created a life peer in 1997, with the title of Baron Molyneaux of Killead.

Unfortunately for me, conscription did not apply to Northern Ireland because there was good reason to believe that republicans would have sabotaged the scheme. Therefore at the age of 20 I had difficulty in obtaining my parents approval to join the Royal Air Force. When Belfast suffered the heavy air raids in spring of 1941 I seized my chance in June of that year. For two years I served in Coastal Command and on transfer to 2nd Tactical Air Force life became even more exciting, particularly under Combined Operations Chief, Lord Mountbatten, when I spent months practicing seaborne beach landings. The high point was the D-Day Assault on Normandy. After landing I drove my Humber Armoured Car to a small assembly area where we had the messy task of removing all the waterproofing which protected the machinery, but not the crew. That completed, the Wing Commander and I headed inland to establish our right to four corn-fields on which our DIY airfield was to be constructed, outside the village of Villons-les-Buissons.

As we approached the site it became clear that squatters, in the form of the 21 Panzer Division, were in occupation and disinclined to vacate. As shells from German 88mms rained down all around us we beat a hasty retreat – sorry 'carried out a tactical withdrawal'.

The Germans were not finally ejected until three weeks later, but by that time our airfield had been constructed on an alternative site at Beny-sur-Mer nearer the coast.

The following eleven months spanned the Normandy break-out; crossing the Seine; Arnhem; the Rhine Crossing; a mad dash over the Keil Canal to Flensberg Air Base to grab and safeguard the experimental rocket aircraft flown back from the Peenemunde area, from which also arrived over 9,000 Luftwaffe personnel escaping from the Russians. The 9,000 must have experienced mixed emotions as they surrendered to Wing Commander R.E.H. Gould and eight other ranks who were nothing like as confident as we looked.

HECTOR MONRO

One of the more senior RAF officers to serve in the House of Commons was Hector Monro, who in 1997 was elevated to the peerage as Lord Monro of Langholm. He was the Conservative MP for Dumfries between 1964–1997, and attained the rank of Air Commodore after the war while serving with the Royal Auxiliary Air Force.

In September 1939 at the age of 17 I wanted to be a pilot in the Royal Air Force. This was quite a step as for five generations my family had all served in Highland regiments. I am glad to say that my two sons do today.

It was a frustrating wait before I could start training via Cambridge University Air Squadron. I do though recall with sadness a hockey photograph taken at school in March 1940. Seven of the XI were killed in the war, including my two best friends.

Flying training in this country or in the USA concluded with a reconnaissance and navigation course which inevitably meant posting to Coastal Command. I flew Catalina and Sunderland flying boats for the rest of the war. As one who was interested in aviation history I grew up on Lindbergh, Amelia Earhart, the Mollisons, and so on. I felt a touch of pride in flying the Atlantic at the age of 20.

There followed anti-submarine patrols over the Atlantic and North Sea from bases in Scotland, before being posted to 240 Squadron based in Madras to continue patrols over the Indian Ocean.

Some of the crews with the squadron did remarkable 34-hour round trips from India to the Gulf of Siam to deliver or pick up special agents working behind the Japanese lines. Landing and take off had to be done on the moonpath and the flights completed at 50 feet. It was always a tense moment if the agent would appear from the shore in a dinghy –or Japanese soldiers!

Later I was home again to transfer to Sunderlands and to deliver new aircraft to India, East Africa and South Africa. A few days in Durban was a great change from wartime Britain!

Then to 209 Squadron in Ceylon poised and ready to play its part in the assault on Malaya and Singapore. This extremely dangerous operation was saved by the Atom Bombs.

Immediately we were flying surrendered parties to Singapore and Hong Kong, and bringing back to Ceylon our own prisoners of war who had suffered so much under the Japanese. They were in a desperate physical state.

For the next 9 months I flew Sunderlands throughout the Far East. Hong Kong, Japan, Java, Australia, Burma and Borneo were all regular trips. Borneo was always popular as we alighted on various rivers and delivered the mail to the local District Commissioner.

When I flew a Sunderland back from Hong Kong to the United Kingdom there seemed little future with the RAF, so I transferred to 603 City of Edinburgh Squadron of the Royal Auxiliary Air Force flying Spitfires. Quite a change!

That began a long association with the Auxiliaries culminating as an Air Commodore and the Hon Inspector General of the Royal Auxiliary Air Force. On my retirement in 2000 I had completed 60 years involvement with flying and the Royal Air Force. I had been lucky to serve with such excellent air crews and ground crews.

Not so many exciting or heroic moments but thousands of hours of flying all over the world. Many memories I shall treasure for ever.

GEORGE MACKIE

George Mackie, who was the Liberal MP for Caithness and Sutherland between 1964–1966, served throughout the war with Bomber Command. As well as being an MP he has also been President of the Scottish Liberal Party and Liberal Spokesman in the House of Lords for such things as Devolution, Agriculture, Scotland, and Industry, after his elevation to the peerage as Lord Mackie of Benshie in 1974.

I joined the RAF in Norwich on 3 September 1939 as a potential Observer (Navigator/Bomb-aimer) in order to get in earlier than I would as a pilot. I was eventually called in early February and after training went to Lossiemouth Operational Training Unit as a Pilot Officer to crew up on Wellington Bombers –a twin-engine plane of geodetic aluminium construction able to take much punishment from enemy fire. This was course No 13 and out of 6 crews, 3 crashed with many of the crew killed in our last week.

My crew was posted to 15 Squadron at Wyton and did several operations over Germany before being sent out to Egypt by way of Malta.

After going considerably off course, we were approaching Malta in daylight when we were attacked by a ME110 and shot it down. I remember this attack because, although much exposed to hostile attack by both Ack Ack and fighters, this was the only time in daylight and, as I was keeping a lookout in the astrodome, I saw the whole episode. Our rear gunner Bob Turner deserves much credit for coolness and accuracy.

In Egypt we joined 148 Squadron and did many ops to Benghazi, Greece, Crete and other areas in the Med.

The operations in the Middle East were often interesting and varied. We bombed fuel tanks in Greece, airfields and shipping. We dropped supplies to guerrilla fighters in the hills of Crete. We bombed armoured columns in the Western Desert and I did a couple of flights with extra tanks to drop agents in Yugoslavia. Perhaps the most interesting and successful was the blocking of the Corinth Canal when we went in at a height of 50ft and planted a 1,000 lb bomb in the opposite bank. Bombing Benghazi was called the milk run.

I came back to UK in 1942 and after a spell as an Instructor went to 149 Squadron on Stirlings. My short time on Stirlings was not satisfactory. The performance of the aircraft had deteriorated. They were mostly employed on mining and I did not get on with the squadron commander, so I accepted a posting to Boscombe Down as a bomb-aimer on experimental work in January 1943. The work there was interesting and I dropped the first 1200 lb blast bomb and also worked on the roly poly bombs used by the Dam Busters.

In September 1943 I heard that my old CO 'Turkey' Rainsford was commander of 115 Squadron on Lancaster IIs with Hercules air-cooled engines. He promised me a crew and possible promotion. I joined the Squadron and captained a crew, the pilot being a flight sergeant, Steve Atkins. Our crew worked well together and I spent the winter of 1943 and spring of 1944 mainly bombing Berlin. All German targets were heavily defended and, in the words of the old RAF joke, 'the natives appeared hostile'. I acted as master bomber for the squadron on a number of targets in France before the invasion.

George Mackie was credited with three operational tours and awarded the DSO and the DFC after his final tour finished in May 1944. He was thereafter appointed a Staff Officer in Bomber Operations in Charles Street and was demobbed on 2 January 1946, after which he returned to farming in Angus before eventually entering into the world of politics.

COLIN TURNER

Colin Turner, the Conservative MP for Woolwich West between 1959–1964, who was made a Knight in 1993, was due to leave Highgate School in July 1939 when he was 17½ years old. He had applied for a short service commission in the RAF, but, due to the outbreak of War, all short service commissions had been cancelled. So, in January 1940 he applied to join the RAF for aircrew training. In June he was accepted and sworn in, but it was not until 28 December that his training began. In May 1941, after passing out at the ITW at Torquay, he was posted overseas for training at an unknown destination.

Our liner joined the famous Churchill convoy to reinforce the Middle East. A few days later in mid Atlantic when our powerful naval escort suddenly disappeared at dawn, we learnt later that the *Bismarck* had crossed our course just 19 miles away but did not see the convoy owing to the terrible weather!

Whilst in Freetown, Sierra Leone, refueling, the liner was hit by a battleship. The repairs took over 2 weeks before our journey recommenced. It was only when we saw Table Mountain that we realized that we were to be trained in South Africa. From July to September there was navigational training at 47 Air School, Queenstown, and at East London during October and November for bombing and gunnery.

Now fully trained as Air Observers, we were sent by liner to the Canal Zone where we spent Christmas 1941 in Cairo. In January 1942 again we were on the move by liner to Mombasa in Kenya. From there we went by train to Nairobi and on into the Highlands. At Gil Gil, which is almost on the equator, we found ourselves in a transit camp for aircrew awaiting training at 70 OTU, Nakuru. At last having found a pilot and an air gunner we started training at Nakuru. Passing out in August 1942, we were posted to 223 Squadron in the Western Desert flying Glen Martin Baltimores, light bombers, in support of the Eighth Army.

Our first operations were during the Battle of El Alamein, where the Squadron operated with a formation of eighteen aircraft, which opened up to cover a wide area pattern-bombing the enemy formations below. In March and April 1942 we were engaged in intensive operations supporting the advance of the Eighth Army in Tunisia. We took part in the final raid in Tunisia and saw white flags as we flew away. In early June the Squadron was involved in the mass air raids on the Italian island fortress of Pantelleria. The entire light bomber force of the Desert Air Force and that of 48th Medium Bombardment Group of the USAF undertook two or three mass raids a day, resulting in the quick surrender of the island.

On 2 July I was commissioned in the field as Pilot Officer. During my interview with the Air Vice Marshal following a discussion about the general tactics employed by the Desert Air Force squadrons, he asked what exams I had passed at school. When I said I had failed school certificate twice, he asked what subject I had failed in. When I said German he roared with laughter and said, 'By Jove, you must hate them, commission granted.'

July and early August saw a further period of intensive operations during the invasion of Sicily. After moving to Sicily in August and to Italy in September the Squadron supported the Eighth Army in its battle up the east coast. Finally, whilst based at Foggia, on 16 December I took part in my final operation, the 83rd.

On one raid on a railway marshalling yard at Catanzaro, Italy, on 7 September 1943, we were supposed to bomb some 6000 feet above the target, but owing to the weather we dropped the bombs from about 1200 feet! As a result of the low-level attack our aircraft was badly hit and the plastic nose in which I was sitting was almost completely blown away and I was wounded by dozens of pieces of plastic. We returned safely to our base in Gerbine, Sicily, on one engine and the undercarriage down, flying alongside the Squadron formation.

Unlike Bomber Command flying over western Europe, the average time of squadron operations was less than 3 hours.

Back to the UK in January 1944 for a long leave. I was promoted to Flying Officer on 3 January 1944 and awarded the DFC in the same year. In May I rejoined my pilot, who had been posted to 527 Squadron calibrating the radar stations on the East Coast. In June whilst flying a passenger from Digby to Thornaby in Durham we had great difficulty in finding the runway. There was 10/10ths cloud at 700 feet and very heavy rain. With almost no visibility and the undercarriage down the aircraft stalled. On hitting the ground I was thrown through the roof of the Blenheim and was found some 55 yards from the aircraft. I broke my spine, left arm and right leg and spent the next 14 months in hospital and rehabilitation centre. I was invalided out of the RAF in September 1945 with the rank of Flying Officer.

PETER SHORE

Peter Shore was Labour MP for Stepney from 1964–1974, Stepney and Poplar from 1974–1983 and Bethnal Green and Stepney from 1983–1997. His political appointments have included being PPS to the Prime Minister; Secretary of State for Economic Affairs, Deputy Leader of the House of Commons, Secretary of State for Trade, and Secretary of State for the Environment. He was created a life peer in 1997, as Lord Shore of Stepney. After the war was over he was sent out to India, where he witnessed – with mixed emotions – the final days of the Raj.

> I was a reluctant warrior. I hated the necessity for war and the militarisation of life that inevitably accompanied it. But I hated Nazism and aggression still more.
>
> Mine was an uneventful war. Still 17, I went up to Cambridge in January 1942, joined the Air Squadron there and waited for the call-up which came in April 1943. After that, for me war service was mainly about training. I managed to fly Tiger Moths in Marshall's airfield outside Cambridge in the early summer of 1943 and thereafter joined the queue at Heaton Park, Manchester, and at Monkton in Canada, before arriving at No 3 British Flying Training School in Miami, Oklahoma, USA.
>
> I learnt to fly first PT 19s, then Harvards but quite late in my course showed a certain unreliability about putting down my undercarriage when coming in to land. So I didn't complete that course, but went instead to Pickton and Belleville in Ontario, Canada, to complete my air crew training as a navigator and air bomber.
>
> Back in England, now a Pilot Officer, in October 1944 there was

still further training ahead –notably a 12-week Operational Training Unit Course on Wellingtons in Moreton-in-Marsh when we crewed up with those –including our Australian pilot –who were, so it was planned, to fly together on Lancaster Bombers. We completed our course and were waiting our next posting when the news came through of the German surrender on 8 May 1945.

We were immediately grounded. The Far East and the War against Japan was the obvious next objective, but Hiroshima and Nagasaki brought that conflict to an unexpectedly early end.

How best to use us now unwanted air-crew? I became a codes and cipher officer and in late 1945, was posted to India and stationed at Yelahanka outside Bangalore. In many ways this was the most interesting part of my war service. The future of India was being actively negotiated and various contingencies, including the possibility of breakdown, were the subject of highly classified messages that I received and de-coded in my Yelahanka office.

I was a passionate supporter of Indian self-government and rejoiced at the wisdom of the Viceroy and his advisers and those who then commanded the Indian Army in securing the not guilty verdicts and immediate release of the many thousands of brave but misguided Indian Army men who, when captured and recruited by the Japanese, formed the Indian National Army to fight for the freedom of their country.

All over India the return of these men to their towns and villages was greeted with widespread rejoicing and acclamation. In travelling across India by rail as I occasionally had to do, and finding the words Jai Hinde (Quit India!) chalked on all of the train carriages and being greeted at every stop by crowds of demonstrating, Indian nationalists, I did feel a certain irony in my position. There I was, clearly in uniform, a representative of the old Order when I myself felt so strongly supportive of the new. But I acquired, in those last days of the Raj, an affection and understanding and respect for India and for the peoples of the sub-continent that I took back with me to Cambridge in October 1946 and which has lasted all my life.

BIBLIOGRAPHY

The following books have been useful, either as a source of reference, or for quotes. In the case of quotes, permission has been obtained from the copyright holders in each case.

Robert Boscawen *Armoured Guardsmen* Pen & Sword Books. Copyright: Robert Boscawen.

Belinda Hadden *Three Chousing Reers!: A life in the day of Reginald Bennett*. The Grey Agency. Copyright: The Grey Agency.

Paul Bryan *Wool, War and Westminster* Tom Donovan Publishing. Copyright: Paul Bryan.

William Deedes *Dear Bill* Macmillan. Copyright: W. F. Deedes.

Douglas Dodds-Parker *Setting Europe Ablaze* Springwood Books. Copyright: Douglas Dodds-Parker.

Stephen Hastings *The Drums of Memory* Leo Cooper. Copyright: Stephen Hastings.

Denis Healey *The Time of My Life* Michael Joseph/Penguin Group. Copyright: Denis Healey.

Roy Jenkins *A Life at the Centre* Macmillan London Limited. Copyright: Roy Jenkins.

John Peyton *Without Benefit of Laundry* Bloomsbury. Copyright: John Peyton

Anthony Meyer *Stand Up and Be Counted* Heinemann. Copyright: Anthony Meyer

Tony Benn (Abridged and introduced by Ruth Winstone) *The Benn Diaries* BCA. Copyright: Tony Benn.

INDEX

274